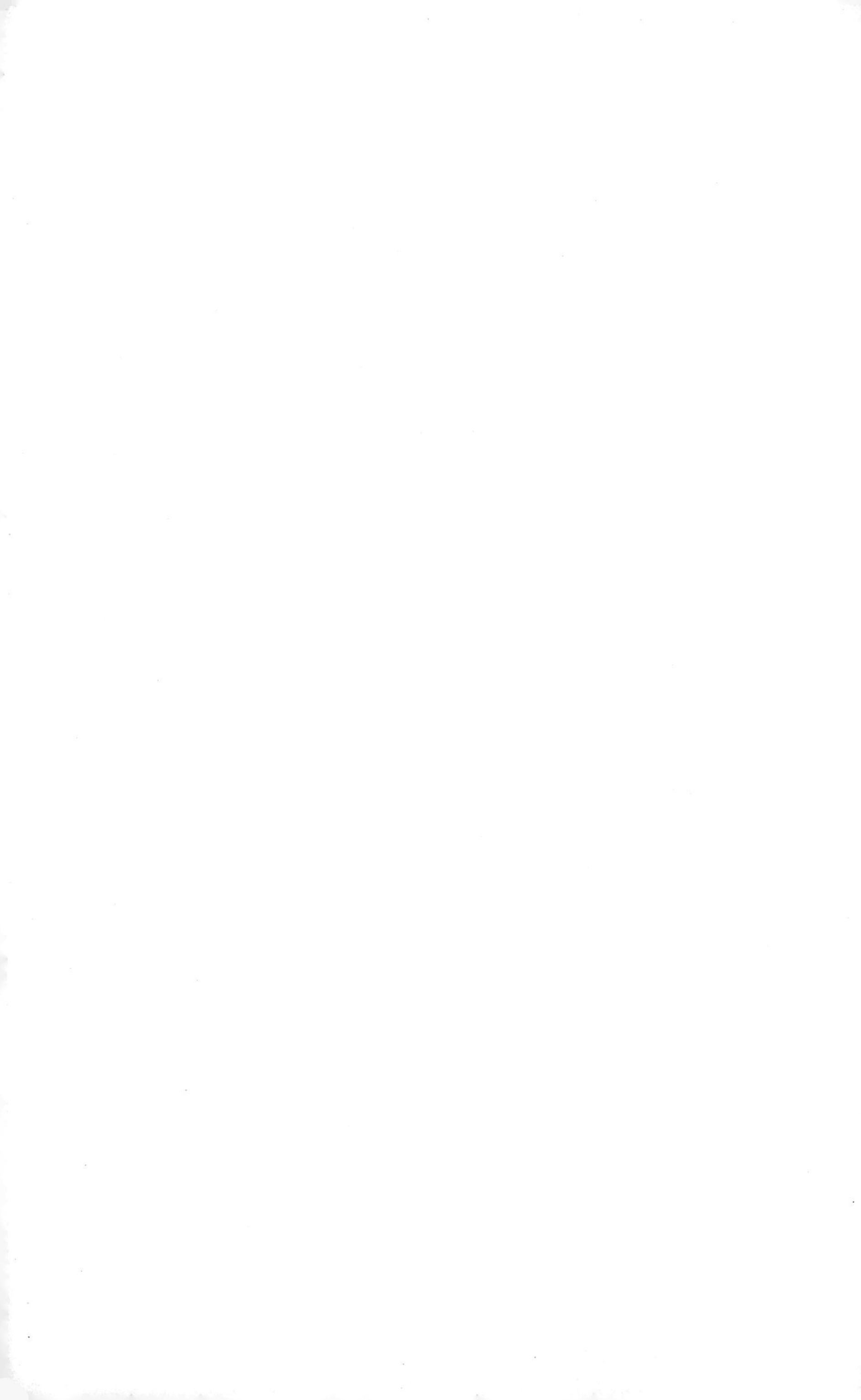

Robert

Lehman

Lectures

on Contemporary Art

Dia Center for the Arts, New York
No. 1

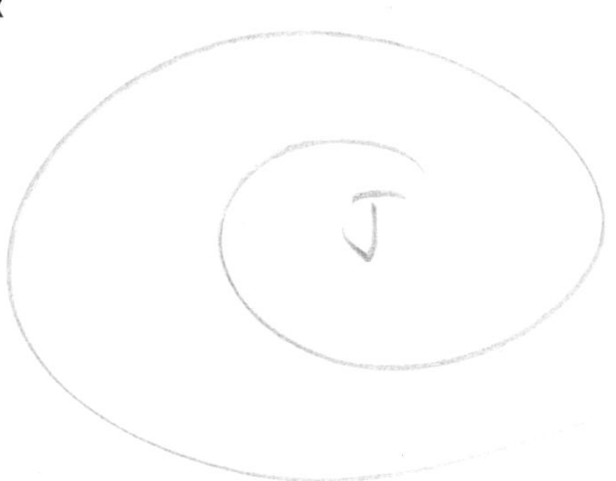

Robert Lehman Lectures on Contemporary Art

EDITED BY LYNNE COOKE AND KAREN KELLY

Printed in the United States of America
by Becotte and Gershwin, Inc., Warminster, Pennsylvania.
First Printing 1996

Library of Congress Number 93-73430
IBSN 0-944521-75-4

Dia Center for the Arts
542 West 22nd Street
New York, New York 10011
212.989.5566

Design by Laura Fields and Bethany Johns Design, New York.

Typeset in Garamond and Gill Sans.

Cover image by Bill Jacobson Studio, New York.

Contents

Preface

Since 1992, Dia has presented the Robert Lehman Lectures on Contemporary Art. As is Dia's Discussions in Contemporary Culture series, The Lehman lectures are an example of Dia's ongoing commitment to critical and intellectual discourse. The long-term exhibitions at 548 West 22nd Street offer a fertile space for discussion. The series was founded with a generous grant from the Robert Lehman Foundation, Inc., and has showcased a distinguished array of scholars, critics, art historians, and artists.

In this premier volume, we have assembled the first nine lectures in the series, and we owe our gratitude to the authors, who were generous with their time as we gathered the manuscripts and edited them for publication for this book. Curator Lynne Cooke has overseen the series since its inception, assisted for the last two years by Stephan Urbaschek, who coordinated the lectures with the contributors. Karen Kelly edited all of the texts, and Franklin Sirmans dedicated himself to the tasks of tracking down photographs and checking facts. We extend thanks to Laura Fields who designed this book in consultation with Bethany Johns. The entire Dia staff has helped prepare for and present the lectures to the public. We would also like to acknowledge the support and assistance of the artists and their galleries. In addition, we are indebted to Brian Wallis, Phil Mariani, and Kristin Jones, who read and reread galleys, offering their thoughtful and insightful editorial comments.

Dia hopes to continue this valuable lecture series into the future and looks forward to publishing unique scholarship such as this volume represents.

Michael Govan, Director

Introduction

LYNNE COOKE

No poet, no artist of any art, has his complete meaning alone.

—T. S. Eliot

The lectures published in this anthology were delivered in response to exhibitions held at Dia Center for the Arts in New York over the past four years. The exhibition program is devised according to a set of governing parameters: each exhibition is devoted to the work of a single artist; each exhibition occupies one floor of Dia's converted warehouse building on West 22nd Street in New York City; and the duration of each exhibition is approximately one year.

Installations of works from Dia's permanent collection are intermittently inserted into this calendar of exhibitions. The presentation of Joseph Beuys's monumental work *Arena* was one such instance. Often, however, the exhibitions take the form of site-specific installations, as artists respond directly to the physical or sociocultural character of the site. Lawrence Weiner, Dan Graham, Robert Gober, and Ann Hamilton variously reacted in this way to an invitation to show at Dia. On Kawara, whose own work is focused around issues of time, responded somewhat differently: instead of addressing the physical site or its history, he engaged with the duration of the exhibition, proposing a series of installations of paintings from his Today series that changed each month the exhibition was on view. Commissions to Katharina Fritsch and James Coleman allowed major new works to be presented to audiences in the United States who knew these artists more by reputation than through sustained contact with their art. And in 1991 Dia's copious spaces permitted Brice Marden to present for close scrutiny a new and monumental series of paintings with related drawings.

The Robert Lehman lecture series was devised to extend the discussion and focus the debate generated by each exhibition. Each lecturer was asked to respond to a specific exhibition: the terms of their responses were left open. The selection of lecturers was guided by a wish to bring to New York renowned historians, critics, cultural theorists, and others whose work was probably best known to the local audience via their publications. In addition, the series offered the possibility of presenting some of the new forms of art history that have burgeoned over the past two decades—of mixing art history with art criticism, since in the contemporary field the two disciplines overlap, and of inviting theorists and scholars from completely different disciplines.

What has been called the New Art History greatly widened the practice of art historians as they built on concepts and theories first articulated in feminist, queer, or gender politics, in film theory, linguistics, or psychoanalysis, or Structuralist and Poststructuralist theory. Likewise, academics from other disciplines have contributed greatly to the discourse surrounding contemporary art, not only at a theoretical level but through writing directly on artworks, as may be witnessed in the work of Roland Barthes, Michel Foucault, Julia Kristeva, and others. In addition, cultural theorists are increasingly participants in the nexus from which the making and the presentation of current art originates.

Stephen Bann is well known for the diversity and breadth of his work, ranging from studies of the nineteenth-century collector John Bargrave to a groundbreaking account of earlier work by Brice Marden to which he brings a singular and refreshing perspective. In this essay, he explores the complex ways in which Marden's recent series of Cold Mountain paintings engages with tradition. Bann's text not only countermands any reading of Marden as a quintessential (late) modernist, an artist whose work explicitly rejects the art of the past, but maps the rich and manifold set of relationships that links this American painter's work to an unexpectedly multifarious set of artistic precedents, precedents that lie at the margins or beyond the borders of the canonical art-historical lineage. Integral to Bann's subtle teasing out of these affinities and allusions is his use of several models in concert with one another. Drawing not only on older works of art but on a range of earlier commentators on art, Bann's elucidation is equally as attuned to the textual aspect of these works as it is to their formal beauty.

Trained in anthropology, Antje von Graevenitz finds placing Joseph Beuys in a tradition of twentieth-century art practice less apt, less illuminating, than considering his practice and aesthetic in relation to terms and concepts borrowed from anthropology. Exploring the parallels between the practice of Beuys and those of a shaman—parallels that the artist himself cultivated—von Graevenitz, however, never loses sight of the fact that Beuys was operating within frames of reference that were inherently modernist, not least those foreshadowed in the art of James Joyce, another of Beuys's mentors.

At first glance, Lawrence Weiner's work appears to break radically with the precepts and fundaments of Western sculptural practice, yet it is precisely that art form that constitutes the basis of his practice: hence, its forms, as much as its materials, supply the norms and points of departure for his work. Anne Rorimer grapples with the radical unconventionality of Weiner's text-based oeuvre by subjecting his installation at Dia to a close and sustained exegesis grounded in a rigorous and deliberately conservative art-historical methodology. By contrast, both Maureen Sherlock and Stephan Schmidt-Wulffen opt for the role of art critic rather than historian, albeit from quite different perspectives. For Schmidt-Wulffen, Fritsch's art is exemplary in its response to certain key issues facing contemporary artists. "What is it that a work of art gives to us in this historical moment?" he asks at the beginning of his lecture. "How can art in a time of a constant flux of imagery and semantic consumerism make an important statement? How can artists today develop images that resist a simple, cursory glance and a quick commentary, and remain in our minds as a presence, forcing us again and again to look for new interpretations?" Whereas Schmidt-Wulffen seeks to articulate what he calls the "secret rules" by which Fritsch confronts such problematics, Sherlock, by contrast, focuses on the thematics that underpin Gober's practice. She traces the evolution of his engagement with sexual politics, with issues of gender and homophobia, and with the AIDS pandemic, to its culmination in the installation at Dia in 1992, locating them within a specifically American heritage, one that has its foundations in the writings of Walt Whitman, Henry David Thoreau, and others.

Dan Graham's preoccupation with architecture as the most social of art forms has long been acknowledged, but seldom has it been so stringently explored in relation to specific architectural precedents. As a practicing architect as well as an architectural historian, John Vinci is particularly well placed to comment on Graham's allusions, debts, and invocations, while the fact that he has also collaborated on certain of Graham's projects—most notably, *Heart Pavilion* for the Carnegie International in 1991—gives him a unique perspective. As witnessed here, Vinci never becomes an apologist for Graham; rather, he uses the opportunity to lecture on his friend's work as further occasion for continuing their ongoing dialogue.

Dot Tuer and James Coleman also have had a longstanding relationship, Tuer being one of the earliest and most insightful writers on the Irishman's art. In this penetrating lecture, she returns again to what is for her the central thematic of his practice: casting the act of seeing into question. Informed by psychoanalyst Jacques Lacan's theories and by Jonathan Crary's analyses of the incarnate viewer, she explores in detail the obsessive yet constantly inventive ways in which Coleman returns to his chosen thematics.

For Ann Hamilton, vision is ineluctably imbricated in the body. However, too often vision is accorded priority over the other senses, and other forms of bodily knowledge, she argues. Susan Stewart teases out the implications of these fundaments in Hamilton's thought in a multifaceted examination of the "relations between the senses, experience, and human work as the transformation and recognition of nature." The breadth of Stewart's references leads her finally to an inquiry of metaphysical import. Yet, such is the dexterity, skill, and tact with which these allusions are interwoven that the result is the very opposite of a display of erudition. Stewart's reading thus neither narrowly fixes Hamilton's installation nor leaves it impossibly open-ended, irresolute, or diffuse. Indeed, her account of the way *tropos* works serves as an analogue for her own interpretive practice: "The associations are not endless—but they are manifold and each carries over meaning.... And this carrying over continually emphasizes the contamination and continuity between...the material and spiritual, the senses and abstraction."

Jeff Wall's training, albeit a brief one, as an art historian informs his approach to On Kawara's Today series. "As the transgeneric or postgeneric moment of painting," the monochrome, Wall contends, is the necessary starting point for contemporary painterly practice: the question then becomes what is put on top of it. Kawara's insertion of a date invokes, for Wall, the obsolete genre of history painting, a terrain long ceded to photojournalism. Tracing a trajectory that maps the various attempts whereby abstract art has sought to retain the structures, if not the representational language, of the higher genres of painting, Wall gives a dazzling account of the dilemmas facing ambitious painters since Rodchenko limned that seemingly impassable boundary marker, his "trimonochrome" *Pure Red-Yellow-Blue Color* in 1921.

T. S. Eliot's assertion, used here as an epigraph, that there is more in or to a work of art than the artist knows or intended, is one with which few contemporary artists would disagree. What they as well as most viewers of their art seek are cogent, comprehensive, and persuasive readings that illuminate or analyze from what can only ever be some of the multivocal perspectives a significant work of art offers. These lectures memorably answer to such expectations, challenging us to return again and again to the works with new interpretations.

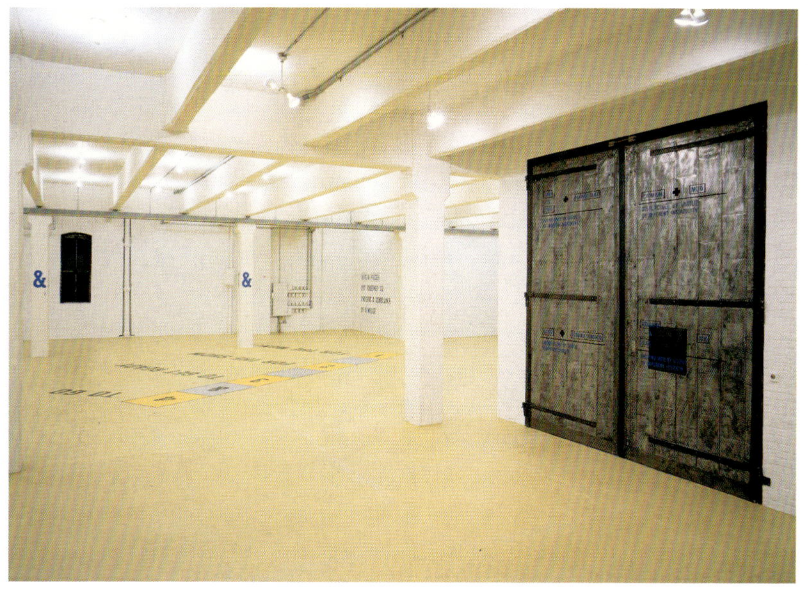

Lawrence Weiner, "Displacement," April 4, 1991–June 20, 1992.

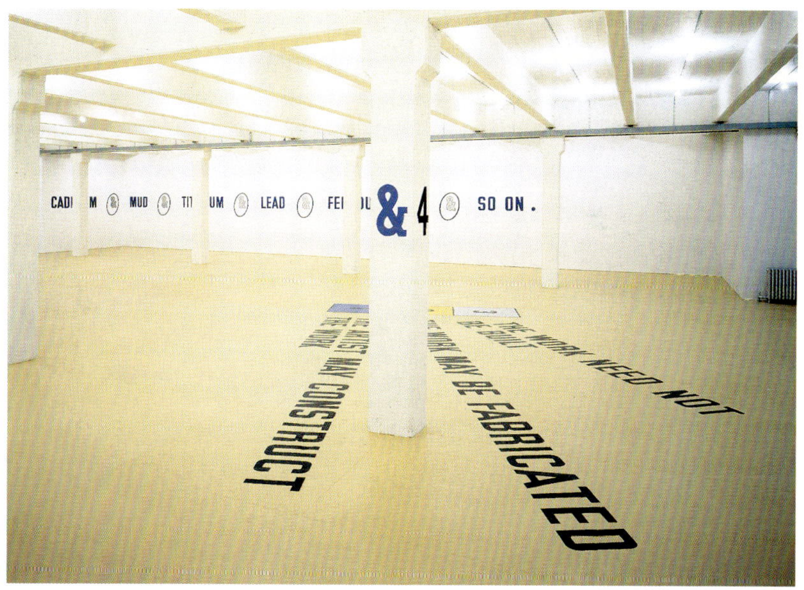

Lawrence Weiner, "Displacement," April 4, 1991–June 20, 1992.

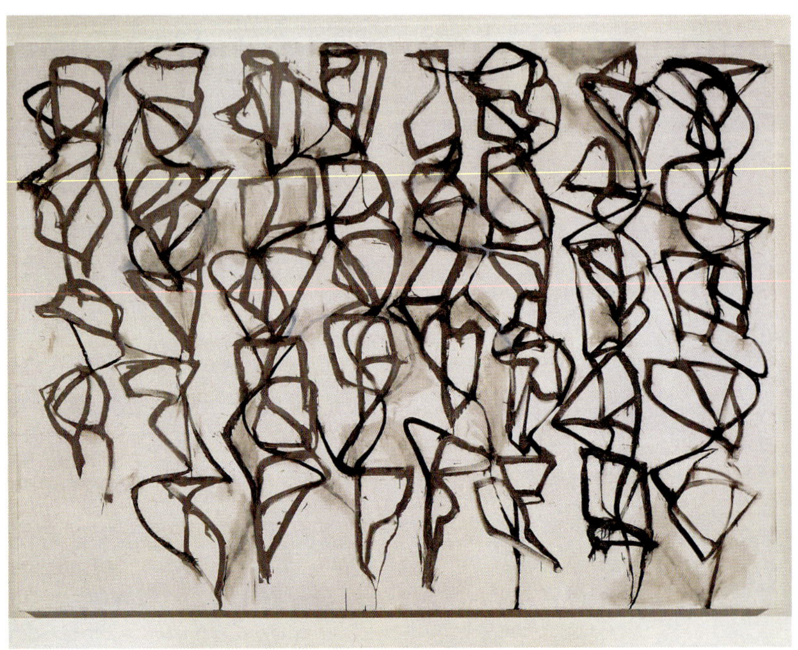

Brice Marden, *Cold Mountain 1 (Path)*, 1988–89, from the exhibition "Cold Mountain," October 17, 1991–May 31, 1992.

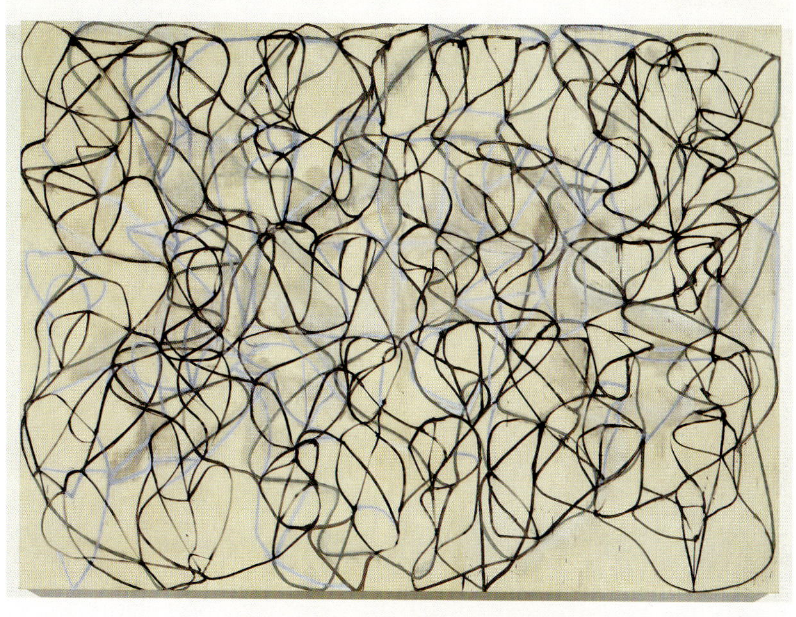

Brice Marden, *Cold Mountain 3*, 1989–91, from the exhibition "Cold Mountain," October 17, 1991–May 31, 1992.

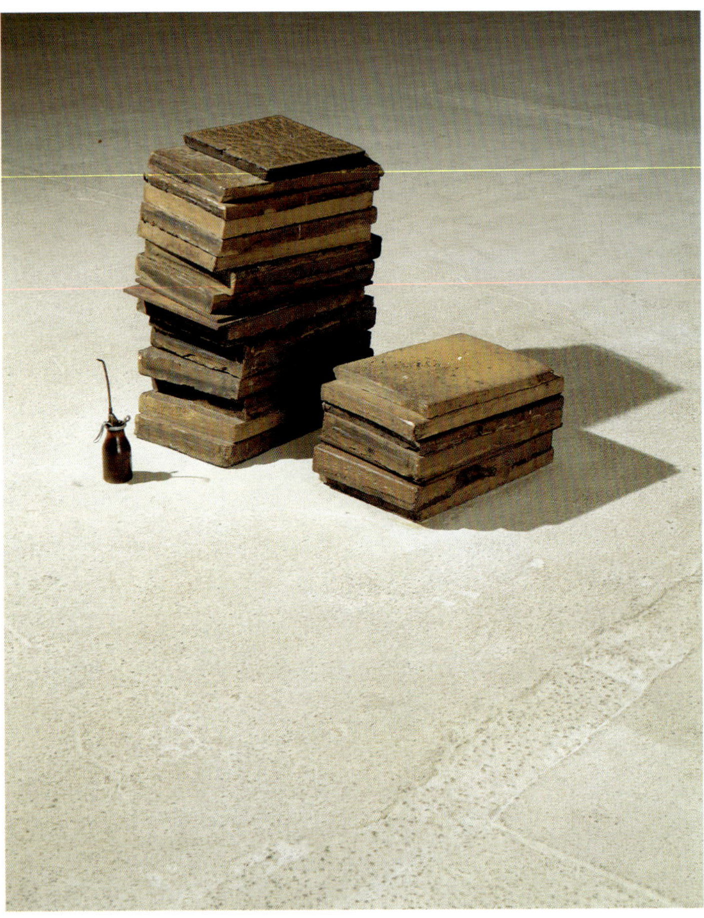

Joseph Beuys, *Arena—where would I have got if I had been intelligent!*, 1947–72, exhibited at Dia January 23, 1992–April 4, 1993.

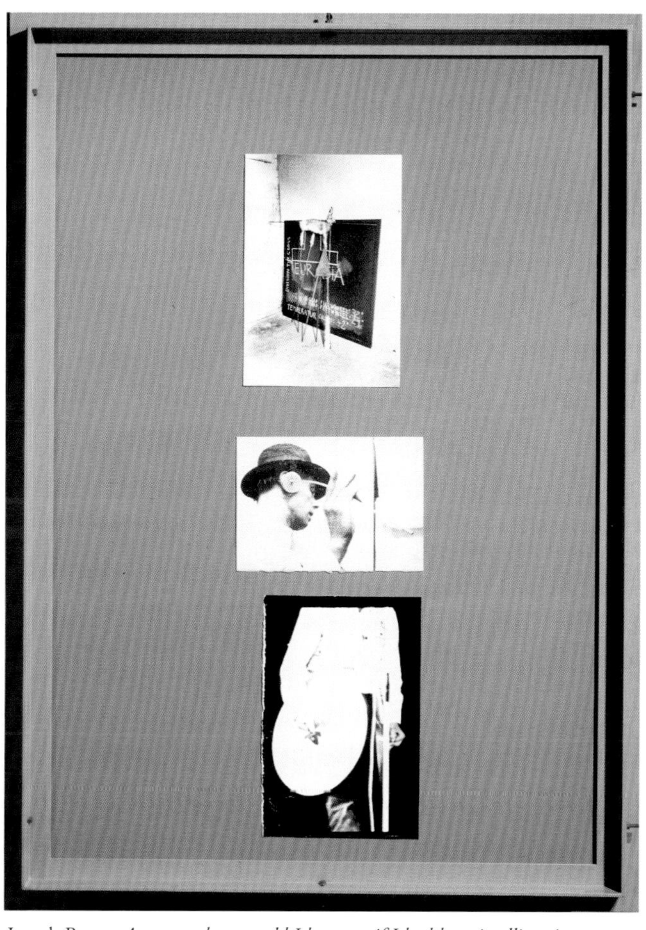

Joseph Beuys, *Arena—where would I have got if I had been intelligent!*, 1947–72, exhibited at Dia January 23, 1992–April 4, 1993.

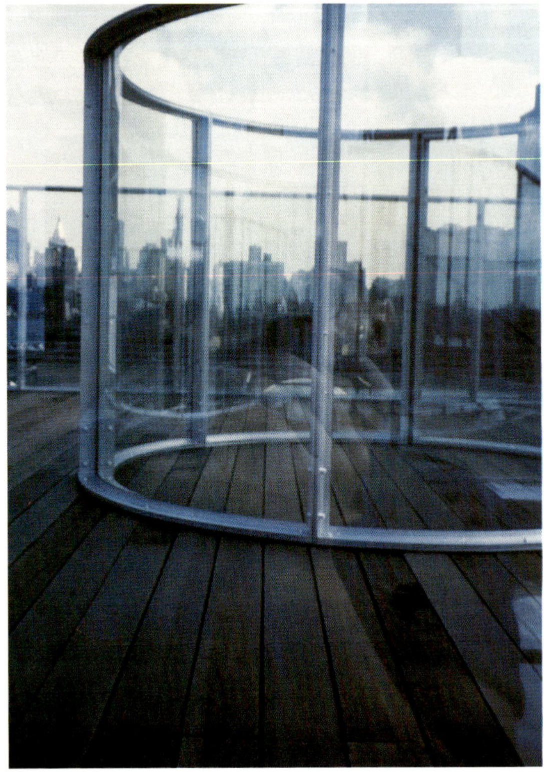

Dan Graham, *Two-Way Mirror Cylinder Inside Cube*, 1981/91, Rooftop Urban Park Project at Dia Center for the Arts, extended exhibition, opened September 1991.

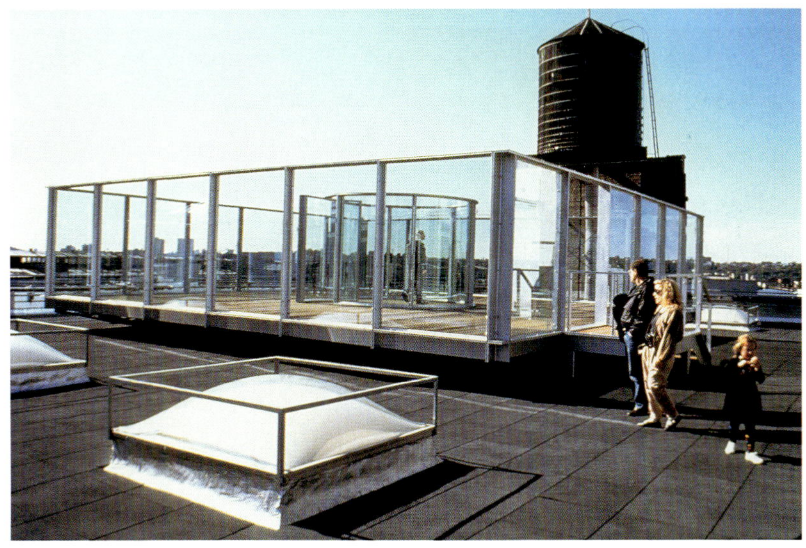

Dan Graham, *Two-Way Mirror Cylinder Inside Cube*, 1981/91, Rooftop Urban Park Project at Dia Center for the Arts, extended exhibition, opened September 1991.

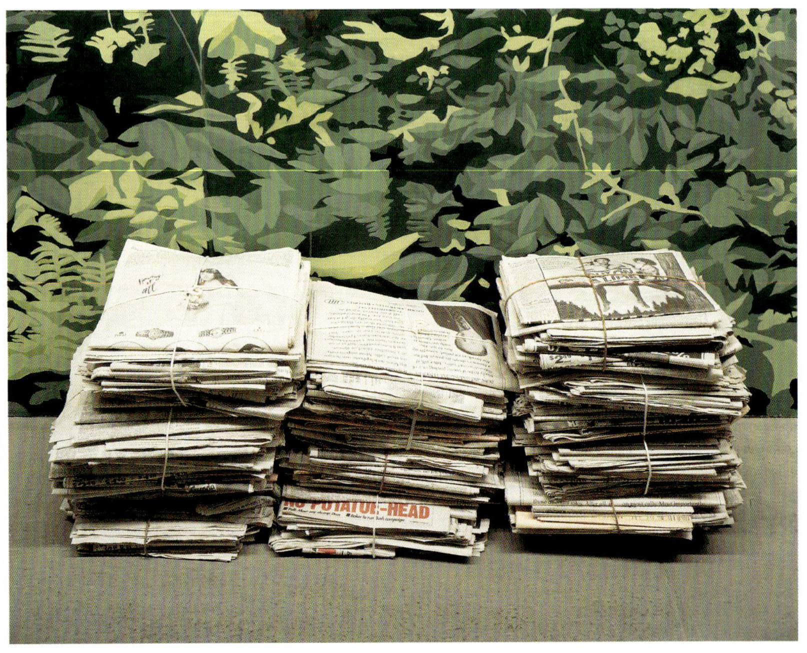

Robert Gober, exhibition at Dia, September 24, 1992–June 20, 1993.

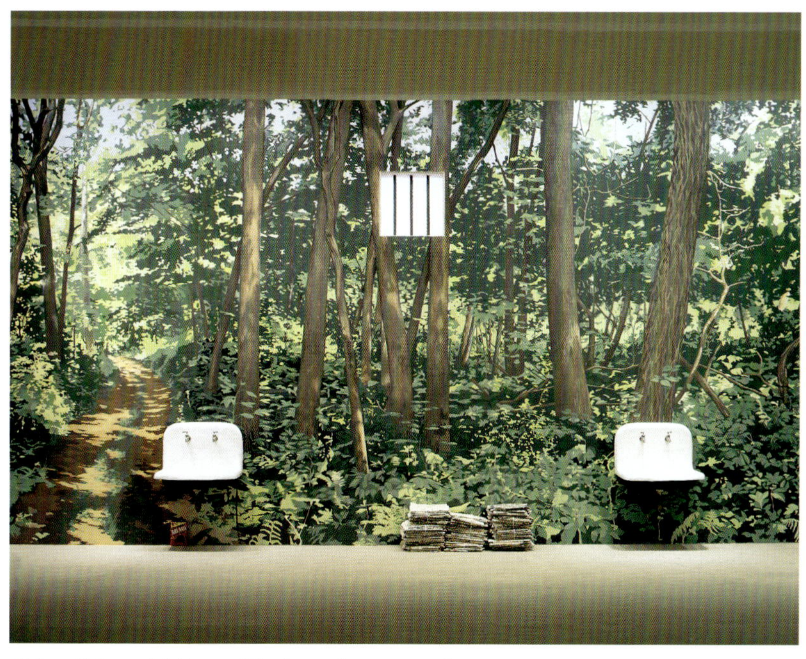

Robert Gober, exhibition at Dia, September 24, 1992–June 20, 1993.

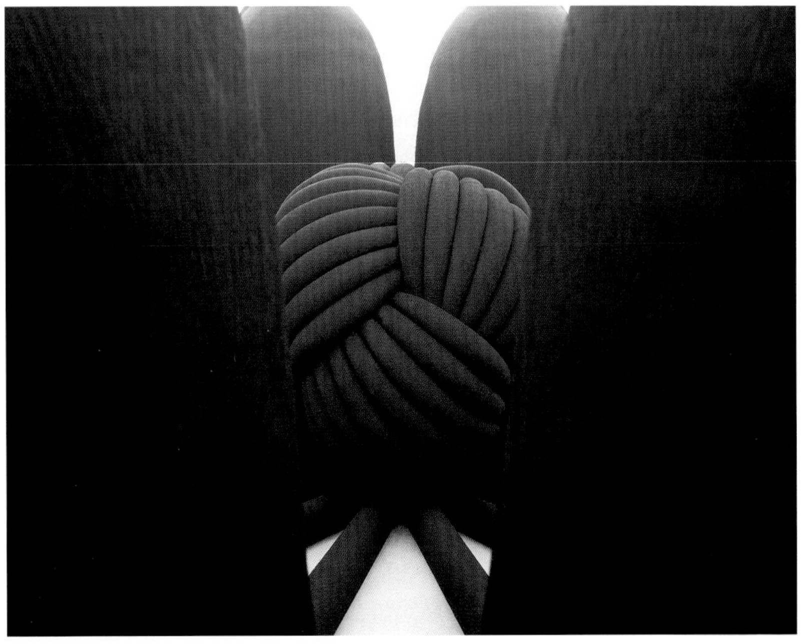

Katharina Fritsch, *Rattenkönig* (*Rat-King*), 1993, exhibited at Dia April 15, 1993–June 19, 1994.

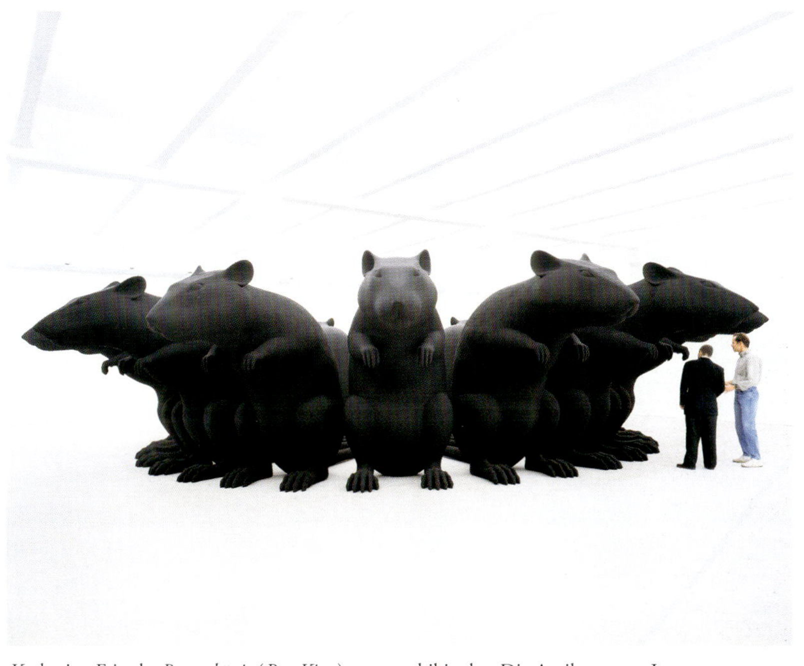

Katharina Fritsch, *Rattenkönig* (*Rat-King*), 1993, exhibited at Dia April 15, 1993–June 19, 1994.

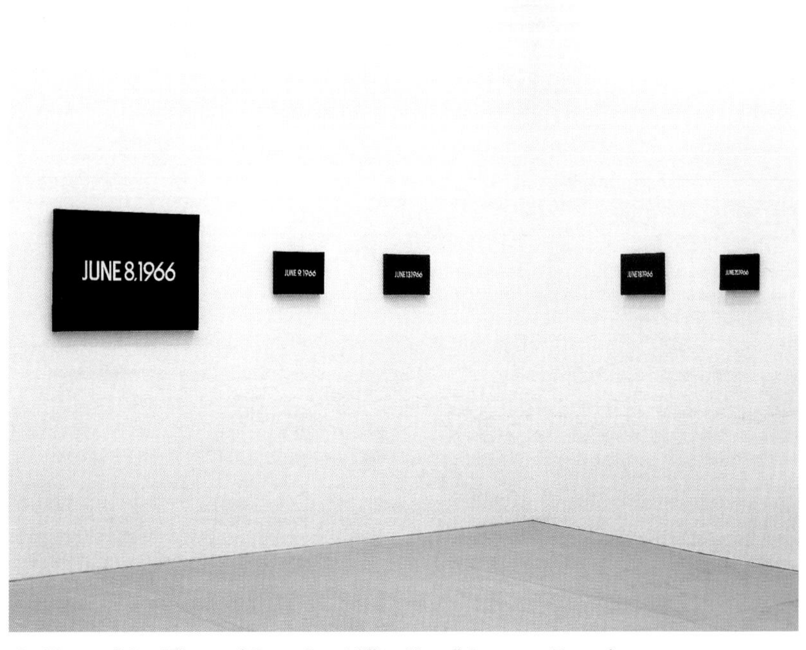

On Kawara, "One Thousand Days One Million Years," January 1–December 31, 1993.

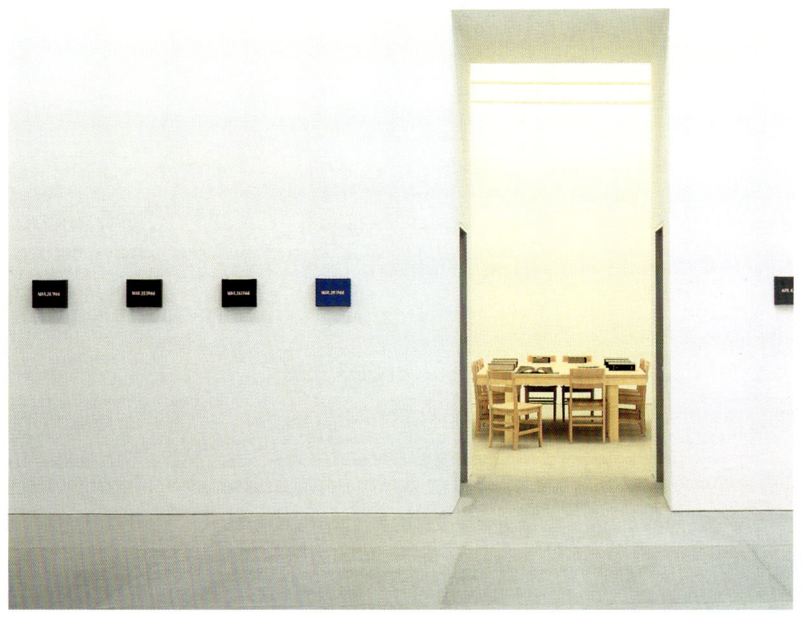

On Kawara, “One Thousand Days One Million Years,” January 1–December 31, 1993.

Ann Hamilton, *tropos*, October 7, 1993–June 19, 1994.

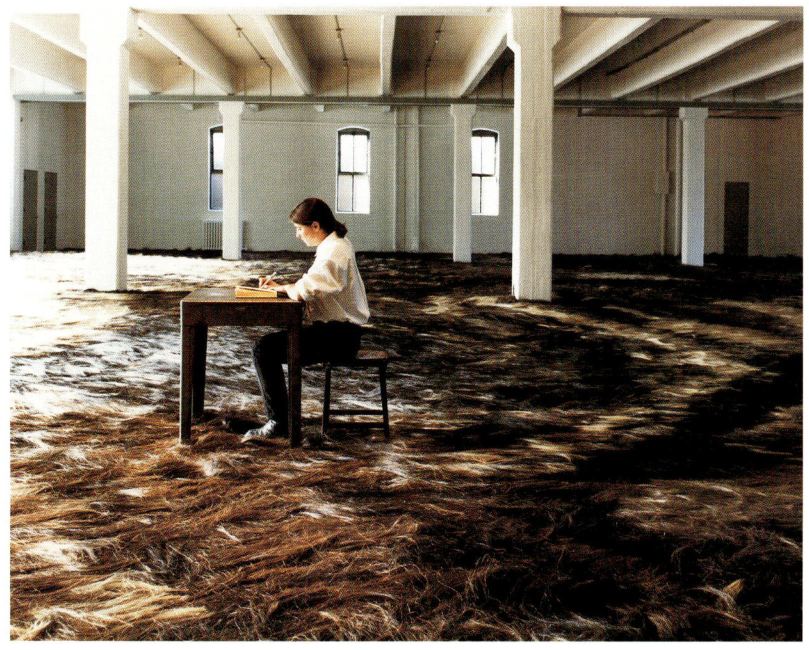

Ann Hamilton, *tropos*, October 7, 1993–June 19, 1994.

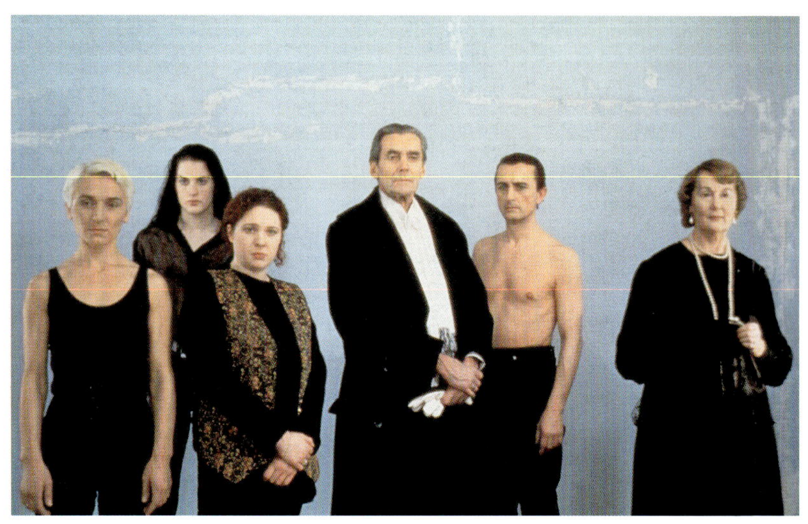

James Coleman, *I N I T I A L S*, 1994, from the exhibition "James Coleman—Projected Images: 1972–1994," April 19, 1994–March 12, 1995.

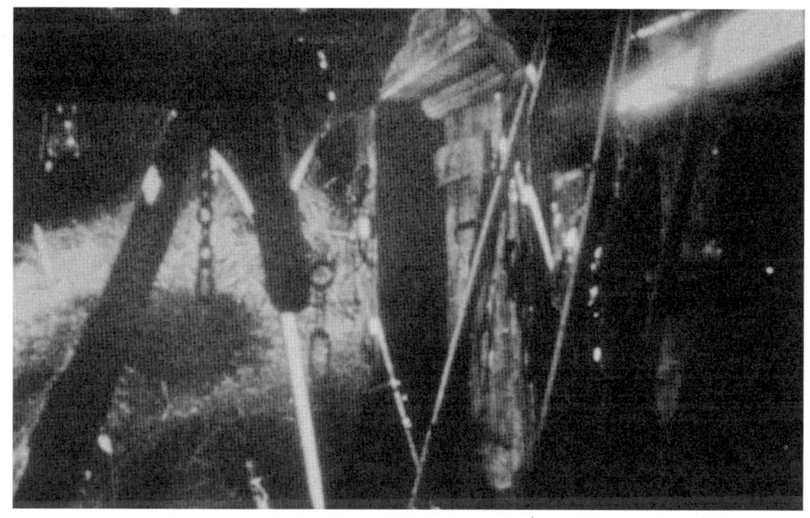

James Coleman, *La Tache Aveugle*, 1978–1990, from the exhibition "James Coleman—Projected Images: 1972–1994," April 19, 1994–March 12, 1995.

Lawrence Weiner: "Displacement"

ANNE RORIMER

Lawrence Weiner came to the radical conclusion in the late 1960s that language could function in lieu of other materials typically associated with making works of art. Since 1968, Weiner has exhibited works that rely on language to be the very substance of the message it delivers, existing as the means to its own end: the production of meaning. While the thematic content of individual works by Weiner derives from the import of words, the presentational format and exhibition context always play major supporting roles. The six works that comprised the exhibition "Displacement" bear witness to Weiner's varied and extensive oeuvre. A brief overview of his career will provide a basis for understanding his contribution to recent aesthetic practice and a framework for considering the significance of "Displacement."

Paintings and sculptures of the mid-1960s embodied references to their own condition as objects within those aesthetic categories. A work like Roy Lichtenstein's *Little Big Painting* (1965), for example, instead of representing an expressive condition or exterior reality, is a flat representation comprised of depersonalized brushstrokes. Similarly Donald Judd's sculptures, stripped of extraneous compositional or figurative elements, thematically address the volumetric wholeness of sculpture per se. At the same time, in the interest of reinvigorating sculptural and pictorial form, a number of artists had begun to reconsider the potential of language vis-à-vis the making of art. Robert Smithson's *A Heap of Language* (1966), for instance, consists of sequentially penciled words, such as "phraseology," "speech," "tongue," "lingo," "English," "dialect," "brogue," or "cipher," all of which relate to language itself. Formed into a moundlike shape, these words create visible form out of language, serving as material objects as well as signifiers. Bruce Nauman's work from this period also uses words to determine concrete, material form. As the color photographs *Eating My Words* or *Waxing Hot* from Nauman's portfolio Eleven Photographs (1966–67) suggest, language, with its potential for double meanings, need not only be used to represent something but can itself be the subject of representation. In *Eating My Words*, the word "words," cut out of bread and spread with jam, is self-reflexively consumed by the artist; the word "hot," in the form of a painted wooden sculpture, is being polished. Works by Joseph Kosuth from his Art as Idea as Idea series (1967) go even further in giving autonomy to language. In these works, comprised of enlarged photostatted dictionary definitions, language is treated like a found object. Moreover, language asserts itself as exactly that which it describes: it is both a verbal description and a photographic depiction of words.

The work of Lawrence Weiner utilizes language *as is*—that is to say, not in predetermined association with any other material support or contextual framework. The words of each work are their own material; they are not subordinate to and do not need to answer to a specific, tangible, physical format for their existence. Nonetheless, while existing exclusively as linguistic constructions, they are designed to be understood as sculpture. As early as 1960, Weiner had begun to challenge the traditional assumptions underlying painting and sculpture. Although nothing remains from his early Cratering Pieces, executed in Mill Valley, California, in 1960, we know that they consisted of gigantic holes in the ground caused by explosions of dynamite. These explosions were conducted by the artist in a youthful attempt to expand the conventional boundaries of sculpture, literally as well as theoretically. By making huge hollows in the ground instead of objects, Weiner sought to test the professed

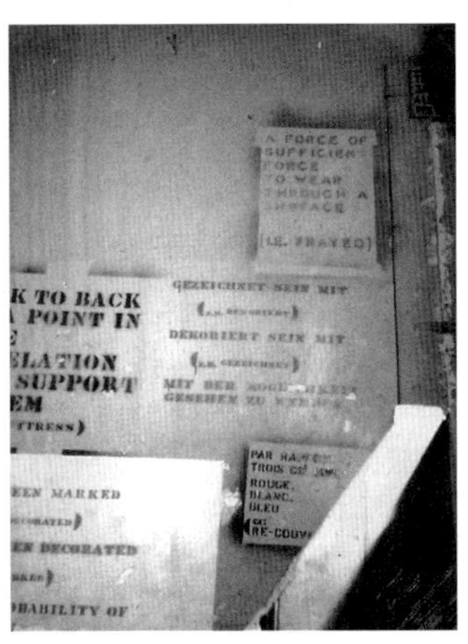

Lawrence Weiner's hallway at 13 Bleecker Street, New York City.

definitions of sculpture as an object contained by its own physical nature within a circumscribed, physical space.[1]

An early untitled work by Weiner consisted only of a partially carved limestone block (dated 1960–62, it now exists in its remade form only). The importance of this block of stone lies in the special relevance Weiner has assigned to it with respect to his initial thinking about art. Perplexed by sculpture's enforced singularity and its confinement to an existence in one time and place, he had not yet found an alternative to this condition. Having chipped away at it for long stretches of time without determinate results, Weiner perceived the block as a record of what simply amounted to ongoing activity. According to the artist, the block helped him to define that "sculpture was about 'put in place' volume or mass," further explaining that "you move it from one place to the other."[2]

In 1964 at the Seth Siegelaub Gallery in New York, Weiner exhibited a series of paintings he called "Propeller Paintings" because of their propellerlike images derived from television test patterns.[3] They are notable for their emphatically colored, blade-shaped forms that overstep the limits of the surrounding rectangle. Here, the painted image tentatively attempts to transgress the boundaries of its own rectilinear format. Some five years later, in a radio symposium, Weiner recalled, "the picture-frame convention was a very real thing. The painting stopped at that edge. When you are dealing with language, there is no edge that the picture drops over or drops off. You are dealing with something completely infinite."[4]

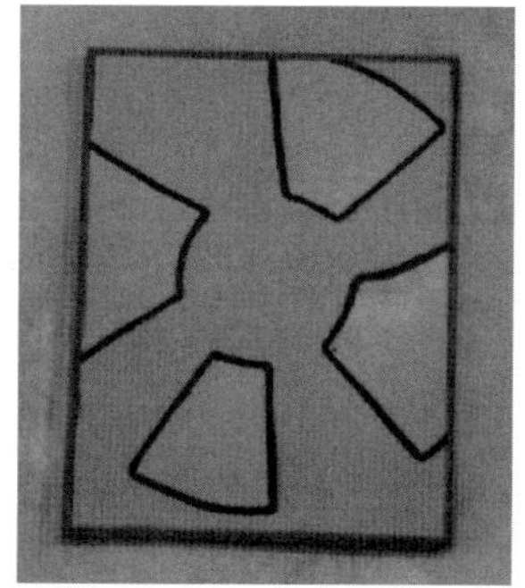

Lawrence Weiner, *Untitled*, 1964.

After the Propeller Paintings, Weiner embarked on a series of paintings that would be his last in the traditional sense of painting as a flat, extant object affixed to the wall. These paintings challenged the requisite uniqueness of a painting or sculpture. In every instance, Weiner violated the painting's rectilinearity by removing a rectangular chunk from its edge. Then he covered the canvas surface with spray paint and added bands of another color to the work's top and/or bottom, as he was trying to create a work as mechanically as possible, and thereby to cover his tracks as the author of the painting. Weiner also asked each prospective owner to select the size and color of the work in the interest of making works that were virtually alike. Yet, he was still left with unique art objects that could not function, as he would have wished, as pure "visual information."[5] Their unavoidable uniqueness inevitably linked them to monetary value.

A one-person exhibition at the Seth Siegelaub Gallery in December 1968 marked Weiner's departure from previously accepted methods of making and exhibiting art. The exhibition was comprised of twenty-four works that, divided into the "general" and the "specific," were printed one to a page in a palm-sized gray book titled *Statements.* Some works had been previously sold and/or constructed and, taken together, suggest the range of content in Weiner's art at that time. There were pieces involving specified materials and their handling, such as *ONE SHEET OF PLYWOOD SECURED TO THE FLOOR OR WALL*, and ones that were more involved with action taken, as in the case of *A DYE MARKER THROWN INTO THE SEA.* Of major note is the fact that the works were shown *only* within the context of the publication and not in any other presentational manner.

Earlier, in the spring of 1968, Weiner had realized that physical construction of his works in language need not be a requirement of the finished work. In the process of installing a sculpture for the now historic outdoor exhibition "Carl Andre, Robert Barry, Lawrence Weiner" (conceived by Chuck Ginnever, organized by Siegelaub, and held on the grounds of Windham College in Putney, Vermont), Weiner discovered that he had placed his work in a vulnerable location.[6] The piece was *A SERIES OF STAKES SET IN THE GROUND AT REGULAR INTERVALS TO FORM A RECTANGLE—TWINE STRUNG FROM STAKE TO STAKE TO DEMARK A GRID—A RECTANGLE REMOVED FROM THIS RECTANGLE.*[7] Weiner decided that, despite any physical damage, the sculpture would remain intact by virtue of the fact that it had been formulated entirely in language by way of the descriptive phraseology, which at this time accompanied and had become a part of his work.

Soon thereafter, Weiner devised the text that has accompanied presentations of his work ever since.[8] It reads:

> The artist may construct the piece.
> The piece may be fabricated.
> The piece need not be built.
> Each being equal and consistent with the intent of the artist, the decision as to condition rests with the receiver upon the occasion of receivership.

By means of this statement, the artist has left the actual, physical realization of any one of his works to the discretion of the person receiving the work, whether that is a spectator, an owner, an exhibitor, or the artist himself. *A SQUARE REMOVAL FROM A RUG IN USE*, for example, was constructed indoors in a home. Weiner went to the owners' residence in Cologne at their request, and cut a square section out of the rug. He thereby created a lacuna rather than, more typically, adding a new objet d'art to their collection. In the spring of 1969, *RESIDUE OF A FLARE ON A BOUNDARY* was implemented by the artist outdoors, under the auspices of the Stedelijk Museum, Amsterdam, for the exhibition "Op Losse Schroeven: Situaties en Cryptostructuren" ("Square Pegs in Round Holes: Structures and Cryptostructures").

For the most part, however, Weiner's works since 1969 have remained in their linguistic state.[9] Generally, these take the form of phrases spelled out on a wall using commercially available, black adhesive Letraset or by using stenciled, drawn, or painted lettering—often in block letters, in recent years. In one of its presentations, the first work in *Statements*, *ONE QUART EXTERIOR GREEN INDUSTRIAL ENAMEL THROWN ON A BRICK WALL*, was applied to an actual brick wall—just as if the enamel had been thrown on (making overt the clear reference to action painting in the work's content). Like the Windham College piece, the majority of Weiner's early works, including those appearing in *Statements*, specify their material form and the manner of their assembly or tions, as in *TRIED AND TRUE, TO THE SEA*, and *WITHOUT OR WITHIN.*

But even while Weiner reduced the verbal content of certain works, he increased their potential for embracing multiple interpretations. Whereas certain works pertain to delimited physical procedures, others are much less explicit. Compare *ONE FLUORESCEIN SEA MARKER POURED INTO THE SEA* to *AND THEN THERE WERE NONE* or *AS IF IT HAD BEEN.* Whereas the fluorescein marker piece stipulates the exact nature of its components, the other two works allow considerable room for individual interpretation. If the phrase "and then there were none" is understood to indicate removal—of whatever and how many of them—"as if it had been" suggests simulation of something that could have existed in any particular form. The fact of prior and conditional being engenders unlimited speculation as to what might be visualized.

For the most part, Weiner's early works represent physically contained, painterly or sculptural situations of a somewhat traditional nature. They may be as discrete as *6 TEN PENNY COMMON NAILS DRIVEN INTO FLOOR AT INDICATED TERMINAL POINTS* or *A 2" WIDE 1" DEEP TRENCH CUT ACROSS A STANDARD ONE CAR DRIVEWAY*, or as dramatic as *A FIELD CRATERED BY STRUCTURED SIMULTANEOUS TNT EXPLOSIONS.* In contrast, his works from about 1970, such as *A CITY DRAGGED*, are less finite in relation to conventional forms of sculpture and its norms of display.[11] Later works, especially those without a grammatical subject, expand the content of previous modes of painting and sculpture in order to express the properties, behavior, or functions of materials, objects, or empirical phenomena.

Weiner treats language in a neutral way as the means to objectively impart information about the verifiable, external world. While certain works are more concrete than others, all of them are grounded in the actuality of observable qualities, processes, conditions, actions, substances, or things. Thus, a piece like *FROM MAJOR TO MINOR/FROM SMALL TO LARGE/[OFTEN FOUND] WITHIN THE CONTEXT OF EFFECTIVENESS*, without explicitly defining an object or entity, is nonetheless physically definitive. Encompassing the multiple facets of reality, Weiner's art deals with both nature and society, but a significant proportion of his works are concerned with aspects of the natural world. Several refer to the surface of the earth (*A BLACK MARK UPON THE EARTH* or *OVER A CRACK IN THE CRUST TO THE OTHER SIDE*), to bodies of water (*A RUBBER BALL THROWN ON THE SEA* or *A DIRECT AFFRONT TO A NATURAL WATERWAY*), to climate (*A GROUPING OF THAT WHICH IS CONNECTED WITH USE IN A TEMPERATE CLIMATE*).

Other works, however, apply to social realities rather than nature. *A SQUARE REMOVAL FROM A RUG IN USE* possesses different connotations from *A TRIANGULAR REMOVAL FROM A TREE,* though both have to do with ideas about shape and alteration.

The intrusion of society into nature underlies an early work titled *3 MINUTES OF 40 lb. PRESSURE SPRAY OF WHITE HIGHWAY PAINT UPON A WELL TENDED LAWN/THE LAWN IS ALLOWED TO GROW AND NOT TENDED TILL THE GRASS IS FREE OF ALL VESTIGES OF WHITE HIGHWAY PAINT.* The words "well tended" invest this particular piece with associations that speak for themselves as to social propriety. A number of years later, in a series of connected works, Weiner distilled certain observations about the place of art in society into generalized phrases that served as the titles of four works: *MADE UNSUITABLE, PUT OUT OF PLACE, CATERED,* and *NOT QUITE DONE.* Furthermore, the four pieces, shown together in 1976 under the heading "WITH RELATION TO THE VARIOUS MANNERS WITH VARIOUS THINGS" allude to circumstances of nonacceptance, dislocation, subservience, and inadequacy.

Weiner's art has at times reflected the idea of political or geographical division. A number of pieces touch on the question of territorial demarcation and, in the process, overcome such separation, such as a relatively early work *AN OBJECT TOSSED FROM ONE COUNTRY TO ANOTHER.* Succeeding pieces address the fact of instated boundaries more directly. *THE RESIDUE OF A FLARE IGNITED UPON A BOUNDARY* remains general, but *THE JOINING OF FRANCE GERMANY AND SWITZERLAND BY*

ROPE or *AN EQUILATERAL ROPE TRIANGLE HAVING BASEL SWITZERLAND GERMANY AND FRANCE AS POINTS* draw the concept of country into the body of the work—not as a political statement but as part of the work's fabrication.

The immense flexibility of language endows Weiner's art with its broad thematic scope. On the one hand, a work by Weiner may operate on a global scale (as witnessed by *REMOVALS HALFWAY BETWEEN THE EQUATOR AND THE NORTH POLE*) and, for all its unfeasibility, be "down to earth" in its concerns. On the other hand, seemingly intangible subjects are rendered concrete through language: *A TRANSLATION FROM ONE LANGUAGE TO ANOTHER* loses its abstract character by virtue of its formulation in material terms.[12] In other works, such as *AN ACCUMULATION OF INFORMATION TAKEN FROM HERE TO THERE* and *AN AMOUNT OF CURRENCY EXCHANGED FROM ONE COUNTRY TO ANOTHER*, an abstract quantity—whether of currency or of information—is converted into a linguistic communication that has been transformed into a representation.

Referential and self-referential at the same time, Weiner's works are what they describe. For this reason, they contend with the subject of their own nature. This is true whether he is dealing with the nature of their inherent properties (as with *RED/AS WELL AS GREEN/AS WELL AS BLUE*), the nature of action exerted by or upon them (as in *THE RATE OF ATTRACTION OF ONE OBJECT TOWARDS ANOTHER AS DETERMINED BY THE DEGREE OF ENCUMBRANCE EXPERIENCED BY EACH OBJECT*), or the nature of their situation (as in *LEFT HERE/PUT THERE/FOR A LIMITED TIME*). The verbal components in Weiner's works—in these cases applied to color, force, and position—not only portray abstract or physical entities in themselves but often include those elements or processes that contribute to the making of art. Weiner's *SOME LEAD TO STAND ON/SOME LEAD TO THROW/SOME LEAD TO HOLD* brings to mind Richard Serra's *Casting* (1969), formed by the successive throwing of molten lead into the angular intersection between floor and wall. Weiner evokes the inherent physicality of lead, which can be stood

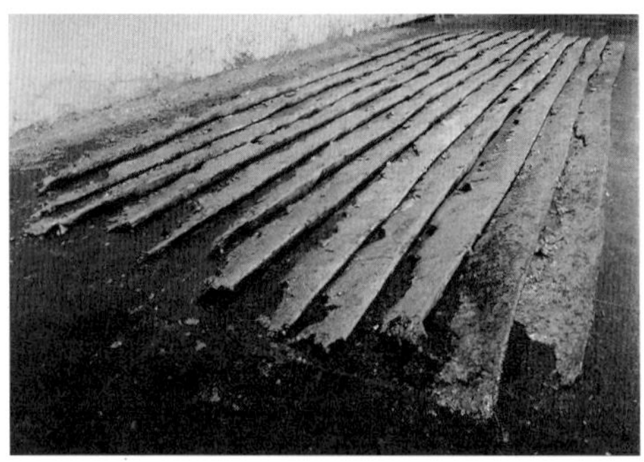

Richard Serra, *Casting*, 1969.

on, held, or thrown, and allows the work to proclaim its own sculptural attributes. Other works in this series involve reference to materials as diverse as wood, glass, and gold.

Weiner sometimes permits the ambiguities of language to enter his work by encouraging the deliberate double meanings found in well-known expressions or figures of speech. By presenting these phrases in isolation, the artist allows the literalizing propensity of language to take over in such pieces as *AROUND THE BEND*, *OVER THE HILL*, or *BESIDE THE POINT*. Free-floating metaphoric associations are not suppressed in these works. Rather, the ability of identical words to produce different levels or kinds of meaning is acknowledged as a means to further enrich a work. However, Weiner does not claim to be investigating the vagaries of language.[13] Instead, he seeks to gain access to all available modes of verbal expression so as to delineate and shape any and all aspects of concrete reality.

Although in principle works by Weiner may be materially constructed, in all cases they first must be registered in the mind's eye and grasped with respect to their linguistic specifications. Because of the way they are embodied in language, they are never conclusive descriptions subject to one static mode of mental or physical perception. And, just as they may be visualized in any number of ways, their presentational format is variable. A work may be delivered vocally—on a tape or record or as part of a film—or made visually manifest by use of the written word. Upon its materialization as text, the work becomes objectified.

While Weiner's first exhibitions took the form of statements in books, after 1972 he began to use the walls of exhibition spaces.[14] Around that time, Count Panza di Biumo, a contemporary art collector in Milan, asked Weiner's permission to transfer several of the artist's works onto the walls of his home, using a system of lettering devised by his architect.[15] Before this request, Weiner had conceived of his works as simply existing on typed sheets of paper. For exhibitions, he had generally pinned the texts to the wall.[16]

The mode of inscribing each work onto the surface of the wall affects its material aspect without interfering with its inherent content. Decisions about lettering, for example, influence a work's visual appearance just as would a frame or vitrine surrounding a physical object. The color, scale, layout, and manner of placing the lettering—at eye level, close to baseboards, or near the ceiling—vary according to the nature of the exhibition, and from piece to piece. Having initially underplayed the role of presentation in his work and still resisting the display of personalized skill in methods of presentation, Weiner has continued to explore different guises for staging his work.[17]

Weiner not only works within the boundaries of the traditionally defined exhibition space, but he was among the first to seek alternative presentational means. As he recently stated, his "major concern has been the use factor of art within a society," and he believes that art "is an attempt to place material which could be used to enrich the daily lives of other human beings."[18] In the late 1960s, in an attempt to reach beyond the confines of the institutional art space, Weiner anonymously stenciled or chalked works onto surfaces in public places or tacked unsigned posters of works on walls around the city. Also, in addition to presenting pieces in books or on posters, which he has designed himself, Weiner has printed many of his works on ephemeral objects not usually associated with the display of fine art.[19] To stress the idea that his art is meant to escape the exclusivity of private possession, he has shown work on and as emblematic stickers, plaques, plates, matchbooks, pins, and other nonprecious, nonart items. Books, posters, and ephemeral items contribute to the democratic principle behind Weiner's aesthetic practice inasmuch as they allow for a greater circulation of the work.[20] Whether set within the conventional exhibition space or inserted into unorthodox visual frameworks, Weiner's work, participating in the discourse of art but functioning

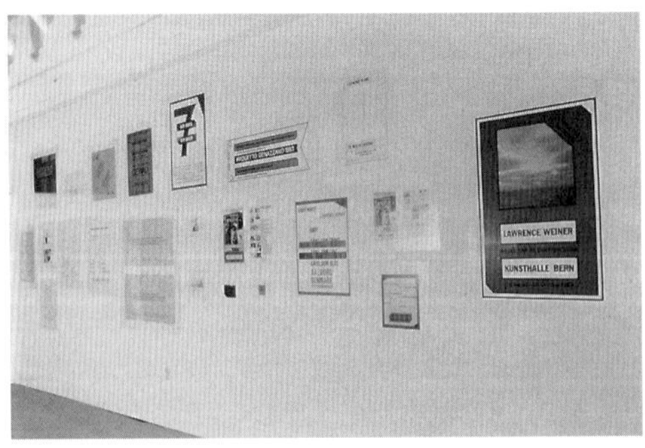

The Lawrence Weiner Poster Archive, Anna Leonowens Gallery, Nova Scotia College of Art and Design, Halifax, 1983.

as language, succeeds in establishing diverse ways of interacting with the culture at large.

All of Weiner's works bond with their physical contexts without being bound by them. Context does not dictate the form of his works, as it does for artists deliberately working with immediate reference to a site, but it may influence the reading of a work. For example, in 1980, Weiner printed *BROKEN OFF*—a work already extensively exhibited—in metallic blue on the upper-left-hand corner of glossy black-and-yellow matchbook covers.[21] As almost anything from tree branches to negotiations can be "broken off," the specific placement of the work fosters one possible understanding of this phrase but does not exclude it from other, future contextualizations.

Additional examples of the impact of context underline how Weiner engenders interchange between the content of a work and the conditions of its placement without fixing any one interpretation. A two-part work conceived for his exhibition at the Leo Castelli Gallery, New York, in 1974 was worded as follows:

BEING WITHIN THE CONTEXT OF REACTION:
UP ON [IN] THE AIR
DOWN ON [IN] THE GROUND

UP ON [IN] THE AIR
DOWN ON [IN] THE GROUND
BEING WITHIN THE CONTEXT OF [A] REACTION

As inscribed on the gallery walls, the work opened a dialogue between itself, its physical context, and its viewers, while having verbally built in the additional context of "reaction," in general, and "a reaction," in particular.[22] Finding themselves within the context of an important contemporary art gallery, located on the second floor of a building and dedicated to the most recent developments in art, visitors might have made a connection between themselves at the moment of confronting this piece upstairs and their reaction to it upon their return to the street. No more than proposing such a reaction in and of itself, the work renders countless variants equally valid.

The geographical context of a work also has bearing on the possible ways of viewing it. A piece created for presentation in Chicago in 1978 invoked the Chicago River[23] that, among other things, can be

> LAID OUT FLAT
> BENT [NOW] THIS WAY
> TURNED [NOW] THAT WAY
> (in effect LOOPED OVER)

For a solo exhibition in Columbus, Ohio, Weiner composed works whose elements corresponded to the properties of the Great Serpent Mound in the Ohio River Valley. Entitled "Mounds & Smooth Cairns," the exhibition referred specifically to the ancient ceremonial formations that grace the nearby area, and included *SOFT MASSES PLACED AND PRESSED TO RISE ABOVE THE SURFACE OF THE EARTH* and *STONE AFTER STONE TO FORM A BRIDGE*.[24] Once again, although conceived for one situation, the work itself retains its adaptability, as witnessed by the reappearance of *STONE AFTER STONE TO FORM A BRIDGE* at the Paris Biennale of 1985. There, the text was discreetly stenciled in yellow

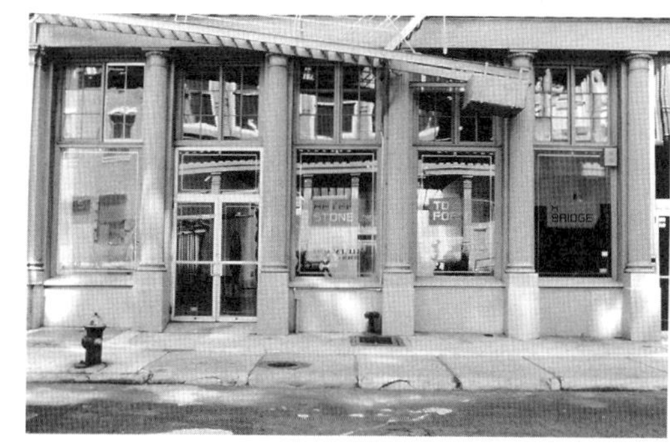

Lawrence Weiner, *STONE AFTER STONE TO FORM A BRIDGE*, Leo Castelli Gallery, New York, 1983.

letters on a stone sculpture installed in front of the exhibition hall at the request of the sculptor himself, thus slanting the words toward another, specific reading.[25] Two years before, this work had been displayed in the window of the Leo Castelli Gallery on Greene Street where it functioned as an interface between the outside and inside of the gallery, as both exterior window dressing *and* the gallery's exhibited content.

Another work that has changed its manner and place of display more than once is *MANY COLORED OBJECTS PLACED SIDE BY SIDE TO FORM A ROW OF MANY COLORED OBJECTS.* Originally made for an exhibition at the Castelli Gallery in 1979, the work soon thereafter entered a group exhibition of recent American art at the Art Institute of Chicago. Several years later, it was featured in Documenta 7 in Kassel, Germany. Instead of installing this piece in the galleries—along with the hundreds of other works selected for this large international exhibition by a team of organizers—Weiner elected to inscribe it above the entrance of the eighteenth-century building used for the exhibition. Giving the impression of being an inscription of universal wisdom that might typically adorn the architecture of the period, the work appeared as if it had always been part of the facade. The same piece was also printed on a removable paper band encircling the exhibition's two-volume catalogue.

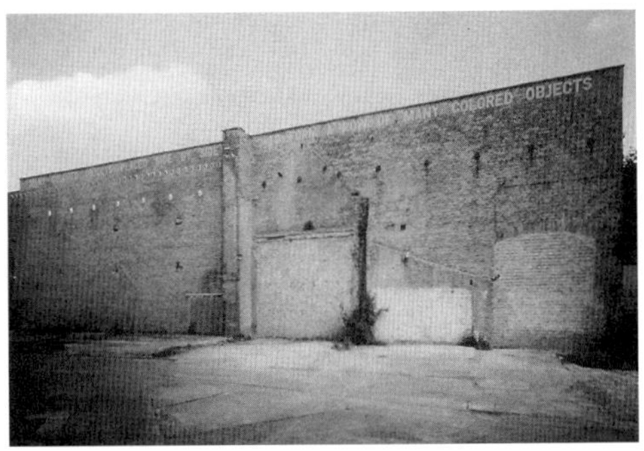

Lawrence Weiner, *MANY COLORED OBJECTS PLACED SIDE BY SIDE TO FORM A ROW OF MANY COLORED OBJECTS*, 1979.

Like every other work by Weiner, *MANY COLORED OBJECTS...* functions as a paradigm of its own construction (with the exact number, color, or placement of objects remaining open) and comments as well on its own immediate circumstance. In Kassel, where the piece subtly lorded over the extensive grouping of works, the reference to the eclectic exhibition could not be missed. Now, in a private collection in Belgium, this work has been painted in blue letters atop a high brick wall where it may be seen outside of the window of its owners' living room in conjunction with the paintings and sculptures of other artists that must be accommodated indoors.[26]

Lawrence Weiner, *AN ARCH AFFORDED IN A WALL OF STONE WITH A KEYSTONE OF CHALK & IMPOSTS OF SLATE,* sticker made for Transmission Gallery, Glasgow, 1991.

By using language to create specific works with their manifold unspecified applications and potential for ubiquitous placement, Weiner frees his work from sole reliance on a particular space. Because of the open-ended, linguistic content of his work, it may be viewed within the structured context of galleries, museums, or private collections, or it may surface outside of this context as well. "Art institutionalizes itself," the artist maintains.[27] Space, for Weiner, means the "entire cultural context," as opposed to "an aesthetically contracted space."[28] Thus rooted in the culture, his works may be uprooted from one situation and transplanted in others. The shifting contexts in which they are shown alter the frames of reference through which his works may be seen. In the final analysis, it is viewers who, informed by both the general cultural context and the particular context in which a work is implanted, determine the work's meaning.

In the fall of 1991, Weiner was invited by the city of Vienna to make a temporary work. The site assigned to him was one of the huge concrete defense towers still remaining from World War II. Weiner chose to use a previously conceived piece, which he painted in two-meter–high silver letters, outlined in black, on a white background on the top of the tower. The tower itself is extremely overbearing and looms—rather bleakly and menacingly—over the houses in the neighborhood. The work, in English on two sides of the tower and in German on the other two sides, reads

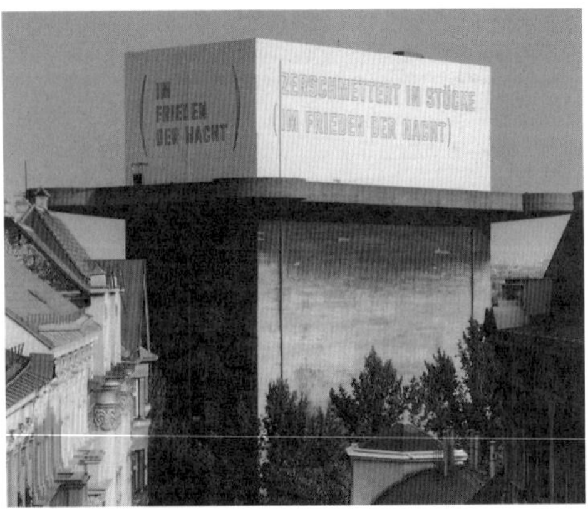

Lawrence Weiner, *SMASHED TO PIECES [IN THE STILL OF THE NIGHT]*, Vienna Arts Festival (defense tower in Esterházypark), 1991.

SMASHED TO PIECES [IN THE STILL OF THE NIGHT]. In German, the word "still," which in English means "calm," also means "peace." Although Weiner's installation designs and color schemes are generally arbitrary, for this work, they were not. The colors of the lettering alluded directly to the colors of the SS uniforms worn by the German troops. If the phrase "smashed to pieces in the still of the night" conjures up various juxtapositions of violence and quiet, the Viennese context emphatically engenders specific associations with the destruction wrought by the Second World War.

While thematically addressing the three-dimensional material world, Weiner's works do not impinge on three-dimensional space. A series of five works for a 1987 exhibition at the Arts Club of Chicago titled "5 Figures of Structure" nonetheless and paradoxically directly addressed sculptural monumentality. One of the pieces, inscribed in large letters outlined in charcoal, read "*ONE SLAB PUT TOP TO BUTT OF ANOTHER SLAB SET ABOVE ANOTHER SLAB SET TOP TO BUTT WITH THE GROUND.*" All the works in the exhibition spoke about slabs put in relation to each other and in relation to the ground. Since a slab is one of the fundamental units of architectural construction, the five Arts Club works were about building in its most basic state. But a slab, as a form of marker, can also refer to a tombstone or monument. In decisive contrast with their thematic content, the works blended in with the surrounding interior walls. They denied their own potential as sculpture insofar as they lacked not only three-dimensionality but also impositional or overbearing monumentality.[29]

The six individual works in the Dia Center for the Arts exhibition placement. The works *ONE SHEET OF PLYWOOD SECURED TO THE FLOOR OR WALL* and *ONE SHEET OF TRANSPARENT PLASTIC SECURED TO THE FLOOR OR WALL* set definite parameters with respect to what might be located where. In dividing his works in *Statements* between the "general" and the "specific," Weiner thus distinguished between pieces that involve more detailed definitions than others. For example, *ONE SHEET OF CLEAR PLEXIGLAS OF ARBITRARY SIZE AND THICKNESS SECURED AT THE FOUR CORNERS AND EXACT CENTER BY SCREWS TO THE FLOOR* is more precise as to where it is to be fastened than the two preceding pieces, and *ONE 14 OZ. AEROSOL CAN OF ENAMEL SPRAYED TO CONCLUSION DIRECTLY UPON THE FLOOR* gives more specific information than simply *AN AMOUNT OF PAINT POURED DIRECTLY UPON THE FLOOR AND ALLOWED TO DRY.* Whether general or specific, however, a work by Weiner can exist at any time—or the same work may be on view simultaneously in different locations—no matter what its size or what amount of material is required, or how it is supposed to be carried out.[10]

A study of Weiner's work in its purely linguistic state shows how he has put language to use as a material. In so doing, he has made literal fabrication "immaterial" to the perception of individual pieces. While words account for the content of the work, the rules of grammar provide a structural framework. Weiner's works rely mostly on verbs (in the form of participles, past participles, or infinitives), as well as adjectives, adverbs, or prepositions. Taken either singly or in combination, these parts of speech convey action, condition, or change in states of being. Works may also include subjects denoting things and indirect objects denoting how or where, such as *A WALL STAINED BY WATER* or *A CUP OF SEA WATER POURED UPON THE FLOOR.* Other works, such as *A RIVER SPANNED,* dispense with the indirect object. And by 1970, works like *IGNITED, FERMENTED,* or *DISPLACED* had eliminated all but the verb. While Weiner's subsequent works have often continued to be comprised of long phrases, in other cases, they have been pared down to minimal verbal or adverbial designa-

"Displacement" together encapsulate Weiner's essential working approach and outlook. Already by 1968, Weiner had articulated the idea of sculpture as a displacement rather than a placement. At a symposium at Windham College in Vermont, held in connection with the 1968 outdoor sculpture exhibition mentioned earlier, Weiner stated,

> The idea of building a piece of sculpture outdoors has always intrigued me...I'd liken it to walking in the woods, when you come upon a gravestone that is half buried. Now, if a piece of sculpture can exist within a landscape in that sense, whatever is around the landscape is heightened and brought out. It's a matter of what you can displace with what you are doing to the place.[30]

In short, making sculpture for Weiner is more a question of displacement than of placement, since addition implies subtraction. That is to say, the placement of one element of/in the w/hole involves the removal of another and vice versa.

At Dia, Weiner underlined the fact that the six pieces made expressly for this exhibition were grouped together within the specified confines of a particular installation—in other words, that their manifestation on the walls of this institution was staged. To mark the entryway into the exhibition, he provided what might be described as a fashion runway or hopscotch gameboard, to establish the mise-en-scène. A departure in his installation methods, this floor piece served as a special display feature, allowing visitors to "jump into" viewing the works. It also provided a pointed yet off-the-cuff reference to money and exhibitions, as well as to the conception of art as a game with a particular set of rules. Weiner also painted his standard statement of intent on the floor. Numbers, separating the three main points of the statement, assumed an independent visual presence against their respective rectangular spaces. Only the phrase "each being equal and consistent…," treated parenthetically, was excerpted from the concluding sentence of the statement. Parentheses—sometimes used in other works demarcated and represented the physical space by means of a textual sign.

To tie the gallery elements together, Weiner numbered the columns sequentially and signified their separateness by also painting ampersands on each one. The designated portions of the architecture thus retained their discreteness while simultaneously being linked together. Sign and design merged with the totality of the work's presentational format. In this way, numbers, like words, functioned as both sign and symbol within the broader architectural framework of a literal and institutional structure and an all-encompassing presentational design. Although the six works included in the installation were made specifically for the Dia exhibition, the group may be broken up for individual inclusion in other exhibitions or for purchase on their own. With its endless possibilities for expressing concrete circumstances that might "present a semblance of a whole," the work *BITS & PIECES PUT TOGETHER TO PRESENT A SEMBLANCE OF A WHOLE* served as an introduction to "Displacement."

A silvery metal, working freight elevator door, existing within the exhibition area at Dia and conveniently divided into four sections, provided Weiner with a found backdrop for the presentation of four of the works. Painted in blue on the door, these works dealt with color, mass, and movement in one form or another. The upper-left-hand section contained *SAND & SILVER + FERROUS OXIDE / HAVING SPACE BY VIRTUE OF INHERENT MOVEMENT.* Ferrous oxide is a black, easily oxidizable powder made from iron that takes on a rusty cast. The upper-right-hand section contained *CADMIUM + MUD / DISPLACING BY VIRTUE OF INHERENT INSTABILITY.* Cadmium by itself is a bluish-white, malleable, ductile, toxic, bivalent metallic element used mainly in protective platings, but also in paint to produce a brilliant blue, yellow, or red color. *WATER + FERROUS CONCRETE / ENCOMPASSING BY VIRTUE OF INHERENT DENSITY* was painted on the lower-left-hand corner of the door. In this case, concrete contains iron and thus would be colored a brownish-red or terra-cotta hue. And in the lower right, Weiner painted *TITANIUM & LEAD + AIR / MOVING INTO BY VIRTUE OF INHERENT VOLITION.* Titanium, an element that is white when used in paint, and lead, a bluish-white metallic element, are both well known for their use in paint. Despite their chemical constitution, however, none of these works are representations of chemical reactions but are representations of material interactions.

According to Weiner, the representation of color was the reason for putting these materials together. As a grand finale for the exhibition, he strung together the names of materials associated with paint and paint color across the long stretch of wall beyond the elevator to read: *CADMIUM & MUD & TITANIUM & LEAD & FERROUS OXIDE & SO ON....* The guiding factor underlying his initial decision to refer to lead or titanium, for example, had to do with their light-producing capacity. While both of these are white, and while cadmium lends itself to the creation of bright primary colors, mud assumes an earthy tone as does ferrous oxide when it rusts. The four works on the elevator door highlighted the materialization of color. But, although it directly pertained to color and paint, the work should not, as Weiner himself has cautioned, be confused with painting as such.[31] Rather than taking the exhibition space for granted, Weiner took charge of the entire room at Dia as a receptacle for placing work. He thereby succeeded in explicitly elaborating upon and extending his usual procedures of presentation, which are tied in with and may echo—but ultimately are distinct from—the material content of the work being presented.[32]

Concomitant with the presentation inside of the architectural context of the exhibition space was the presentation of the works in the accompanying book. The publication served as a handbook or, in Weiner's words, a "field book" for the exhibition, and permitted the works to be portable. With its inclusion of preliminary, working drawings for the exhibition, it also may be considered a workbook. It offers additional and pertinent meditations by the artist such as *THE AMOUNT OF DISPLACEMENT IS DEPENDENT UPON THE SIZE OF THE HOLE AFFORDED.* In essence, the publication adapted the Dia installation to the space defined by the pages of a book—with numbers identified with chapters rather than columns, for example—and in this way it simultaneously records, contains, and presents that which it is as a book as well as that which it was as an *exhibition* and a grouping of works.

Since 1968, Lawrence Weiner has employed words as units of construction in the formation of works. These works are not about language nor is language, as a means, an end in itself. Even though the representational medium of language serves many causes within and outside of the realm of art, the final goal for Weiner is the making of art. Traditionally relegated to the separate domain of poetry and literature, language has been adopted by Weiner for use within the context of visual art as a vehicle for rendering insight into perceived reality. As the artist maintains,

> Art is not a metaphor upon the relationships of human beings to objects & objects in relation to human beings but a representation of an empirical existing fact. It does not tell the potential & capabilities of an object (material) but presents a reality concerning that relationship.[33]

The use of language, which may be placed anywhere while maintaining its visual and material autonomy, has made it possible for Weiner to redefine the conventional relationship between a material object and its spatial setting, without recourse to arbitrary gesture or personal expression. Without intruding into three-dimensional space in the manner of traditional sculpture, his works engage the endless facets of reality that they endeavor to expose and explicate. In resisting illusionistic modes of representation and escaping mandatory allocation to any one place, they reinterpret and reinvigorate the traditional categories of painting and sculpture while transcending the bifurcation of these terms.

March 26, 1992

NOTES

With special thanks for their comments to Cora Rosevear, Staci Boris, Andrea Kirsh, and Richard Quinn.

1. See Lynn Gumpert, "Lawrence Weiner: Interview by Lynn Gumpert," in *Lynda Benglis, Joan Brown, Luis Jimenez, Gary Stephan, Lawrence Weiner: Early Work* (New York: New Museum of Contemporary Art, 1982), p. 45. According to Weiner, "the craters came about as a way to make sculpture by the removal of something rather than by the normal intrusion of things."
2. Ibid., p. 49.
3. Interestingly enough, Donald Judd, as art critic for *Arts Magazine*, wrote, "[the] paintings work well. Weiner is able, but isn't on his own yet." See D.J. [Donald Judd], "Lawrence Weiner" [review: Siegelaub Gallery], *Arts Magazine* 39, no. 5 (January 1965), p. 64.
4. Lawrence Weiner, quoted in Lucy Lippard, ed., *Six Years: The Dematerialization of the Art Object from 1966 to 1972* (New York: Praeger Publishers, 1973), pp. 131–32.
5. Lawrence Weiner, quoted in Willoughby Sharp, "Lawrence Weiner at Amsterdam," *Avalanche* (Spring 1972), p. 71. Weiner's desire for pure "visual information" without contamination by commercialism should not be confused with the fact that his works are meant to be sold. Weiner does not rule out selling work, but rather endeavors to question preconceptions about the unique object of art and the factors that account for its "preciousness" and monetary worth such as whom it is by, its age and authenticity, availability, etc.
6. See Weiner's account in Lynn Gumpert, "Lawrence Weiner," p. 45.
7. This and all following works from the years 1967–77 are titled as listed in *Lawrence Weiner: Works* (Hamburg: Anatol Av and Filmproduktion, 1977).
8. See Benjamin H. D. Buchloh, ed., *Lawrence Weiner: Posters November 1965–April 1986* (Halifax: The Press of Nova Scotia College of Art and Design and Art Metropole, Toronto, 1987), p. 173. As Buchloh specifies in "The Posters of Lawrence Weiner," Weiner's so-called "declaration of intent" was published for the first time in *Art News* in the fall of 1968 before being published again in the catalogue for Seth Siegelaub's group exhibition, "January 5–31, 1969."
9. For the first exhibition of its kind, in which all works were realized by a variety of individuals, see *Lawrence Weiner: Werke & Rekonstructionen/Works and Reconstructions* (Bern: Kunsthalle Bern, 1983). Weiner explains: "All of the work that's been presented

publicly has the possibility of being built...I'm basically a studio artist. I play with materials, I'll build a piece...I see that as research." Quoted in Gumpert, "Lawrence Weiner," p. 50.

10. Weiner's works are dated according to the year of their first public presentation.

11. Weiner recounts that this work was carried out by him at the time. Having rented a boat for the day, he pulled a dragnet all around the city of Stockholm.

12. See Eric Cameron, "Lawrence Weiner: The Books," *Studio International* 187 (January 1974), p. 5. As Cameron suggests, the material referred to in this work is language itself.

13. Weiner works with translators in order to present work in other countries in languages other than English.

14. Weiner presented a work in the book *Carl Andre, Robert Barry, Douglas Huebler, Joseph Kosuth, Sol LeWitt, Robert Morris, Lawrence Weiner* (New York: Siegelaub/Wendler, 1968)—a group "exhibition" also known as the "Xeroxbook."

15. See Weiner's account in Gumpert, "Lawrence Weiner," p. 48.

16. For a one-person exhibition at the Leo Castelli Gallery in 1972, Weiner simply mounted the invitation card on the wall. During those years, his works were printed on the mailed announcement.

17. For his exhibition "Sculpture" at ARC/Musée d'Art Moderne de la Ville de Paris in 1985, Weiner used handwriting. This writing was not his own, however. Seeking to share the labor involved in "installing" a work, he succeeds in avoiding any intrusion of a personally expressive "touch" that might be traceable to the hand of the artist.

18. Lawrence Weiner, quoted in David Batchelor, "I Am Not Content: Lawrence Weiner interviewed by David Batchelor," *Artscribe International* 74 (March/April 1989), p. 50.

19. For an analysis of Weiner's early books, see Cameron, "Lawrence Weiner: The Books," pp. 2–8. See also Dieter Schwarz, *Catalogue Raisonné, Lawrence Weiner: Books 1968–1989* (Cologne: Verlag der Buchhandlung Walter König and Le Nouveau Musée, Villeurbanne, 1989).

20. See Buchloh, ed., *Lawrence Weiner: Posters November 1965–April 1986.*

21. The words were imprinted for Weiner by another artist, Louise Lawler, who had been using texts on matchbook covers as part of her work.

22. For a discussion of this work in relation to this exhibition, see Susan Heinemann, "Lawrence Weiner: Given the Context," *Artforum* 13, no. 7 (March 1975), pp. 36–37.

23. This work was exhibited at the Renaissance Society at the University of Chicago in 1978. See Naomi Gilman, "The Printed Brushstroke," *Grey City Art Journal* (3 February 1978), p. 7. According to Weiner, he "was fascinated by the idea that the Chicago River originally was made to swing around to accommodate the city's garbage flow."

24. See Edward Leffingwell, *Mounds & Smooth Cairns: An Exhibition by Lawrence Weiner* (Columbus: University Gallery, Ohio State University, 1984).

25. The sculptor was the German artist Ulrich Rückriem.

26. Weiner's oeuvre may simultaneously be owned privately and shared publicly (through publication and/or exhibition with the owner's permission). Weiner, however, has assigned a certain percentage of his works to a personally designated category of ownership titled "Collection Public Freehold." Works in this collection may not be purchased by an individual or institution since he has designated them as belonging to the common domain.

27. Lawrence Weiner, quoted in Robert C. Morgan, "A Conversation with Lawrence Weiner," *REALLIFE*, nos. 11/12 (Winter 1983), p. 36.

28. Lawrence Weiner, quoted in Sharp, "Lawrence Weiner at Amsterdam," p. 71.

29. Discussed further in Anne Rorimer, "Sculpture: Figures of Structure, the Work of Lawrence Weiner," in *5 Figures of Structure—Lawrence Weiner* (Chicago: The Arts Club of Chicago, 1987), n.p.

30. Lawrence Weiner, quoted in Lippard, ed., *Six Years*, p. 47. The symposium was moderated by Dan Graham, who began by saying, "One of the concepts I want to introduce is the idea of place."

31. Lawrence Weiner, telephone conversation with the author, March 1992.

32. As a humorous flourish, not as a work per se, Weiner labeled the two restroom doors next to each other with the words "us" and "them"—causing confusion in some cases!

33. Lawrence Weiner, quoted in Clive Phillpot, ed., "Words and Word Works (4 pages)," *Art Journal* (Summer 1982), p. 122.

"A Cold Coming": Brice Marden's Wager with Tradition

STEPHEN BANN

"A cold coming we had of it,
Just the worst time of the year
For a journey, and such a long journey:
The ways deep and the weather sharp,
The very dead of winter."
And the camels galled, soor-footed, refractory,
Lying down in the melting snow
There were times we regretted
The summer palaces on slopes, the terraces,
And the silken girls bringing sherbet.
Then the camel men cursing and grumbling
And running away, and wanting their liquor and women,
And the night-fires going out, and the lack of shelters,
And the cities hostile and the towns unfriendly
And the villages dirty and charging high prices:
A hard time we had of it.
At the end we preferred to travel all night,
Sleeping in snatches,
With the voices singing in our ears, saying
That this was all folly.

—T. S. Eliot, "Journey of the Magi" (1927)

The first five lines of "Journey of the Magi" are adapted by T. S. Eliot from a sermon by the English seventeenth-century divine Lancelot Andrewes and are printed with quotation marks in the text. Eliot incorporated the words without any overt acknowledgment, except for the slight strokes of those quotation marks. Moreover, he contrives an almost imperceptible transition from Andrewes's language to his own, maintaining the same cadences and the same studied diction, which is suspended between two worlds—that of the seventeenth-century bishop and that of the modernist poet. Why does Eliot engage in this half-veiled identification with a figure of the past? His well-known text "Tradition and Individual Talent," published seven years before "Journey of the Magi," suggests at least part of the answer.

In that earlier essay, Eliot inveighs against the myth—so tenacious in "English writing" at that time—that the valuable element in a poet's work is the individual or original component, that which differentiates it from its predecessors. On the contrary, Eliot maintains, "If we approach a poet without his [*sic*] prejudice we shall often find that not only the best, but the most individual parts of his work may be those in which the dead poets, his ancestors, assert their immortality most vigorously." Tradition, Eliot argues, is not something that can be taken for granted: "It cannot be inherited, and if you want it you must obtain it by great labor."[1] It is no paradox that "the historical sense" is the precondition of any valid contemporary statement. Or, as Eliot graphically puts it in a single formula: "No poet, no artist of any art, has his complete meaning alone."[2]

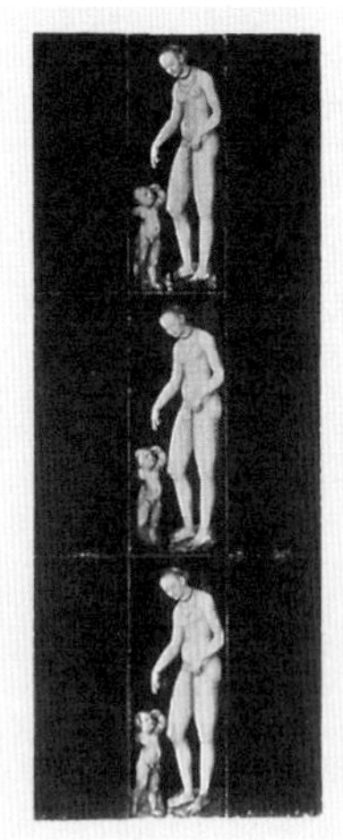

Brice Marden, *Homage to Art 13*, 1973.

My justification for starting this discussion in Eliot's territory resides only partly in the admission that he is talking not only about poets, but about "artist[s] of any art," but also in the fact that after art historian Meyer Schapiro defended Abstract Expressionism in his address "On the Humanity of Abstract Painting" (1960)[3] at a famous meeting of the American Academy of Arts and Letters, Marcel Duchamp developed his own defense of modern art from the basis of Eliot's "Tradition and Individual Talent." Most important in this connection, however, is the fact that Brice Marden's series Homage to Art, which I first saw in the mid-1970s, seems to put the artist's relation to tradition into an inescapably provocative and fascinating form, one that risks being dismissed as mere mannerist play with the icons of European classical painting. Marden's gesture could be viewed, as I suggested in 1976, as "a perpetual reshuffling of the cards of *Post-Renaissance* painting, a dealing of these cards across the table on which the 'modern' card is always fated to remain face down."[4] Yet the whole issue lies in whether indeed those cards *are* "face down"—whether or not the vibrant black graphite surfaces of the abstract rectangles not only balance but interpret and prolong the deep olive varnished ground color of Cranach's *Venus and Cupid* (1509) or the dusky tones of Goya's *Marquesa de Solana* (1794–95). To revert to Eliot's "Journey of the Magi" and to transpose the terms of comparison, does Marden's "quotation" set up its own cadences, its own diction suspended between two worlds, which defines the conventional limits of the two separate discourses, as do Eliot's quotation marks?

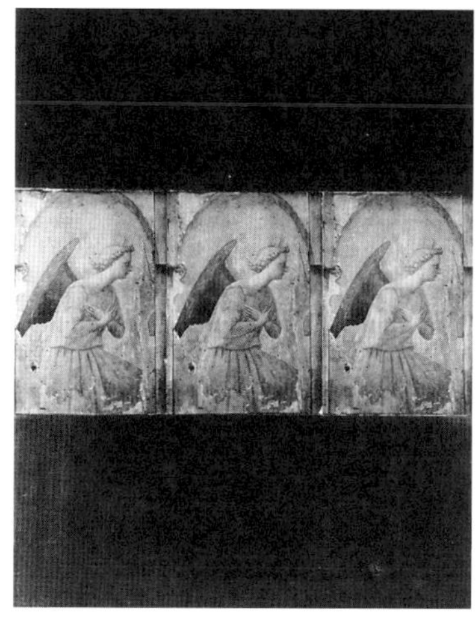

Brice Marden, *Homage to Art 14*, 1974.

This question places at the forefront of this discussion of the Cold Mountain series an issue that frames Marden's career to date and underlines the profound engagement of his art: How is a relationship to tradition, a "historical sense" as Eliot puts it, conveyed in a period that has ostensibly lost its free commerce with the symbols of past art? In 1960, art historian Meyer Schapiro spoke of a far-reaching change in what he called the "norm of the human," which had taken place over the course of time. In Schapiro's analysis, the transition is not simply away from a richly symbolic figuration toward an impoverished abstraction. As a vital transitional stage, lesser genres are vested with the values of humanity. "Not long ago only the heroic, the mythical, and religious were admitted to high art," Schapiro wrote. "But more recently, "it became clear

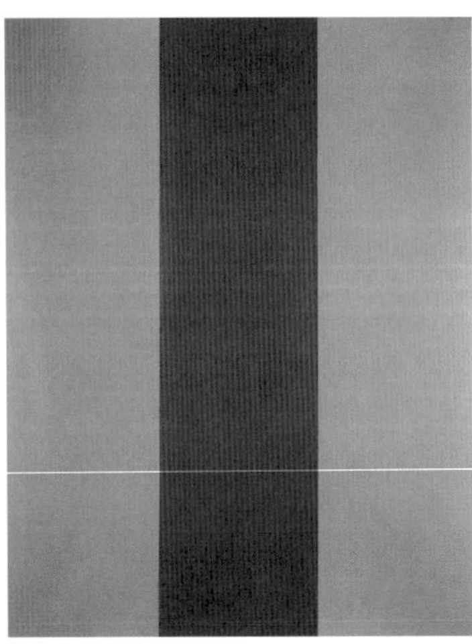

Brice Marden, *Pumpkin Plumb*, 1970/73.

that a scene of common life, a landscape or still life could be as great a painting as an image of history or myth."[5] It is this kind of argument that might underpin the character of Marden's early paintings from the 1970s, at least one like *Pumpkin Plumb* (1970/73) that has a title implying a connection with the genre of still life. For Schapiro, Cézanne in particular marked the coming of a post-classical mode, imposing "the conviction that in rendering the simplest objects, bare of ideal meanings, a series of colored patches can be a summit of perfection."[6] Works like Marden's *Pumpkin Plumb* might be seen as a striking example of this incorporation of the Cézanne tradition, adopting what might be called his change of key from the major to the minor mode. The achievement in Marden's early work of a special color effect, dependent on a distinctive technical procedure, consolidates this identification. In his study of Cézanne, English critic Roger Fry wrote of *Compotier, verre et pommes* (1877): "The paste under his hands grows to the quality of a sort of lacquer, saturated with color and of an almost vitreous hardness."[7] Overriding the difference between the still life and the contemporary abstract painting, then, is the achievement of a finish. In Cézanne's case, this is the result of a change from the use of a palette knife to "the accumulation of small touches of a full brush"; in Marden's case, it is the development of a special procedure whereby the oil medium is mixed with beeswax and turpentine ("The mixture is then applied to the canvas with a brush and worked over so the medium and paint are thoroughly mixed and evenly cover the shape."[8])

Yet, the argument that Marden's work achieves a relation to a tradition that has already been bracketed off by Cézanne does not carry conviction if we take into account his more recent paintings, in particular, those from the last seven years. The Cold Mountain series must be framed within another reading of tradition. In the course of the last few years, art theorists and art historians have been devoting more care and attention to unraveling the lines of derivation and affiliation between painters and their past, expanding the problematic so acutely raised by Eliot into a more thorough and particularized examination of the mechanisms by which the artist simultaneously overcomes and identifies with a tradition. The French nineteenth-century painter J.A.D. Ingres has been favored in this respect. In his study *Tradition and Desire from David to Delacroix*, art historian Norman Bryson comments on the way Ingres worked through his relationship to Raphael, the paragon of the High Renaissance, through a strategy of appropriation and reversal; Raphael's mistress, La Fornarina, turning her back discreetly toward us, becomes the recurrent *baigneuse* of Ingres's painterly career.[9] In *Painting as an Art*, art historian Richard Wollheim claimed, in more directly Freudian terms, that Ingres's need to elevate and placate his own father was the motivating force behind much of his most characteristic work; hence, the arcane classical subject of *Antiochus and Stratonice* (1840) becomes explicable as it is based on the story of a king who yields his rights over a young and beautiful wife to his love-sick and pining son, and the bourgeois icon *Monsieur Bertin* (1832) is illuminated by the discovery that Ingres could only paint it because he observed after innumerable frustrating sessions the ingratiating spectacle of the patriarch Bertin being kind to his sons.[10]

Wollheim's analysis focuses on a relationship to the biological father in which the artist must idealize and placate his parent and precursor through unremitting work (in this case, the work of perspectival imbrication that can be detected in the intricate composition of *Antiochus and Stratonice*). Bryson focuses instead on the relationship to an ideal father, Raphael; here, Ingres resembles the appropriation artist of recent Postmodern theory, whose sign of identification is accompanied by an equally dramatic sign of refusal, or at least disjunction. Unfortunately, however, neither of these nineteenth-century models is quite adequate in an investigation of Marden's work: not that of Wollheim, for there is no doubt that it is the art and artists of the past that are summoned up in these understated modern equivalents; and certainly not the Postmodern posture of Bryson's analysis, for Marden is a painter whose career has been devoted to avoiding an appropriative or disjunctive strategy. On one hand, Marden's painting certainly follows consequentially upon that apparent evacuation of meaning marked by the painting of Manet. Even a summary comparison between two famously antithetical works, Goya's *The Third of May, 1808* (1814–15) and Manet's *Execution of the Emperor Maximilian* (ca. 1867), makes clear in what way the narrative complexity of the image has been foreclosed by Manet's deadpan strategy; instead of a confrontation which seeks (however ambiguously) to involve our assent to perennial human values of liberty and oppression, we are faced with a confrontation whose values have to be sought elsewhere—in the implicit comment on the foreign policy of the French imperial regime—if they are not sought for, and seen, in the striking light and dark tonalities of the paintwork.[11]

Perhaps we have to deal in Marden's work with not one continuous relationship to tradition but two stages that are, in essence, separate, divided by the period of crisis in the early 1980s that Marden himself has pointed to as a watershed in the production of his works. On a recent visit to the Boston Museum of Fine Arts, I was struck by the way a museum label explained the circumstances of J.M.W. Turner's painting, *Fishing Boats with Hucksters Bargaining for Fish* (1837/38). Turner intended his work to provoke direct comparisons with French and Dutch paintings of the seventeenth century. In this particular case, the precedent was a work by F. N. van de Velde, *A Rising Gale* (ca. 1700). The label indicated that this was, in fact, Turner's second

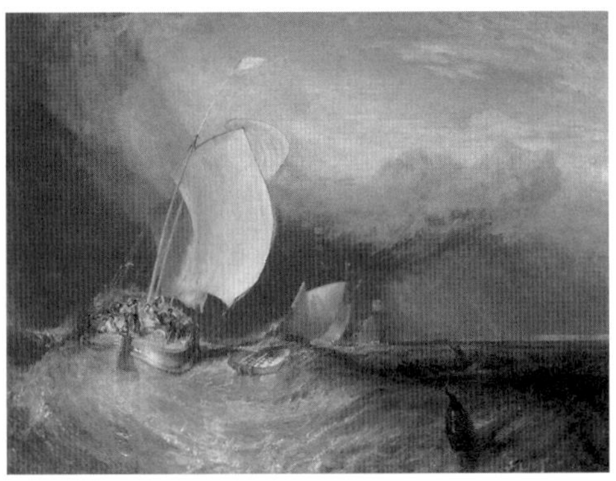

J. M. W. Turner, *Fishing Boats with Hucksters Bargaining for Fish*, 1837/38.

attempt to come to terms with the prestigious old Dutch master, and the label suggested a way to characterize the difference. In the first instance, as a young painter in 1801, Turner was trying, as the text said, to "emulate" the Dutch master; but in the second case, over thirty-five years later, his concern was to "challenge" the illustrious precedent. Let's not be too concerned about the particular connotations of those two words—"emulate" and "challenge"—but bear in mind the relationship to the pictorial model, to tradition. Quite apart from the pictorial relation to van de Velde, *Fishing Boats* has other claims on our attention with respect to its relation to tradition. Here, the label's unusually fine description raises two key points: "The churning of the waves is rendered in skeins of paint so subtle as to defy description. In the foreground, a boat that appears to be of gold seems to spring from the painter's imagination as it swoops through a very powerful sea." The beautifully apt reference to skeins of paint and an equally well-judged remark that the little boat in the foreground appears to be "of gold" are applicable to the watershed in Marden's work in the early 1980s and its relation to tradition.

Having visited Marden's exhibition "Connections" at the Boston Museum of Fine Arts in 1991, I valued the opportunity to see a selection of his work beside paintings by Zurbarán, Goya, and many others, of whose relevance to Marden's work I was already aware. What was truly fascinating was the inclusion of an Andean headcloth from about A.D. 1000–1400. The pre-Columbian textile was, as the curator noted in the exhibition brochure, an example of "deceptive simplicity masking a complex technique or visual pattern.... Once the gauze-

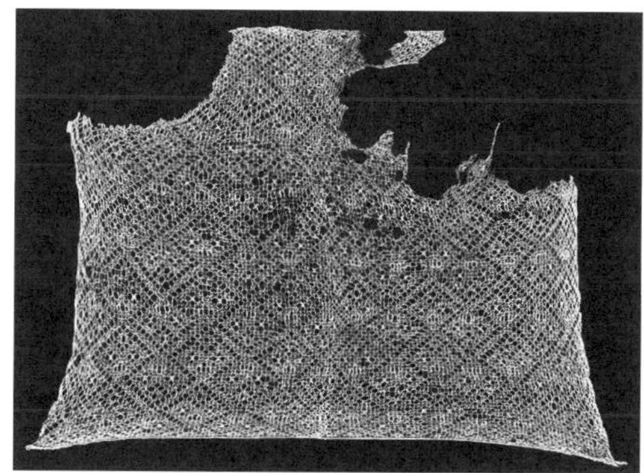

Fragment, Late Intermediate Period, Peru. 45 x 32 inches. Gift of Mrs. Samuel Cabot. Courtesy Museum of Fine Arts, Boston.

like cloth is spread out, the subtle pattern of interlocking diamonds, defined by the larger 'holes' in the fabric, is discernible."[12] In this context, such an artifact was not merely a picturesque addition to the works on exhibit but a convincing illustration of the historical connection between painting and weaving. In his *Fenêtre jaune cadmium*, art historian Hubert Damisch highlights a more substantial reason for connecting the processes. He derives a new way of looking at the contemporary art of Piet Mondrian and Jackson Pollock by drawing on such sources as Gottfried Semper's learned *Treatise of 1863* on the derivation of all arts and crafts from the original techniques of weaving. In so doing, Damisch astonishingly evokes a form of painting that is no longer governed by superimposition of layers but by the interweaving of brushstrokes, as suggested by Balzac's tale *The Unknown Masterpiece* (1834).[13] Marden's recent paintings, culminating in the Cold Mountain series, manifest precisely such skeins of paint. The tessellation of brushstrokes in the early panel paintings, applied in the interest of uniformity of surface, has been supplanted by an open work of long curving strokes that collect the linear texture into a loose weave, here and there countering an almost gravitational pull toward the ground.

The second remark about Turner's *Fishing Boats*—that "the boat appears to be of gold," the result of Turner's technical wizardry with yellow pigment—is also worthy of our attention. In Book Two of his fundamental treatise *On Painting* (1435), the Italian Renaissance art theoretician Leon Battista Alberti reminds his readers that the hallmark of the modern (that is, Renaissance) painter is to achieve the *effect* of gold using other colors:

> Certain people employ gold in an immoderate fashion because they think that gold confers a certain majesty on the tale. And those people, I am far from approving of them. Moreover, if I wanted to paint Virgil's Dido all resplendent with gold...I would try to render such an abundance of gold rays as would strike the eyes of those who see her, but through colors rather than through gold. As it is for his colors that an artist merits most admiration and praise, you can easily see that if you put

gold on a flat panel, the majority of the surfaces which ought to have been represented as clear and brilliant appear somber to the spectator, and certain others, perhaps, which ought to have been more shadowy, appear more luminous.[14]

Alberti's comments are extremely revealing, with regard to both their aesthetic implications and to their implicit view of the artist's relation to society. As art historian Michael Baxandall has pointed out, the use of precious metals and pigments was governed, even up to the time of the Renaissance, by contractual obligations that obliged the artist to use materials to a certain stipulated value. The artist's own status as a craftsman was legally sealed specifically to prevent him from cheating on his commission. Alberti saw the difficulty in combining the new realism in the treatment of light and shade with the incongruous sheen of precious metals. But he also recognized that if the artist could create the effect of gold without using gold, he could emancipate himself to some extent from his earlier servile status. Gentile da Fabriano's *Adoration of the Magi* (1423), on the cusp between International Gothic and early Renaissance painting, demonstrates the force of Alberti's point. Unlike Eliot's questing and questioning Magi, Gentile's wise men are emissaries to Christ's birthplace, weighed down with the exotic gifts, whose value is distributed metonymically over the painting's surface in the form of gold leaf. It is also tempting to accept art historian Pierre Francastel's interpretation that the young man at the center—who is placed to receive the admiration usually destined for the Christ child—represents the self-assured young commissioner of the altarpiece, Palla Strozzi, the pampered beneficiary of a fortune accumulated through commerce in Oriental silks and fabrics.[15] Gentile's picture, therefore, represents the possibility of a double reading, almost an ironic reading, in which the narcissistic young man who has paid for the tribute vies with the symbolic focus of the composition. But it also represents a stage in the process whereby the overt signs of value in the work are converted, step by step, into signs of the artist's personal genius, a value that can endow pigments of little worth with the "merit" attaching to their new status.

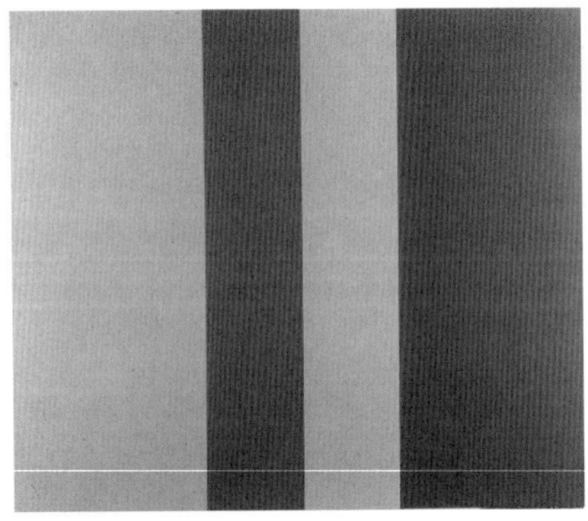

Brice Marden, *Interrogatio*, 1978.

It has always seemed right to insist—as have writers as varied as Jean-Louis Schefer, Marcelin Pleynet, and Julia Kristeva—on the determining role of color in finally overturning or, to be more exact, undermining from within the linear determinants of what the Renaissance called "legitimate perspective." The five works of Marden's remarkable Annunciation series represent both a validation and an extension of this broad historical view.[16] The series comprises five stages in the process of the Virgin Mary's acceptance of the annunciation. In the Renaissance, these five stages were expounded by Florentine preaching friars as a way of concentrating the minds of their congregation on the sacred mystery: *Conturbatio* (a troubled state of mind), *Cogitatio* (reflective state of mind), *Interrogatio* (self-questioning), *Humilitatio* (humbling of the self), and *Meritatio* (the acceptance of self-worth and, therefore, the angel's message). But Marden's series is not iconographically coded in any hard and fast way. Rather, it indicates Marden's adherence to a modernist line of descent that includes, at the very least, the names of Cézanne, Henri Matisse, Mondrian, and Ad Reinhardt. Indeed, Marden's sketch of the total series as a kind of permutational set recalls a late sketch of 1966 by Reinhardt, setting out the overall logic and development of his paintings to date.[17] In the longer term, it bears witness to the post-Renaissance artist's historical acquisition over five centuries of a personal investment in color. The affective liberation of color, its emancipation from symbolic, perspectival, or

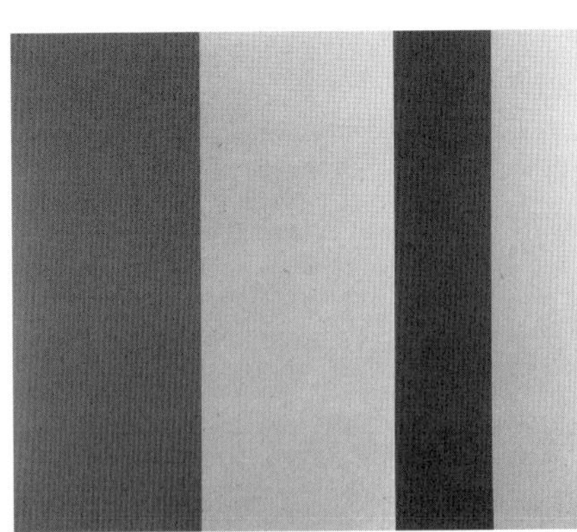

Brice Marden, *Meritatio*, 1978.

social determinants, is powerfully celebrated in works that refer in their titles and in their quasi-permutational structure to the symbolic and rationalistic structures of a previous age.

By placing himself in this tradition, Marden contradicts Schapiro's point in "On the Humanity of Abstract Painting" that "a scene of common life, a landscape or still life could be as great a painting as an image of history or myth." Against this Promethean, humanist view of contemporary art, works like Marden's Annunciation series form a perplexing exception to the rule. Why would a contemporary artist evoke the stages of the annunciation as described by a fifteenth-century friar? The simple answer is that the artist had been reading the work of Michael Baxandall.[18] But that gives rise to another question. Not just why does a contemporary artist read Baxandall's work, but why does he see its concepts as a possible part of his own operation and development? Highlighting the historical role of color broadly answers this question. However, it needs closer investigation, as the shift in Marden's work from the early panel paintings to the Cold Mountain series is closely bound up with the historical project in which he was involved.

In retrospect, the Annunciation series seems significant not only as the culmination of Marden's panel paintings but also as the indication of a new level of subjective investment in the history of art and culture in general. Schapiro's text gives the sense, however unintentionally, that the modern artist now inhabits a demythologized realm, insulated from the heroics of the distant past. But Marden realized that the primitive, archaic, and religious dimension of culture was precisely what the painter had to investigate, not as a merely antiquarian quest but as a way of identifying and exposing the ideological, subjective, and sexual investments of the present day. To evoke this dimension, art critic John Yau has remarked that the form of the assembled panels of Marden's next substantial work, the astonishing *Thira* (1979–80), resembles that of a lintel. This is consonant with the fact that the word *thira* means "door" in Greek. "We are either travelers poised on the threshold of a temple, whose light (sign of divine presence) has been extinguished, or we are ancient worshippers witnessing the aftermath of a cataclysmic event,

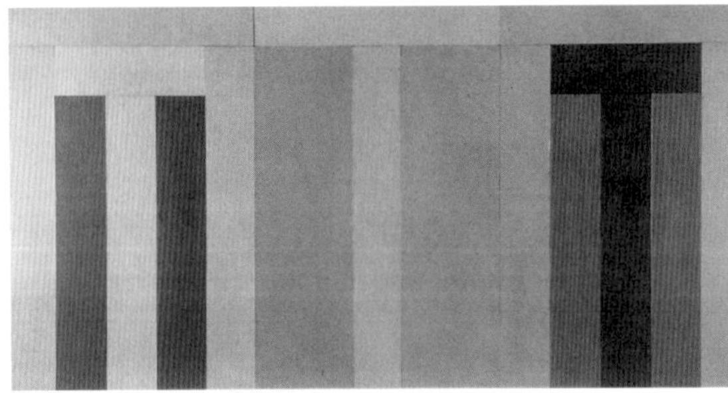

Brice Marden, *Thira*, 1979–80.

such as an eclipse," Yau writes. But the reference is even more ambiguous than this. In addition to the explicit references to Greek architecture, the configuration of panels also alludes to "both Calvary and the three-armed cross of the Old Testament. By embedding Christian symbols within Greek ones," Yau claims, Marden "reverses the flow of history."[19] The objective of this almost bewildering concatenation of symbols is, therefore, both to deconstruct history and to bring history into the present in its deconstructed form. As Yau notes,

> *Thira's* colors mime earth, sky, and the polychromed surfaces of Greek architecture. Its self-sufficient distillations are emblematic of Marden's understanding of a crucial period in the development of our consciousness. It is visual re-visioning of the transition from Matriarchal utterances (the oracle) to Patriarchal dominance (the priests). It is the priests, after all, who extinguished the oil lamp of the oracles, and forced them to repeat what they were told.[20]

Though *Thira* has the power to transfix the observer, what Yau is describing is the continuing exploration that led Marden to the Cold Mountain series and will, no doubt, lead him beyond.

In *Thira*, Marden attempted both to reverse the flow of the Judaeo-Christian, Graeco-Roman tradition and to collapse it from within. By the time *Thira* was painted, Marden had developed an alternative focus to his life in New York, living in Greece for part of the year. During a lecture in February 1992 in London, Marden made a telling remark. He said in the period around 1980 he was "going to Greece to learn how the West went wrong."[21] The line may have been meant as a joke insofar that it referred to a time when Greece was ruled by a military government, but its meaning went deeper than that. Marden spoke of his conviction that the Greek myth of Apollo and Python, symbolizing the victory of the male over the female principle, was the antique record of a disastrous turning point in Western culture, the consequences of which are with us today. This achievement of a secondary vantage point, from which values are, in Nietzsche's term, "transvalued," is a clue, I believe, both to the temporary setback in Marden's career in the early 1980s, and to his extraordinary accomplishment in the years following. But, in order to see why his art had to change—why, for instance, the crucial Chinese reference worked its way into the Cold Mountain series—we must take a wider view of the cultural context he was beginning to open up.

To return briefly to Eliot: as an American poet living in England, Eliot pursued the exact opposite strategy. He traveled abroad precisely to find and adopt the patriarchal, Graeco-Roman, Judaeo-Christian tradition. The preface to his collection *For Lancelot Andrewes* (1928) includes the famous declaration that his point of view is "classicist in literature, royalist in politics, and Anglo-Catholic in religion."[22] In the poem "Journey of the Magi," Lancelot Andrewes is a privileged source with whom to identify, since he believed in going straight from the "Signe" to the "rich Signatum." As cultural critic Andrew Ross has observed in *The Failure of Modernism*, the journey of the Magi as described by Eliot is a straight and narrow path: the Wise Men "resist 'the silken girls bringing sherbet' and follow the signs to their proper conclusion."[23] There is no place here for either the ambiguity of the sign or questioning the very meaning of the quest on which the Magi were embarked.

Contrasting with the example of Eliot is that of Cy Twombly, an American artist of the older generation. He has demonstrated what French theorist Roland Barthes called, in an essay devoted to him, "the wisdom of art."[24] Twombly established himself in Rome not to become "a classicist, an imperialist, and a Catholic in religion," but to stage his drama of selfhood within the mythic context of the Mediterranean world. The prime characteristic of Twombly's work involves "straying signs"—signs slightly detached from reference by the informality of their graphic traces. Yet, his work also involves quite specific transformations of mythic and historical materials. In his *Nike Androgyne* (1981–83), for example, he alludes to the Greek custom of personifying Victory in terms of a godlike figure, the best-known version being the *Winged Victory of Samothrace* exhibited in the Louvre. Twombly's Victory, however, emerges from a palimpsest of lines, in which the wing motif appears to be struggling to assert itself. And, in selecting this particular attribute from among those assigned to the Victory, Twombly invests the whole image with the troublesome sign of sexual ambiguity.[25]

However far Twombly may be from Marden in most respects, he is closer to him than any other American painter precisely because of the way he has developed this alternative focus for his practice as an artist. Both Twombly and Marden are involved in an artistic exploration that derives from the heartland of Western culture and from the type of selfhood that culture has produced. Both also experiment with the notion of a new equilibrium of male and female principles. In Twombly's case, this is explicitly connected with androgyny; in Marden's case, it is linked to the conflict between patriarchy and matriarchy. And Marden has even adopted Twombly's mode of "straying signs." As opposed to the dense condensation of symbols in Marden's *Thira*, we now have the endless variations and displacements of the Cold Mountain series.

My discussion of the Chinese referent in the Cold Mountain series has been reserved until this point, precisely to frame it within the cultural context of Marden's earlier work. Why, after all, would Marden use the name of an eighth-century Chinese poet of the Tang dynasty who left the court and retired to a mountain community of Buddhist monks and hermits? What is the point of Marden's Orientalism? Above all, there should be no connection to what art critic Robert Hughes refers to as "wind-bells and Bay-area Zen" or the decades of "bad abstract painting based on Chinese and Japanese ideograms."[26] If one looks carefully at the "Journey of the Magi," the story of the Magi seems like the epitome of a self-congratulatory Orientalist myth; the wisdom and riches of the East are drawn West for an event which founds their history upon a new and irreversible basis. Certainly there can be little doubt that Gentile's *Journey of the Magi*, in Francastel's subversive reading, is a testimony to the grandeur and conspicuous display of Renaissance Florence, which attracts the rich fabrics of the East like a magnet, and fills the Strozzi warehouses with salable commodities. Even more, Eliot's sober, modernist revision of the journey is based, as we have seen, on the denial of the plurality of the sign and a foreclosing of any stray element that would detract from the univocal ideological message: no "silken girls bringing sherbet" to him.

Marden's wise man is a Chinese sage; his journey is not westward but inward—both geographically and subjectively. His methodical practice of calligraphy, in strict form, with couplets of verse arranged vertically on the page, avoids the dualism between script and representational signs that is the Western inheritance; it is easy to see why Marden was so enamored of it. In the last resort, the achievement of these works is only comprehensible if we place it within a development of pictorial representation that has nothing to do with Chinese art: the tradition of Turner's "skeins of paint," of Balzac's "unknown masterpiece," uncannily anticipating the faceted planes of Cézanne—the tradition of Cubism and of Jackson Pollock. Marden's ability to raise the issues of ideology and cultural tradition, briefly evoked here, depends radically on his secure stance within a history of painting that has not ceased to renew itself in its productive transformations both in the modern period and beyond.

This means that the Cold Mountain series must, in one sense, be seen in traditional terms. Or, rather, it should be seen as a daring experiment, which in the end reinforces a traditional source of value. In the London lecture, Marden spoke of the advice of the German gallery director Michael Werner, who suggested that he paint directly on white, just as he drew on white paper. Now, this was both good and bad advice—good in the sense that it liberated Marden's technique and made the analogy with calligraphy and the Chinese poem all the more immediate; bad in the sense that it neglected the all-important pictorial issue of the relation of figure to ground, which could not be left simply as a relation of positive and negative. One can trace the development in the series from the first painting, *Cold Mountain 1 (Path),* 1988–89, where the calligraphic element is most stressed and the ground most neutral, to the much richer effect of *Cold Mountain 3* (1989–91), where a longer period of preparation indicates a much more intensive treatment of the surface. Indeed, Marden himself pointed out that this work had a particularly fine yellow ground color. I would reiterate Alberti's point that "admiration and praise" is due to the painter who creates the effect of the glow of gold without having to utilize the material. Here, as in Turner's storm-tossed fishing boat, the lattice of brushstrokes creates the effulgence of light in its most resonant and brilliant form.

In 1976, I wrote that Marden's work to that date demonstrated what the English aesthetic critic Adrian Stokes called the "carving approach," as opposed to the "modeling" approach. Marden's already declared fascination with the Mediterranean and, in particular, his choice of the title *Adriatics* for a recent portfolio reminded me strongly of Stokes's view that Renaissance painting, as well as sculpture, developed from the effect of "light on stone" and the endless fantasies the imagination might project upon that luminous, sun-drenched field. In the early 1970s, Marden wrote of the experience of sailing in the Adriatic: "remember the slow smooth movements of a big boat on the water."[27] In the London lecture, he mentioned the fine linen canvas of the Cold Mountain paintings, on which the brush moved "like [it was] skating." He also used the image of Prometheus fashioning things out of clay, and spoke of the danger of "imposing" too much upon the painting. Perhaps what connects all of Marden's work—from the panel paintings to the Cold Mountain series—is this search for an otherness in his materials and more than that, what Stokes calls, in relation to Cézanne, "a precise love and a passionate identification with what is other, insisting upon an order there, strong, enduring, and final *as being an other thing,* untainted by the overt gesture, without the summary treatment, without the *arrière-pensée* of thinking 'makes it so.'"[28] In his 1935 study *Stones of Rimini,* Stokes noticed a distinct change in the art of his times: "Already there are painters who disdain the molding properties of oil paint, who so to speak, prefer to polish and scratch their canvases like the carver his stone."[29] In his own Mosaic Studies (significantly titled) of the 1970s, Marden demonstrated his wish to have both a polished surface and a tessellated, woven structure. In the fullness of time, in the Cold Mountain series, he has shown, in a way that could not have been predicted, how both those aims could be combined and reinforced in a wholly original way. It was a "cold coming," perhaps, but its outcome not folly but wisdom.

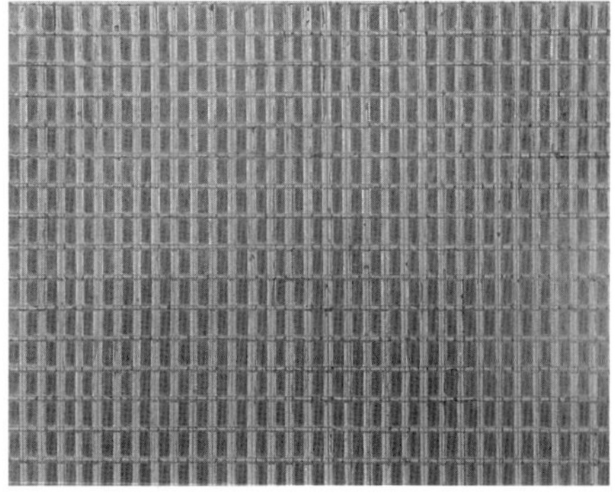

Brice Marden, *Mosaic Study #2*, 1978.

May 14, 1992

Notes

1. T. S. Eliot, "Tradition and Individual Talent," in *The Sacred Wood* (London: Methuen, 1927), pp. 48–49.

2. Ibid.

3. See Meyer Schapiro, "On the Humanity of Abstract Painting" (1960), reprinted in *Modern Art: 19th and 20th Centuries* (New York: G. Braziller, 1978), pp. 227–232.

4. Stephen Bann, "Adriatics—à propos of Brice Marden," *20th Century Studies*, nos. 15/16 (December 1976), p. 118.

5. Schapiro, "On the Humanity," p. 227.

6. Ibid.

7. Roger Eliot Fry, *Cézanne: A Study of His Development* (1960; repr. Chicago: University of Chicago Press, 1989), p. 41.

8. Brice Marden, quoted in Diane Waldman, "Technical Statement," *Brice Marden* (New York: Guggenheim Foundation, 1975), p. 28.

9. See Norman Bryson, *Tradition and Desire from David to Delacroix* (Cambridge: Cambridge University Press, 1984).

10. See Richard Wollheim, *Painting as an Art* (London: Thames and Hudson, 1987).

11. See Stephen Bann, "The Odd Man Out: Historical Narrative and the Cinematic Image," in *The Inventions of History: Essays on the Representation of the Past* (Manchester: Manchester University Press, 1990), pp. 171–199.

12. Deborah Kraak, "An Andean Headcloth Chosen by Brice Marden for His 'Connections' Project," in *Connections: Brice Marden*, leaflet (Boston: Museum of Fine Arts, 1991), n.p.

13. See Hubert Damisch, *Fenêtre jaune cadmium, ou, Les dessous de la peinture* (Paris: Seuil, 1984), pp. 11–46, 278–297.

14. Leon Battista Alberti, *De Pictura (1435)* (Paris: Macula, 1992), p. 203. Translation from the French is mine.

15. See Pierre Francastel, *La Figure et le lieu: l'ordre visuel du Quattrocento* (Paris: Gallimard, 1967), p. 85.

16. See *Brice Marden: Recent Paintings and Drawings* (New York: Pace Gallery, 1978); and Stephen Bann, "Brice Marden: From the Material to the Immaterial," in *Brice Marden: Paintings, Drawings, and Prints 1975–1980* (London: Whitechapel Art Gallery, 1981), pp. 6–14.

17. See Ad Reinhardt's *Personal Sketches of Paintings* (1966) in Margit Rowell, *Ad Reinhardt and Color* (New York: The Solomon R. Guggenheim Museum, 1980), p. 29.

18. See Michael Baxandall, *Painting and Experience in Fifteenth-Century Italy: A Primer in the Social History of Pictorial Style* (Oxford: Clarendon Press, 1972).

19. John Yau, "A Vision of the Unsayable," in *Brice Marden: Recent Paintings and Drawings*, exhibition catalogue (London: Anthony D'Offay Gallery, 1988), n.p.

20. Ibid.

21. Brice Marden, "Patrons of New Art," lecture given at the Tate Gallery on February 26, 1992.

22. T. S. Eliot, *For Lancelot Andrewes: Essays on Style and Order* (1928; London: Faber, 1970), p. 7.

23. See Andrew Ross, *The Failure of Modernism: Symptoms of American Poetry* (New York: Columbia University Press, 1986), pp. 32–38.

24. See Roland Barthes, "The Wisdom of Art," trans. Annette Lavers, in *Calligram: Essays in New Art History in France*, ed. Norman Bryson (Cambridge: Cambridge University Press, 1988), pp. 166–180.

25. See Stephen Bann, "Wilder Shores of Love: Cy Twombly's Straying Signs," in *Materialities of Communication*, ed. Hans Ulrich Gumbrecht and K. Ludwig Pfeiffer (Palo Alto, Calif.: Stanford University Press, 1994), pp. 198–213.

26. Robert Hughes, "Lines That Go for a Walk," *Time* (4 November 1991), p. 96.

27. Quoted in Bann, "Adriatics—à propos of Brice Marden," p. 128.

28. Adrian Stokes, *Critical Writings* (London: Thames & Hudson, 1978), vol. 2, p. 174.

29. Ibid., vol. 1, p. 244.

The Old and the New Initiation Rites: Joseph Beuys and Epiphany

ANTJE VON GRAEVENITZ

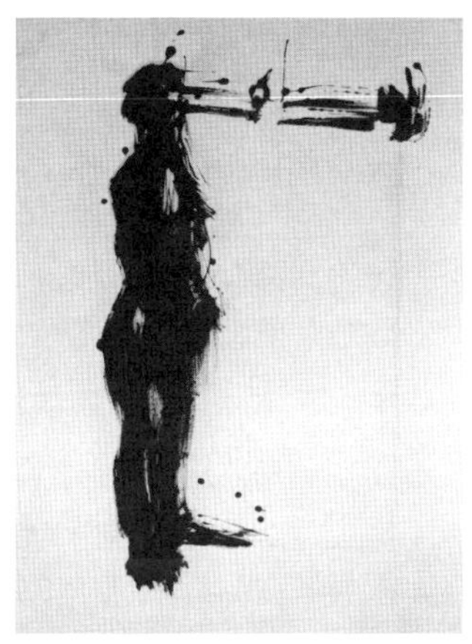

Joseph Beuys, *Schamane* (*Shaman*), 1963.

Peoples entrust their shamans with the task of mentally and physically healing them by mediating between the spirits and humans. In Western culture, these tasks have been divided among various professions: doctors take care of our physical well-being, while teachers, priests, and artists deal with our mental welfare. We do not call these men and women shamans, perhaps because in our culture belief in good and evil spirits has been given up for the most part, and therefore there is no need to communicate with a spirit. But, in his art, the German artist Joseph Beuys often broached the subject of shamanism. In a drawing of 1963, for example, energy radiates from the head of the shaman.[1] Along with other artists, including Terry Fox and Michael Buthe, Beuys assumed the role of shaman in order to heal the deficiencies of the art audience—a lack of fantasy, creativity, feeling, or love, and an imperfect understanding of the relation between the body and mind in nature. It is the goal of the artist as shaman to reawaken all of those slumbering forces to help an individual to heal himself. An important difference can be recognized between the conventional shaman, who believes that outside forces provide healing, and artists as shamans, who believe in self-healing.

Compare, for example, a drawing by the shaman Jenemeyer Jurek Samojedes with a drawing by Beuys titled *Eurasian Drawing* (1953). Interpreting the signs in Beuys's drawing is nearly impossible,

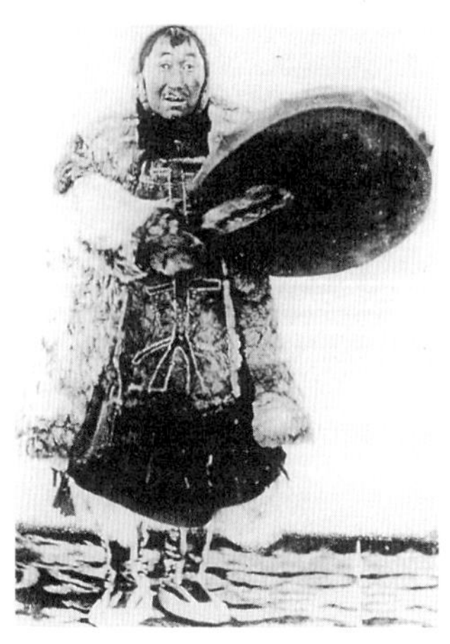

Shaman Jenemeyer Jurek Samojedes.

whereas motifs on the drawing by the shaman can easily be recognized. In Beuys's drawing, a figure can be discerned, though the meaning of it can only be clarified by comparing it with another drawing by the artist titled *Urschlitten, Schädel und Bewusstseinzeichen* (*Primordial Sled, Skull, and Sign for Consciousness*), 1955. Pressing his thumb above the drawn sled, the artist admitted to me in 1980 that an energy or spirit was being represented there that caused the sleigh to move. This explanation also informed his large installation, *Das Rudel* (*The Pack*), 1973, showing sleds trailing behind a Volkswagen bus. Each was packed with felt, a lamp, and some fat—items for people in emergency, brought out for healing. When I asked Beuys about his role as shaman, he stated, "I use this ancient figure to express something of the future. I say that the shaman stood for something that was able to unify spiritual and material things. When we use this figure in materialistic times, we point toward something in the future. Important in this is only that I took up the role of shaman to express a tendency as a return toward the past."[2] The question is, then, whether he found a new language for the shaman, or whether he took over its ancient symbolic language?

In many interviews, Beuys clearly opposed the use of certain terms. He did not like symbols, for example, nor did he work with associations and analogies. By 1968, he had stated, "I do not want to interpret, because then it would seem that the things I do are symbolical, and they are not."[3] Once, in conversation, he repeated that associations were suspect; he was looking, he said, for relations between matter and mind, making apparent only the things that already had meaning in their own right. He wanted to emphasize forgotten things. Art critics dealing with Beuys's work struggle to find the appropriate term for this expanded "art-notion," as Beuys called his work. Perhaps the word might be "emblems" since his works combine both the image and the real objects? But this term denies specific use of images by Beuys, for the elements in his artworks do not directly depict something; they *are* the things themselves in their own reality. *Erdtelefon* (*The Earth Telephone*), 1969, combines the notion of a real telephone and its natural equivalent for nature: straw in a lump of earth, Beuys's vision of an animal's mode of communication. The *Fettstuhl* (*Fat Chair*), 1964, was originally titled *Initiationsobjekt* (*Object of Initiation*) in a 1960 drawing, and is composed of fat—Beuys's deposit of energy—placed on a chair with an antenna on the arm and inferred communication. It is even more difficult to apply the term "emblem" to Beuys's actions. Perhaps it might only be applied to the composition of the props or to certain gestures within an action, which occurred sparsely and slowly as in a tableau vivant. But it seems impossible to combine all of his motifs into one total and complete emblem. Instead, a new approach for understanding his method is necessary. We must, therefore, discuss his work as a rite of passage and examine the ways he dealt with the work of James Joyce.

In the role of a shaman, Beuys used his actions to transform the spectator. As with his photographic multiple titled *La revoluzione siamo noi* (*We Are the Revolution*), 1972, he seemed to say: "We are the revolution ourselves, we should begin by altering ourselves."[4] A believer in the principles of the French Revolution—liberty, equality, and fraternity—Beuys's ultimate goal was to free man from repression by society and egotism. He believed that liberation would be attained through the development of creativity and that only in creativity would all three revolutionary principles converge. Thus, creativity was the essence of human existence, and

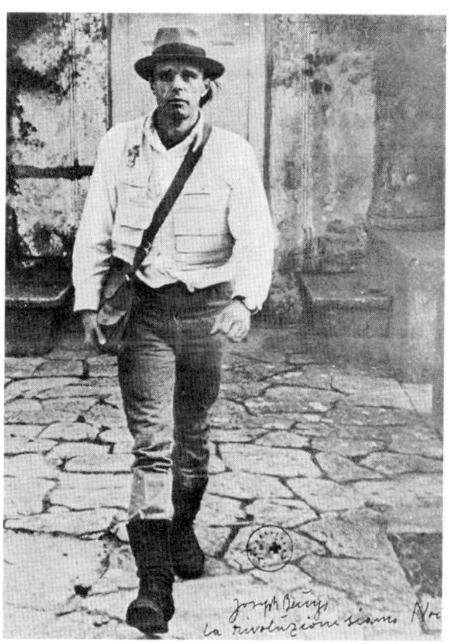

Joseph Beuys, *La revoluzione siamo noi (We Are the Revolution)*, 1972.

in order to develop it, man needed an understanding of the forces of nature within a social context: "I see myself as an enlightener of the real relations in the world. The artists should not invent something, but discover relations."[5] For this reason, he wanted to employ form as a "living substance." This "social sculpture," as he called it, could be aimed at man, who would become free, equal, brotherly, creative, and endowed with wisdom about the world. In relation to this truly sublime task, Beuys developed strategies that involved education, discussions, "plastic" art, and, in particular, performances that took the form of rituals derived from cults.

These performances have been seen as rites of passage. But they are very different from traditional rites of passage, either those described by ethnographers or those handed down to us in mystery plays, fairy tales, stories in opera, drama, and film.[6] In general, all those rites have narratives that develop in three stages: separation, transition through trial, and reintegration. This classic initiation rite could not occur without some sort of humiliation, obstruction, repression, or suffering; on this point all the main scholars in this field—Arnold van Gennep, Mircea Eliade, and Victor Turner—agree.[7] Van Gennep sees the structure of initiation as a process of these three stages: first, separation from the ordinary surroundings; second, transition and change during the trial proper; and finally, the reintegration of the purified person in the normal social network where he or she has to prove him- or herself again. Turner, however, does not believe that this third stage takes place. He sees only a continuation of life enriched by the experience of transition, the initiated bearing this experience in mind, thinking about it, and knowing that it can never be denied.

How can we relate this social process to the work of Joseph Beuys? Beuys never put the viewer through trial zones, like Bruce Nauman did with his "corridors" or "double cages." Nor did Beuys in the course of his performances inflict any bodily pain. Nor did he himself go through any arduous trial, though his own life was, in fact, painful enough at some stages (his airplane crash in World War II or his artistic crisis during the years 1956 and 1957, for example). But Beuys almost never subjected the audience to an arduous or painful experience. Perhaps the one exception, *Projekt Vlake,* took place during a large outdoor exhibition in Arnhem, The Netherlands, in 1971. The project consisted of an invitation to the public to bike a hundred miles, from the train station at Yerseke-Kruiningen to the farm "Cattle Place" in Vlake, Zuid-Beveland. At "Cattle Place," visitors could see the place to which Beuys had occasionally retreated during his artistic crisis.[8] Visitors could also listen to a tape recording of extracts from Julien Green's diary and memories of the van der Grinten family about Beuys's life. The work sought to establish a real form of identification with Beuys's crisis, both in content and artistic methodology. The work created for the visitor the conditions for the stages of a rite of passage: separation and transition. In the exhibition itself in Arnhem, a color film taken from the perspective of an anonymous and invisible cyclist was shown. In this way, the desired strategy of direct identification was even stronger, for the visitor himself had to act out the crisis of the artist.

But none of Beuys's own ritual acts really translated an initiation rite into a logical and therefore understandable process. Beuys was working with transfers, or, as he preferred to call them, "transformations." "I am interested in transformation, transubstantiation. I am looking for the borderlines of the Religious/Spiritual. Making transformations is a movement of alchemy, religion," he said during a conversation in 1982.[9] He worked with ritualistic acts that had an emblematic character, acts in which only he himself knew the different layers of meaning. Every gesture, even the most realistic and practical ones, had its transferred meaning. It was sometimes difficult for other Fluxus artists to understand what Beuys was doing, because the acts were focused on more concrete, literal, and therefore deliberately silly aspects of their performance.[10] In executing George Brecht's *hammerklavier* (piano) in 1969, Ben Vautier literally hammered nails into the keys, making double noises. Of course, no one could play the instrument afterward, but that was the aim. Fluxus artists like Brecht wanted to damn the old cultural symbols; they wanted to purify the all-too-strictly academic and bourgeois culture and then bring it back to real life. This important

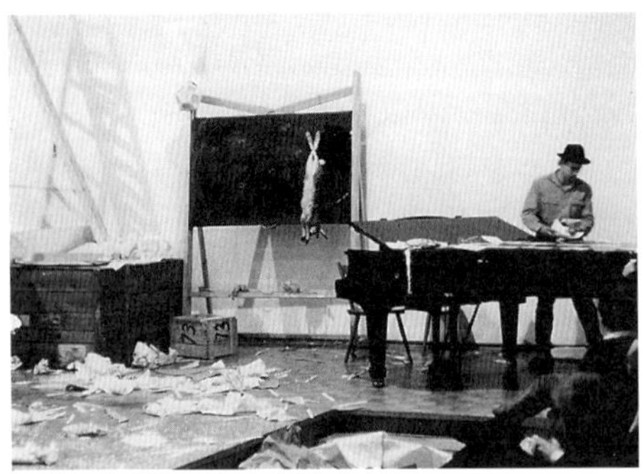

Joseph Beuys, *Sibirische Symphonie* (*Siberian Symphony*), 1963.

difference between Beuys and other Fluxus artists was always apparent. While Beuys worked with transformations, the others employed the concrete and the literal.

Even in Beuys's first Fluxus concert in 1963, *Sibirische Symphonie* (*Siberian Symphony*), his action contained important relics, or *sacra*, as if in homage to a Siberian shaman.[11] These *sacra* were retained in later actions, though altered now and then. Loosely following Richard Wagner, the *sacra* might be called a *leitmotif*, for the *Siberian Symphony* was a sort of music as well. Concerning this first performance, Beuys stated, "the *Siberian Symphony* was in itself a composition for piano. It began with a free movement that I composed myself and then I blended in a piece from Erik Satie; the piano would then be prepared with small clay hills, but first the hare would be hung on the slanting blackboard. In each of these small clay hills, a bough would be placed, then, like an electrical overhead wire, a cable would be laid from the piano to the hare, and the heart would be taken out of the hare. That was all; the hare was actually dead. That was the composition, and it had for the most part sound; then something would be written on the blackboard."[12] The hare, the slate, the transmitter, and the so-called electrical wiring in the action were the *sacra* to the initiation rite of the hare.

A creative being, a builder of tunnels, vulnerable and nomadic, the hare was to Beuys a general metaphor for man. Beuys *took* the heart of the hare, literally and figuratively, in the piece. The old culture, in the shape of a wing, ripped the hare's heart out and caused its death. Mounds of clay and branches were meant to transmit forces from nature. Natural and creative forces in Beuys's experimental sounds enlightened the hare, who replaced a man—in this case, the spectator. Beuys had often explained why he chose the hare as an incarnation of man's fast-moving and nomadic existence: "The hare is the same as the deer, but in a completely different way more specialized on the forces of blood, it has a strong attraction to woman, birth, and the monthly period, to the chemical changes of the blood as a whole."[13] Beuys typically interpreted the digging of tunnels into the earth as digging into the mind or reincarnation. Man also must penetrate into matter, laws, and work. As he told Caroline Tisdall, "I am the hare."[14]

In his drawing *Therapeutisches Basismodell* (*Therapeutic Basic Model*), 1964, Beuys used a reddish-brown substance—which he explained later as an organic material—to draw a colored circle on brown paper with the letter *h* next to the sign for equality.[15] Here, the hare is the organic substance sui generis. In his role of shaman, Beuys simulated the death of this initiated animal to stimulate the spectator into *becoming* the initiated, the one who would question the coming new culture, the Fluxus culture. When the viewer felt the need to ask questions, Beuys felt the ritual had been successful. At that point, the viewer's thoughts become the real artwork: the *Siberian Symphony* was simply the *tool* for the artwork. Rites of passage in Beuys's work were thus transforming acts, executed upon himself or upon certain objects, never aggressively, repressively, or violently.[16] In so doing, Beuys worked with combinations of objects of various materials. Their explicit meaning was often not immediately clear to the audience, but soon the audience would discover similarities between the objects and their key values, and make connections between their principles. Only then would one suddenly see the "storyline" of the performance.

In his action *Eurasienstab* (*Eurasian Staff*), 1967, Beuys recalled his wartime experiences on the frontlines in the East. The work encouraged the unification of what he called "the men of the East and the West." The "staff" reached across Europe from East to West, so to speak, taking central Europe as its axis, as one can see in detail in the upper-right corner of Beuys's drawing titled *Eurasian Staff*. Beuys characterized Western man as rational and analytical, overestimating the value of science and technology, Eastern man, on the other hand, he saw as caring more for intuitive thinking, and

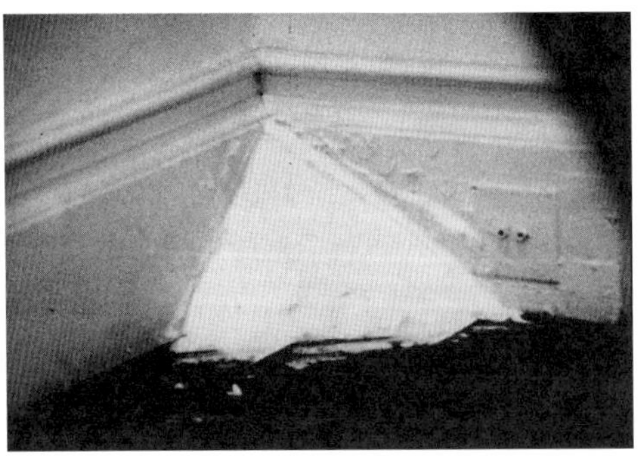

Joseph Beuys, *Eurasienstab* (*Eurasian Staff*), 1968.

using imagery to help him judge the world in a meditative way. Beuys hoped passionately for a merging of these two human characteristics. The unification would result in the ideal Eurasian culture. He named his performance *Eurasian Staff,* and it was performed in cooperation with the composer and organist Henning Christiansen in the Galerie nächst St. Stephan in Vienna. The following year, at the Wide White Space Gallery in Antwerp, twenty minutes of the eighty-two–minute performance were enacted for the camera only. The complete project was called *Fluxus Organum.*[17]

With the organ music as his accompaniment in the gallery, Beuys attached a lump of fat to a chimney with a spatula, which was then left in the fat. Shoe soles were laid out in the form of a cross. On these soles, the so-called East-West nomad identified the four directions: East, West, South, and North. These directions were meant not only as geographic pointers but also as directions of the mind. On the floor, four wooden bases placed at ninety-degree angles were wrapped in felt. Beuys then tied iron and felt soles to his shoes. Fat smeared onto the soles enabled Beuys, the traveler, to move. Fat was smeared on his clothes, as well, providing his body with enough energy and warmth with which to travel. A magnet in his pocket was a metaphor for the forces that enabled movement. The trial of the East-West man portrayed here might be understood, therefore, as a confrontation with physical and spiritual coldness. These might be conquered with energy for physical and mental movement. Attaching a lump of fat in the upper corner of the room and in the opposite bottom corner, Beuys implied that the room itself required a deposit of warmth for the traveler. Fat in the form of a triangle or a pyramid was synonymous for Beuys with thought, production, and the creative act. Fat and its form were thus synonyms for energy and thought. Both were brought together here, radiating from the corners in three dimensions.

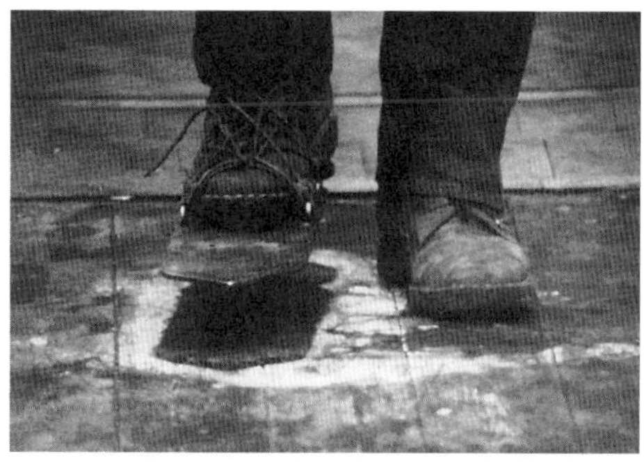

Joseph Beuys, *Eurasienstab* (*Eurasian Staff*), 1968.

Lifting the four beams, Beuys erected a standing quadrangle in the narrow space of the gallery. Then, from a linen cloth, he unwrapped a rod of copper about twelve feet long, the "Eurasian staff" itself. Beuys pointed the rod repeatedly toward each corner of the quadrangle, symbolizing a connection between man—represented by Beuys alone—and all dimensions of a spiritual space. Raising his left foot a little from the floor, Beuys then stood still, rigid, for some time. Was he finding balance on the slippery floor, another test to be mastered, so to speak? When the balancing act was over, Beuys lifted a magnet from his foot and put it in his pocket for use as a compass. Beuys then put tallow at the back of his knee, again to aid travel in mind and space with additional energy. He shifted the copper rod from one beam to another, then returned to his original position and, concentrating, he covered his forehead with the back of his hands—a pose of meditation, for imagination, perhaps, doubtless a suggestion of thought. In fact, immediately after, Beuys wrote on the floor the words "image-head," "motion-head," "parallel process two," and "the moving isolator." Certainly, "image-head" might be taken as a reference to the gesture of covering his forehead, and, both alluding to an intuitively creative process or inner picture, apparently relating to a spiritual movement in outer and inner dimensions. In both processes, spiritual movement and physical movement occur simultaneously and run parallel in the room, which then might explain the phrase "parallel process two." Beuys once told Caroline Tisdall:

> "The Moving Isolator" relates to the chalk drawing on the floor in *Eurasienstab* (*Eurasian Staff*), the drawing near the shoes

> made of felt and iron. Normally, the insulator is considered as neutral. It's a dividing principle, meaning both, mental and social insulation (felt). If you think of the insulator as being in movement, then you get something else. You move away from the idea of a static element that divides one potential from another. It's the idea of using movement to break through insulation (mental and social). I feel that the insulator has been underestimated, and that from it one could create a new energy field. This is a physical speculation but it's psychologically right.[18]

With parallel intentions, a shaman uses natural elements as mental categories. Beuys, again balanced on one foot, his hands folded behind his back, represented both the director who created the whole setting, and the hero of the libretto. The audience could identify with him only as a hero.

Eurasian Staff was a kind of staged story that had nothing in common with the reality of the room in the gallery. It was a story told in fragments that included healing materials, fragments of movement, sacred objects, and written words. All these fragments needed some explanation before it was possible to construct a coherent story. One might compare this kind of interpretive emblematic theater production to the stage productions of Peter Sellars. But at this time, the method was still radically different. Beuys walked through Eurasia alone, using the rod like a shepherd's staff, an instrument of thought, pointing out the dimensions of the space and initiating the rebirth of lost values, which could turn the coldness of the room and of thought into warmth. Eurasian man must save the dying Western culture. In the same year, Beuys wrote in the program of the German Student's Party,

> Art is from its nature the straw that flows from the ambiguity, the confusions and schizophrenias of our time, and solves the coldness and rigidity. Its effect, which everyone is capable of achieving, or has to be made capable of is, the real condition of healing and development of all spheres of human existence, for progress and intensity of science and technology, in professions, in everyday labor.[19]

"Everybody is an artist," he stated.[20]

However easy and straightforward Beuys was in laying out a party program, he never made it easy to interpret his performances. The audience was required to undertake a considerable amount of work, abstracting and synthesizing in order to understand. But, the shaman who performs emblematic acts in any ritual does not worry whether he is understood or not; he performs a ritual act developed by the collective society. Beuys did hope, however, that the audience would decipher the hidden meanings in his actions. In 1983, he stated:

> We have to address people as thinking beings. And when one speaks of addressing people as thinking beings, one must clearly have in mind thought on all different sorts of levels. But, when it is the aim of art to, let us say, to convey to man an image of his own being, then one has to tell something and go the road of thoughts that develop a larger image than just this rationalistic and materialistic image of thinking. For higher forms of thinking are intuition, inspiration, and imagination, these capture the notion of image directly.[21]

Is it justified to use the term *sacra* for the objects that Beuys used in his transformations? The ethnologist van Gennep uses the term "sanctuary" when he compares the strategy of a rite of passage with a mystery play. Phases of transformation in rituals were introduced by touching certain *sacra* or by certain gestures with a transferred meaning, as in the medieval Catholic church when people rubbed their ears with spittle to open them up to the content of the religious belief.[22] Beuys consistently used objects and gestures that suggested an opening of the body for incoming messages. His work *Baumwollfilter* (*Cotton-filter*), 1961, might be thought of as such an instrument. His installation *Zeige Deine Wunde* (*Show Your Wound*), 1972, originally shown in an underground walkway in Munich, also worked in this way. Beyond the influence of the mystery play tradition, the work of James Joyce had a decisive influence on Beuys.

In the early 1950s, Beuys read *Finnegan's Wake* and, a short time later, Joyce's earlier works, including *Dubliners*, *A Portrait of the Artist as a Young Man*, and *Ulysses*. Between 1958 and 1961, Beuys

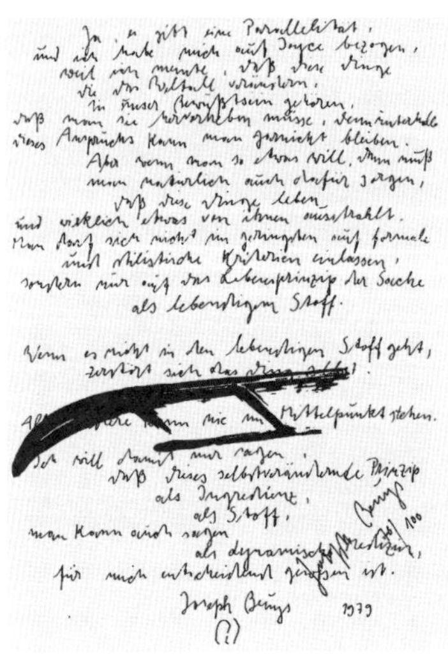

Joseph Beuys, *James Joyce* (multiple), 1985.

added two chapters, nineteen and twenty, to *Ulysses* in the form of drawings made in his notebooks.[23] Beuys considered the intuitive and fluctuating values, so typical in Joyce's novels, instrumental for creativity. Beuys stated that he saw in Joyce a companion who also had portrayed the physical and spiritual elements in things. "We speak too little about that which in Joyce intersperses things with life and radiant force," Beuys argued.[24] It was Joyce himself who termed this aspect of his work an "epiphany." Though epiphany has a religious connotation, originally meaning God's revelation and appearance in nature, Joyce secularized it. Already in *Dubliners*, Joyce no longer used "epiphany" only in its meaning as a sudden emergence of transcendental meaning, above the reality of the narrative. In the novella *Stephen Hero*, Stephen defines the notion of epiphany as a sudden spiritual manifestation when "soul" or the "whatness" of an object leaps up from the vastness of its appearance.[25] Joyce was referring here to the moment in which one realizes that there is a metaphoric potential in an object, a gesture, or a phrase.

Beuys once defined the relation between Joyce's work and his own in the following way:

> There indeed are similarities, and I was inspired by him because the things that change the cosmos belong to our consciousness, they have to be brought to the fore, because one cannot deny this claim. But when one wants this, one obviously has to see to it that these things come to life and that there is a radiation from them. One simply cannot rely upon formal and stylistic principles, but one has to regard the principles of the case as a living material.[26]

Thus, it is not sufficient to see Beuys's work as simply an application of emblematic material or as a collection of metaphors and symbols, though we are accustomed to seeing principal aspects of artistic expressions that are not purely mimetic as symbolic. Beuys said, "I have always chosen those forms, dimensions, and kinds of material that to my mind expressed a connection of energies, a constellation of energy, whether it will serve as movement and energy of heat, as a chaotic principle, out of which the particular arises, as in the case of the corner with tallow, where the material functions in a prismatic and geometric way."[27] He was interested in working with "live substances" and, we can add, with material and acts that could arouse in his spectators a revelation about their own existence and result in an epiphany.

This was a modernistic vision, of course. An initiation through art was Beuys's first aim; the second was understanding life. A shaman might help the newly healed person find the right way for the future—the reintegration of the initiated, the third stage of van Gennep's classification of rites. In contrast to the shaman, an artist has no control over what effect his work might have on spectators. It is this lack of responsibility that allows the Western artist to use the forms and meanings of initiation rites. These rites of passage and the role of shaman are only part of the artwork, never meant in a literal sense, only as a model for a subsequent situation in the real circumstances in which the spectator lives. Shamanism in art has no reality. Art makes an offer of knowledge to humanity; the offer can be accepted or denied. The spectator might distill a meaning about life, but he or she has no real obligation to act upon that knowledge. Beuys was working on a language that would create that obligation, one that would change life in a direct way and would stimulate the spectator to develop the forces of his own creativity.

Taking on the role of teacher, missionary, and even part-time politician, Beuys rarely accepted the idea that art was only a model for reality and that its influence was only indirect. "We have seen the idea that art and the essence we derive from art may have a decisive influence upon life," Beuys stated.[28] So paradoxically, he accepted the ambiguous character of art. But here Beuys remained loyal to his principle of liberty. Since he could not really work

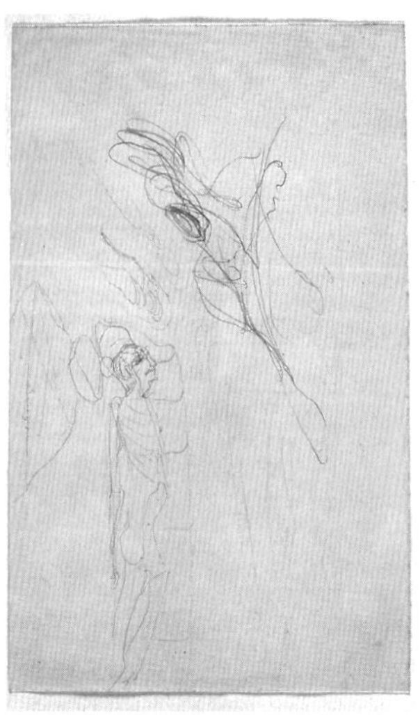

Joseph Beuys, *Initiation*, 1953.

therapeutically, he appealed to the spectator to develop his own creativity and vitality. His aim was sublime, wanting no less than to cross all the restrictive borders of civilization. The spectator was a starting point in the process of transformation, but he or she had to start the machinery on his or her own. Or to quote Beuys, the viewer had to begin his or her own "resurrection." In a drawing titled *Initiation* (1953), two figures seem to represent a soul resurrecting. Beuys's work was based on his hope for the potency of art. Even the theme of death was to him a force of metamorphosis, regeneration, and purification.

Beuys's aim might be seen in the tradition of the modernist artist of the nineteenth and twentieth centuries, who attempted to realize social utopia directed toward the individual. Not a leader in a hierarchical sense nor a dominating shaman, Beuys attempted to teach us innate intelligence in conjunction with acquired knowledge. His model of a rite of passage is consequently linked to the third and fourth stages of ritual as described by the ethnologist Victor Turner: in the end, one has to digest the knowledge and live on.

September 24, 1992

Translated by Martin Adrichem.

Notes

1. This idea seems to have an old tradition. On the right side of the second shrine of Tutankhamen in the Egyptian Museum in Cairo, figures are presented in gold relief, as if their heads are connected to sun balls. It looks as if this substance is radiating from their heads to the sun or vice versa.

2. Erika Billeter, "Joseph Beuys," in *Mythos & Ritual in der Kunst der 70er Jahre* (Zürich: Kunsthaus Zürich, 1981), p. 89. In *Die Zeit* on February 26, 1986, Beuys called himself a shaman. See also Axel Hinrich Murkin, *Joseph Beuys und die Medizin* (Münster: F. Coppenrath Verlag, 1979).

3. See Jaap Bremer, *Museum Journaal* 13 (1968), p. 73. See also Antje von Graevenitz, "Gedankengang zu einem Ofenloch," in *Schwarz*, ed. Hannah Weitemeier (Berlin: Frölich & Kaufmann, 1981), p. 135.

4. In 1991, one of my students, Heike Fehlbrügge, in her paper "Beuys and the Revolution," recognized the similarity between Beuys's shoulder bag and the bag Eugène Delacroix painted belonging to a boy in his picture *La liberté guidant le peuple* (*Liberty Leading the People*), 1830, Musée National du Louvre, Paris. She interpreted the boy's bag as useful for ammunition, and Beuys's bag as a possible container for creative ideas. See also *Die Sekretärstasche*, plate 382, in *Joseph Beuys: Die Multiples*, ed. Jörg Schellmann (Munich: Edition Schellmann and Schirmer/Mosel Verlag, 1992), p. 303.

5. Joseph Beuys, quoted in von Graevenitz, "Gedankengang," p. 137.

6. See Antje von Graevenitz, "Der Eurasienstab von Joseph Beuys," in *Joseph Beuys: Eurasienstab*, ed. Anny de Dekker (Antwerp: Wide White Space Gallery, 1987). See also Antje von Graevenitz, "Erlösungskunst oder Befreiungspolitik: Wagner und Beuys," in *Unsere Wagner: Joseph Beuys, Heiner Müller, Karlheinz Stockhausen, Hans-Jürgen Syberberg, Essays* (Frankfurt am Main: Fischer Taschenbuch Verlag, 1984), p. 34.

7. See Arnold van Gennep, *The Rites of Passage*, trans. Monika B. Vizedom and Gabriella Caffee (Chicago: University of Chicago Press, 1960); Mircea Eliade, *Rites and Symbols of Initiation*, trans. Willard R. Trask (New York: Harper & Row, 1965); and Victor Turner, *The Ritual Process: Structure and Anti-Structure* (London: Routledge & Kegan Paul, 1969).

8. See Caroline Tisdall, ed., *Joseph Beuys* (New York: The Solomon R. Guggenheim Museum, 1979), p. 18.

9. Joseph Beuys, quoted in von Graevenitz, "Erlösungskunst oder Befreiungspolitik," p. 34.

10. See Götz Adriani, Winfried Konnertz, and Karin Thomas, *Joseph Beuys: Life and Work*, trans. Patricia Lech (New York: Barron's, 1979), pp. 108–109.

11. See van Gennep, *The Rites of Passage*, p. 82.

12. Joseph Beuys, quoted in Adriani, et al., *Joseph Beuys*, pp. 91–92.

13. Joseph Beuys, quoted in *Joseph Beuys: Zeichnungen 1947–1959* (Cologne: Schirmer Verlag, 1972), p. 10.

14. See Helmut Gebelein, *Alchemie* (Munich: E. Diederichs, 1991), p. 47. An alchemistic illustration depicts an artist running behind a hare who is "searching the inside of the earth" (Stephan Michelsberger, *Cabala* [1616]).

15. See Ludwig Rinn, "Joseph Beuys: Gute Cascadere sind sehr gesucht," in *Joseph Beuys: Zeichnungen, Objekte* (Bremerhaven: Kunstverein Bremerhaven, 1978), p. 8; *Joseph Beuys: Werke aus der Sammlung Karl Ströher* (Basel: Kunstmuseum, Emanuel Hoffmann-Stiftung, 1970).

16. See von Graevenitz, "Erlossungskunst oder Befreiungspolitik," p. 45.

17. See de Dekker, ed., *Joseph Beuys: Eurasienstab.*

18. Joseph Beuys, quoted in Caroline Tisdall, "From a Telephone Conversation," in *The Secret Block for a Secret Person in Ireland* (Oxford: Museum of Modern Art, 1974), n.p.

19. Joseph Beuys, quoted in "Alle mensen zijn kunstenaar," *Museumjournaal* 14 (December 6, 1969), p. 294.

20. Joseph Beuys: "Jeder Mensch ein Künstler" (from discussions at Documenta 5, 1972, recorded by Clara Bodenmann-Ritter, 1975).

21. Joseph Beuys, quoted in Theo Altenberg and Oswald Oberhuber, eds., *Gespräche mit Joseph Beuys* (Vienna: Hochschule für Angewandte Kunst Wien Klagenfurt, 1988), pp. 75–76.

22. See van Gennep, *The Rites of Passage.*

23. See Adriani, et al., *Joseph Beuys* p. 73.

24. Joseph Beuys, quoted in ibid., p. 20.

25. Richard Ellmann, *James Joyce* (1959; repr. New York: Oxford University Press, 1982), p. 87.

26. See Joseph Beuys, *James Joyce* (1984), in *Joseph Beuys: Die Multiples* (Munich: Edition Schellmann, 1992), p. 376.

27. Erika Billeter, "Joseph Beuys" in *Mythos and Ritual in der Kunst der 70er Jahre* (Hamburg: Kunsterverein Hamburg, 1981), p. 90.

28. "Werkstattgespräch: Joseph Beuys, mit Hanno Reuther," in *Joseph Beuys: Werke aus der Sammlung Karl Ströher*, pp. 37 and 40.

Dan Graham: Sculpture as Architecture, Architecture as Sculpture

JOHN VINCI

Elements of Architecture

In Dan Graham's earliest published works, photographs, video installations, and writings, the subject of architecture is a recurrent theme. In "Homes for America," published in *Arts Magazine* in 1966, Graham analyzes "large-scale 'tract' housing 'developments'" which "constitute the new city."[1] After describing the mass production techniques of the real-estate developer and the limited choices given to the consumer, Graham concludes:

> Both architecture and craftsmanship as values are subverted by the dependence on simplified and easily duplicated techniques of fabrication and standardized modular plans. Contingencies such as mass production technology and land use economics make the final decisions, denying the architect his former "unique" role. Developments stand in an altered relationship to their environment. Designed to fill in "dead" land areas, the houses needn't adapt to or attempt to withstand Nature. There is no organic unity connecting the land site and the home. Both are without roots—separate parts in a larger, predetermined, synthetic order.[2]

Color photographs taken in the years 1965–69 illustrate the ironic and seductive aspects of tract housing and introduce Graham's observations concerning glass, reflectivity, and social phenomena observed in popular culture. Video works, such as *Present Continuous Past(s)* (1974), incorporate mirrors within an enclosed room. In this piece, mirrors are placed on two full adjacent walls within the installation, along with a video monitor with an eight-second delay that

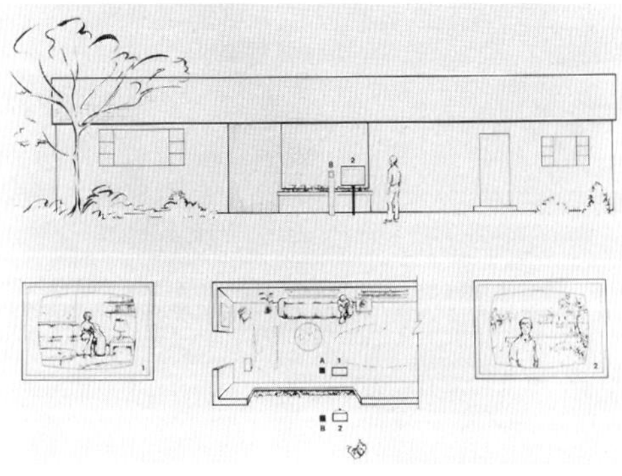

Dan Graham, *"Picture Window" Piece*, 1974.

allows viewers to see themselves eight seconds ago and yet "reflect present time."[3] With this work, Graham began his long-term involvement with glass in various forms, such as insulated glass (for sound attenuation), mirrored glass (for reflection), and clear glass (for illusory effects).

In *"Picture Window" Piece* (1974), a television monitor is placed outside the picture window of a suburban house. A camera continuously records the interior of the house, while a camera on the exterior videos the scene outside for display on a monitor indoors. The viewers indoors see the exterior through the window, while simultaneously viewing themselves inside their home. Persons outside can also view those inside the house by looking through the window, at the same time seeing themselves as they appear from the window. Graham later explained the role that architectural elements play in this work:

> The video camera/monitor is analogous to the window; they both mediate inside and outside space, but from an architecturally (socially) controlled vantage. These openings define a perspective on the other space by their exact size and shape (frame) and what part of the other space is in view at the central area of their picture plane.[4]

A photograph by Graham, *A Typical "Picture Window" from a Dutch Private Home*, further illustrates his statement. In "Conventions of the Glass Window," a related text featuring the "Dutch private home" photograph, Graham observes that "the glass window, like the Renaissance painting, creates a picture plane that places the world at a measured distance for the viewer on either side."[5] Additional architectural references, such as frame, glass, and window, play a prominent part in his ensuing works. *Public Space/Two Audiences* (1976), no longer incorporating video as a component, consists of two rooms divided by transparent thermopane (sound-insulating glass), which may be entered by one of two doors. The end wall of one of the rooms is mirrored. Once inside the work, as Graham explained,

> A spectator in the room with the mirror can choose several alternative ways of looking: he may look only at his own image in the mirror; he may observe himself in the mirror, [while] observing his relation to his group; he may, as an individual, observe in the mirror the other audience (seeing himself in relation to the other audience and perhaps the audience observing him at the same time as he observes them); he may, feeling himself a collective part of the audience, observe both audiences observing each other.... The spectator is made socially and psychologically more self-conscious...the observer becomes conscious of himself as a body, as a perceiving subject, and of himself in relation to his group.[6]

With *Public Space/Two Audiences*, Graham created an architectural structure that functioned as an environment for the observation of social and psychological behavior. *Square Room Diagonally Divided* (1978) offered an architectural variant of *Public Space/Two Audiences*; in it, Graham observed the major impact glass has had on contemporary society. In his essay, "Glass Used in Shop Windows/Commodities in Shop Windows," Graham continued his exploration of the use of glass:

> The glass used for the showcase, displaying products, isolates the consumer from the product at the same time as it superimposes the mirror-reflection of his own image onto the goods displayed. This alienation, paradoxically, helps arouse the desire to possess the commodity.... Under capitalism, just as the projected ego is confused with the body image in the mirror, so that ego is confused with the commodity.... The commodity reflects his desire for a more complete, "better self" identified with the alter *ego*.[7]

In another essay in the same publication, "Glass Buildings: Corporate 'Showcases,'" Graham wrote:

> At the same time that glass reveals, it conceals. If one looks into a glass showcase, one can have the illusion that the container is neutral, without apparent interest in the content of what it displays; or, conversely, the appearance of what is contained can be seen as a function of the qualities of the container itself.[8]

He concludes:

> A building with glass on four sides gives the illusion of self-containment; while it seems apparently open to visual inspection, in fact, in looking through glass on all sides, the particular, focused-upon detail, the "interior" is lost (one looks *through* and not *at*) to the architectural generality, to the apparent materialness of the outward form, or to "Nature" (light, sun, sky, or the landscape glimpsed through the building on the other side).[9]

Graham's early interior installations (through 1978), though relying on architectural devices, promoted social interaction while bringing psychological interrelationships to the fore. His photographs and essays focused on the properties of glass, as well as on the ramifications of its use in society.

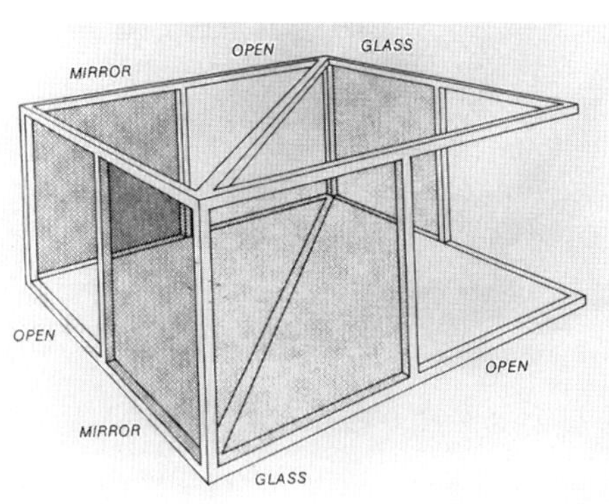

Dan Graham, drawing for *Pavilion/Sculpture for Argonne,* 1978–81.

Graham's proposals for pavilion/sculptures after 1978, translate the elements derived from his installations and writings and transform them into independent works of art. *Pavilion/Sculpture for Argonne* (1978–81), was commissioned as a companion piece for a

U.S. government–funded building at Argonne National Laboratories, twenty-eight miles southwest of Chicago, through the "% for Art" program. The building, semicircular in plan, was sheathed in reflective glass and opaque, green-and-white checkered glass-curtain walls. Confronted with the prospect of placing a work of art within or near this massive, aggressive building, Graham chose instead to place the pavilion several hundred feet away, in a wooded area beyond the building's parking lot:

> The sculpture/pavilion is aligned to the point where the building's front facade ends and its left side begins to curve. It is also aligned to the curve of the access road on its other side. It can be seen either from a car (where it is larger in scale than the Administration Building behind it) or approached on foot. Its orientation is such that the two interior mirrors catch the sun's reflection during the morning, creating a prismatic reflection in relation to the angled, sun-reflecting elements of the building. The diagonal element of *Pavilion/Sculpture for Argonne*, if extended toward the building, would perpendicularly bisect the diagonal floor plan of the building.[10]

Pavilion/Sculpture for Argonne is related to *Square Room Diagonally Divided* in plan and size. However, by virtue of its placement in an exterior setting, the framework and its related structure function as a support for the reflective glass, thus adding another dimension to Graham's work. The metal structure, seven and a half feet high by fifteen feet wide by fifteen feet long, is partially glazed on all sides with seven-and-a-half-foot-square sections of either mirrored or transparent glass. Clear glass divides the interior diagonally; unglazed portions allow the spectator to view the pavilion as a work of art and to relate to other spectators as a cohesive group. Besides reflecting nature, the pavilion also reflects the Argonne Administration Building, thus fulfilling its requirement as a sculpture for the new building. Graham's design not only achieved the goal of the commission but, through his use of cosmic devices—i.e., the reflective glass, the perceived line created by the diagonal element of the framework, and socio-psychological interaction—Graham created a unique and original work of art.

Architect/Sculptor Relationships: Contrasts and Conflicts

Dan Graham's site-specific sculpture for Argonne succeeds in relating to its site and to the object (the Argonne Administration Building) through the use of reflection and a line in space, thus avoiding the conflict of the sculpture's subservience to the building and creating a more balanced relationship between the two. Architecture and sculpture are united, yet separate, without tangible interventions.

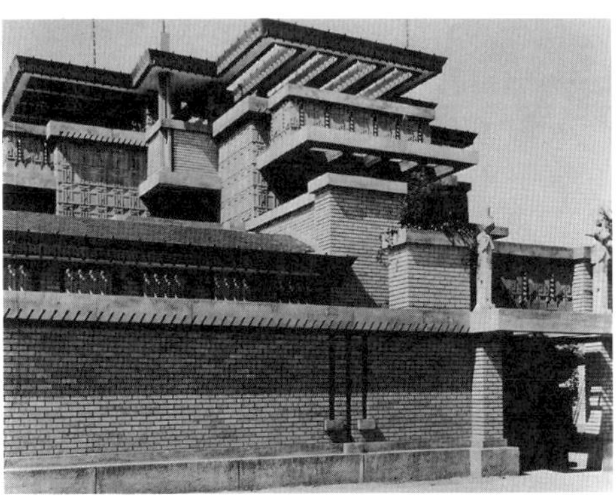

Frank Lloyd Wright, Midway Gardens, Chicago, 1915–17.

Sculpture's use in relation to public buildings by most major twentieth-century architects contrasts with Graham's approach. For instance, attempting to embellish his Midway Gardens (1915–17) as a place of culture, Frank Lloyd Wright commissioned Alphonso Iannelli to design "sprites" to line the tops of the wall piers. The completed sculptures were controlled and perhaps even designed by Wright, and the roles of architect and sculptor (modeler) remain ambiguous to this day. In another project, Iannelli was hired to design a sculptured relief for the interior frieze of George Elmslie's Woodbury County Courthouse in Sioux City, Iowa (1917). Unfortunately, Ianelli's *Order and Disorder*, an interpretation of the Ten Commandments, proved too risqué, as it contained realistic depictions of murder and adultery. Since the sculptor refused to change the images, the sculptures were omitted from the project. In this case, the architect, rather than creating a dialogue between sculpture and architecture, opted to avoid the conflict altogether.

In his German Pavilion in Barcelona (1928–29), Ludwig Mies van der Rohe placed a sculpture by Georg Kolbe off-center in a reflecting pool within the pavilion walls. Originally he was not interested in that particular work but could not locate a sculpture by Wilhelm Lehmbruck or another more important sculptor in time for the building's dedication. In essence, the sculpture was used merely as architectural decoration.

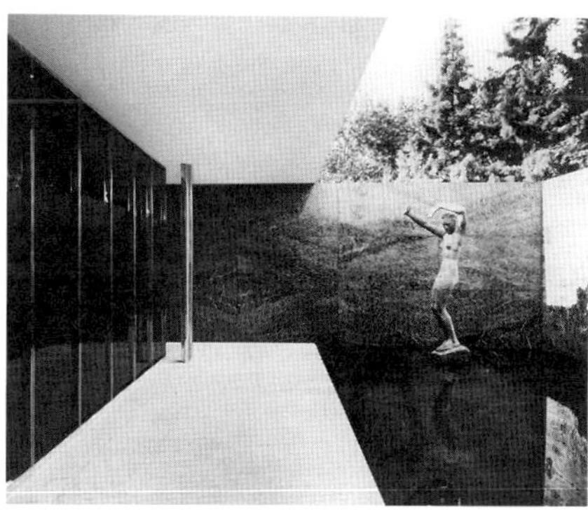

Ludwig Mies van der Rohe, German Pavilion, Barcelona, 1928–29.

During the 1960s and '70s, the placement of sculpture in public plazas became popular. Often, as in the case of Graham's Argonne pavilion, they were commissioned to comply with publicly funded arts programs. In 1972, Claes Oldenburg designed *Bat Column*, a gigantic latticed baseball bat, for the General Services Administration Building in Chicago. Confronted with the backdrop of a large, austere building with reflective glass-curtain walls, Oldenburg placed the sculpture vertically in front of the building on a narrow, amorphous plaza, in an attempt to relate his work to the massive building. The success of the work lies not so much in its relationship to the building, but rather as a comment on traditional monumentality.

Two recent works by Bruce Nauman are closer in concept to the Graham work. Architectural structures built of poured concrete, they each serve to direct the viewer into and through their respective buildings. At the University of New Mexico in Albuquerque, Nauman's sculpture *The Center of the Universe* (1988) was placed at a junction of several paths to the campus buildings. This forces pedestrians to experience Nauman's pavilion. Cross-shaped in plan and in section and measuring fifty feet by fifty

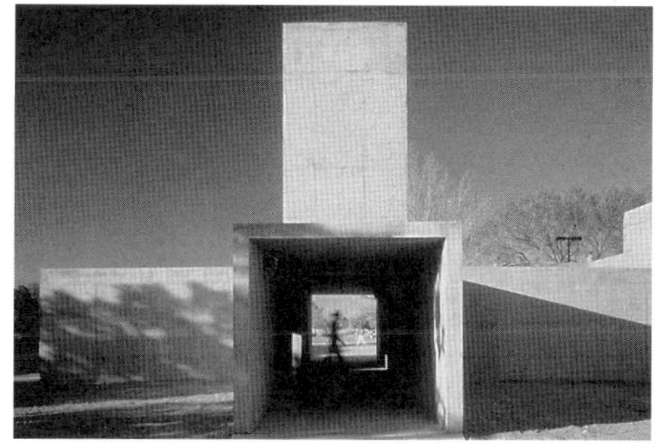

Bruce Nauman, *The Center of the Universe*, Albuquerque, 1988.

feet by fifty feet, the structure consists of three tubes (ten feet by ten feet by fifty feet) intersecting perpendicularly at their centers, similar in form to the object used in the game of jacks. Openings, oriented in opposite directions, frame views of the exterior in the direction they are facing: the vertical tube is open to the sky in the upward direction and to the earth twenty feet below in the downward direction. Spectators may enter one end and choose one of three possible exits. They may view the sky by looking upward, or they may contemplate the earth through a grate in the floor.

Nauman's work is site-specific and metaphorical, but its location and function, unlike Graham's pavilion/sculptures, create a confrontational situation for the users. Consequently, attempts have been made to disguise or embellish the structure with nature (plants and ivy). A second work by Nauman, *House Divided* (1983), built in Manilow Park at Governor State University near Chicago, is set in a pastoral setting. Its form, not unlike that of a gable-roofed barn, was also constructed of poured concrete and measures fourteen feet high by thirty feet long by twenty feet wide. Its rectangular floor plan is diagonally bisected by a concrete wall that segregates one half of the interior from the other. The viewer may enter one half and exit through the opposite end; the other half is solid and therefore inaccessible. Nauman's works, while offering sociopsychological situations, refer in their titles to specific metaphors to reinforce their sculptural nature; Graham's works, on the other hand, are interactive not only with the viewer but also with the reflected surroundings.

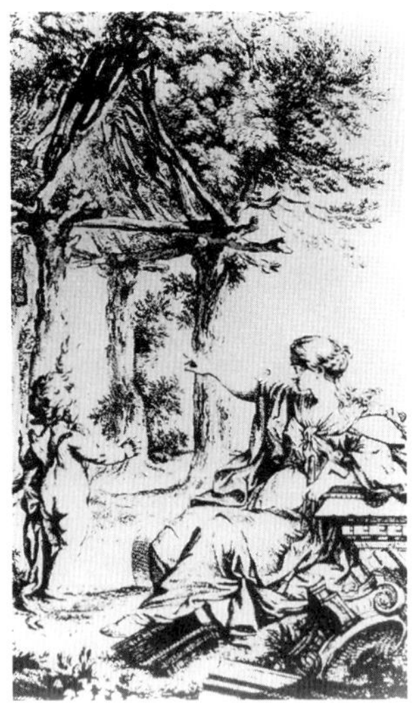

Marc-Antoine Laugier, from *Essai sur l'architecture* (Paris 1775).

Graham's pavilion/sculptures are related to Abbé Marc-Antoine Laugier's "rustic hut" proposed in 1775 as a first principal for architecture. Referencing the earliest classical temples, he felt it encompassed more than a simple structure and represented a microcosm of a larger idea. Graham, with Robin Hurst, wrote in the essay "Corporate Arcadias,"

This elementary hut Laugier set in an Edenic nature, as a critique of the despoilments of the new, disordered bourgeois city. As a model, the hut, a simple shelter, reduced architecture to an absolute elemental base, reflecting an Enlightenment myth of a social arcadia in terms of the urban plan. Simultaneously, the hut evoked two related archetypes: first, Greek architecture's pure, geometric, elementary forms; second, the original derivation of its column from the tree.[11]

Architects/Architecture: Reference Points in the Work of Dan Graham

Laugier's rustic hut is pivotal to understanding the essential architectural nature of Graham's pavilion/sculptures. It informs as well his observations of the work of such architects as Mies van der Rohe, Philip Johnson, Robert Venturi, and Leon Krier. Rational thought underlies and governs the work of van der Rohe. With his two apartment buildings at 860–880 Lake Shore Drive in Chicago (1948–51), often considered the first all-glass-and-steel towers, he devised a method for constructing high-rise buildings inexpensively. Yet, for Graham, they epitomize the image of the corporate "showcase." Structure is the predominant element of these two identical buildings, sited across from Lake Michigan. Steel mullions, attached vertically to the exterior frame at four-foot increments, support the glass and create a modular rhythm on the structure. Often interpreted solely as decoration, the mullions also serve a secondary structural function. The towers, three bays by five bays in plan, are placed perpendicular to one another and staggered to fit the irregular site. This composition was the result of a request from Northwestern University that the buildings not block the lake view from their adjoining site. The project's success lay in Mies's creative solutions conjoining his rational concerns with his artistic sensibilities.

Like Mies's glass towers, Graham's *Two Adjacent Pavilions* (1978–82), installed on the grounds of the Rijksmuseum Kröller-Müller in Otterlö, Holland, consists of two equal framed glass structures that are integrated with their site.[12] This work was placed in a sculpture park, an "arcadian" setting, as Graham notes, that evolved from French and English gardens. According to Graham,

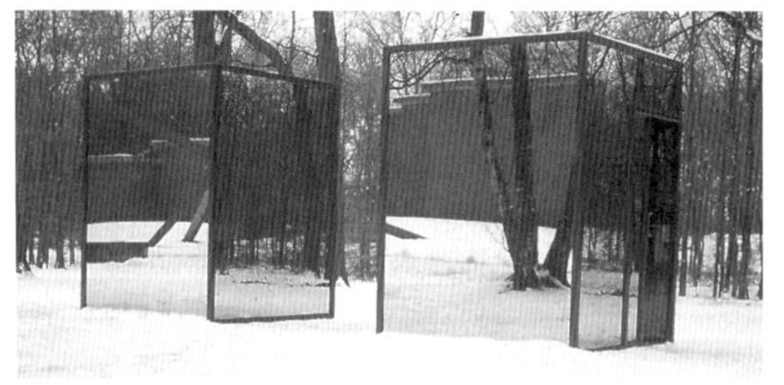

Dan Graham, *Two Adjacent Pavilions*, 1978–82.

"The work places the materials and forms of the modern city—glass and reflective glass with steel supports—in a 'natural' or utopian setting." He further states:

> *Two Adjacent Pavilions* picks up another tradition, the transformation of the horizontal, "curtain-wall," glass office-building into the vertical modern glass museum placed in an isolated country setting...or the bourgeoised variant of the romantic (nineteenth century) "aristocratic" glass house country retreats such as Mies van der Rohe's *Farnsworth House* in Illinois or Philip Johnson's own house in Connecticut.[13]

The relation of Graham's work to the architecture of Philip Johnson and Mies van der Rohe is largely dependent on the social implications of these structures and their settings, and to a lesser extent on their use of similar materials. According to artist and critic Jeff Wall, Graham's pavilion/sculptures play on the "fantasies" associated with the house Philip Johnson designed for himself in New Canaan, Connecticut (1949), and Mies van der Rohe's house for Dr. Edith Farnsworth (1945–51).[14] Wall assigns anthropomorphic values to the presence of these houses in pastoral settings, contrasting the structures as they are alternately perceived in the night and in the day, and attributing vampiric symbolism to the reflectivity of the glass at night. He characterized the opening and closing of the draperies in the

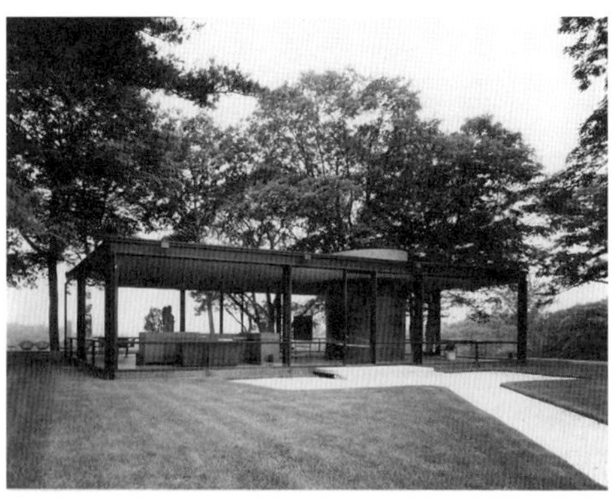

Philip Johnson's house in New Canaan, Connecticut, 1949.

Farnsworth House as a defeatist measure that denies the real boundary at the end of the property. The country houses possess functional characteristics and, by their nature, demand auxiliary methods to assure their usefulness, thus affecting the nature of the architecture. Graham's pavilion/sculptures, on the other hand, rely solely on their reflectivity and transparency and on the interaction between viewer and site, without ultimately having to serve as operative structures.

Mies's aspirations were not, as Wall contends, conceived in a spirit of "self-consciously tragic negativism."[15] On the contrary, he aspired to a higher order of architecture than seemed possible at that time. Mies is often quoted as saying, "Less is more," or as declaring, "God is in the details," expressing a theological attitude toward architecture. In other words, the closer one comes to achieving perfection, the closer one is to God, in the same way that a cloistered nun strives for perfection in her daily life. Mies's architecture has been characterized as embodying Thomas Aquinas's dictum, "Order is the disposition of equal and unequal parts attributing each to its place."[16] The Farnsworth House, which measured twenty-eight feet by seventy-eight feet, was designed with an open plan, free of interior columns. Rooms were formed by freestanding walls and cabinets, evoking what Mies referred to as "universal space," a device developed in his earlier work. The floor of the house, which was suspended four feet above the ground, allowed the structure to be sited close to the river while remaining above the flood plain. The asymmetrically placed stairway provided access to the open porch. The white painted steel and simplified detailing emphasized the perfection of its form.

The house of Philip Johnson, an unwavering disciple of Mies at the time, was conceived in the spirit of Mies and was similar to discarded studies of the Farnsworth House. These two houses are referred to interchangeably by Graham, as well as by Jeff Wall in his essay. Johnson was quoted as saying that the brick floor and round brick core were "derived from a burnt-out wooden village,"[17] although, in fact, the use of brick in his floor patterns resembles the floors in the houses Mies built in Germany in the late 1920s. The "fantasies" defined by Wall instill a creative narrative in relation to both houses, but it is the architectural concept that lies at the foundation of Graham's work. Graham does not aim to be the master of architectural detail, as did Mies, nor is he the arbiter of good taste, as is Philip Johnson. Rather, Graham's pavilion/sculptures depend on their sociopsychological meaning, as well as on the assistance of an architect and/or builder for their visual impact.

In an attempt to break from the "heroic" architecture of the modern movement, Robert Venturi wrote *Complexity and Contradiction in Architecture* in 1962. Published in 1966, this influential book was a reaction against the tenets of modernism. In it, Venturi wrote:

> I am for richness of meaning rather than clarity of meaning; for the implicit function as well as the explicit function. I prefer "both-and" to "either-or," black and white, and sometimes gray, to black or white. A valid architecture evokes many levels of meaning and combinations of focus: its space and its elements become readable and workable in several ways at once.
>
> But an architecture of complexity and contradiction has a special obligation toward the whole: its truth must be in its totality or its implications of total-ity. It must embody the difficult unity of inclusion rather than the easy unity of exclusion. More is not less.

Continuing this premise, he added:

> Orthodox modern architects have tended to recognize complexity insufficiently or inconsistently. In their attempt to break with tradition and start all over again, they idealized the primitive and elementary at the expense of the diverse and sophisticated. As participants in a revolutionary movement, they acclaimed the newness of modern functions, ignoring their complications. In their role as reformers, they puritanically advocated the separation and exclusion of elements, rather than the inclusion of various requirements and their juxtapositions.[18]

Venturi's litany of contradictory aspects of architecture, both current and historical "at varying levels of program and structure,"[19] concludes:

> ...is not Main Street almost all right?...And it is perhaps from the everyday landscape, vulgar and disdained, that we can draw the complex and contradictory order that is valid and vital for our architecture as an urbanistic whole.[20]

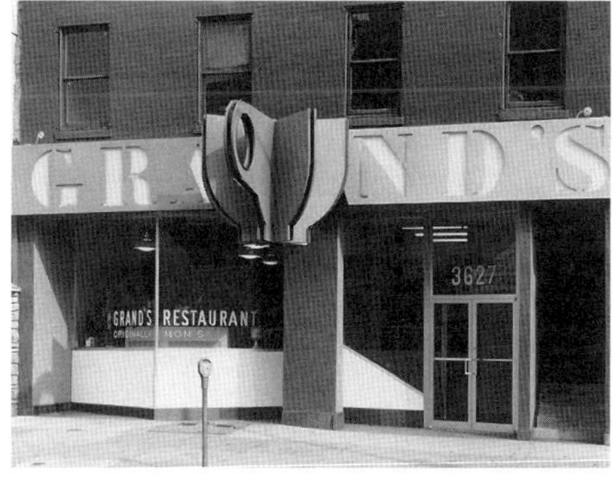

Venturi, Scott Brown and Associates, Inc., Grand's Restaurant, Philadelphia, 1967.

Accompanying the publication of Venturi's thesis were illustrations with text of his proposed and executed projects. One of the earliest projects depicted was the 1967 renovation of a restaurant in West Philadelphia, once known as Mom's, in which two storefronts were combined to form a single interior. Venturi's device of hanging a large porcelain cutout of a coffee cup at the junction of the two storefronts and incorporating large stenciled backlit letters—"GRAND'S"—across the entire facade integrated the composition. This modest project enforced the dualities expressed in *Complexity and Contradiction in Architecture* and marked a pivotal point in Venturi's architectural development. With this project, he introduced an element of vernacular architecture by adhering to the modest character of the restaurant, with its ordinary furnishings, and incorporating Pop Art by means of the giant cup, bright colors, and super graphics, derived from the work of Jasper Johns.

Guild House, Friends Housing for the Elderly (1960–63) in Philadelphia was Venturi's first major building. With the incorporation of decorative concepts and with the deemphasis of the structural elements in favor of the brick veneer, Venturi entered a new era in architectural expression, consciously acknowledging the "decorated shed." He maintained the urban character of this six-story apartment building by placing the majority of the apartments and a public meeting area on the front facade, facing south, on the active streetscape. Using setbacks, he not only achieved the maximum length of the street facade exposure but also emphasized its impact. The central facade, four bays wide, features an entry divided by a structural column which, encased in a monolithic, polished, dark gray granite, emphasizes the entrance; white glazed bricks are used for further enhancement. The floors above the entrance have recessed balconies, and the top floor terminates in a nonstructural arch, pointing to the veneer of the plain, brownish-red brick wall. Perforated metal panels form the balcony railings and a large decorative television antenna tops the central composition. The otherwise plain, recessed facades are interrupted with overscaled but modestly designed double-hung windows; one course of white glazed brick demarcates the unadorned masonry walls.

In reference to his mother's house in Chestnut Hill, Pennsylvania (1962), Venturi stated:

> This building recognizes complexities and contradictions: it is both complex and simple, open and closed, big and little; some of its elements are good on one level and bad on another; its order accommodates the generic elements of the house in general, and the circumstantial elements of a house in particular. It achieves the difficult unity of a medium number of diverse parts rather than the easy unity of few or many motival parts.[21]

Without attempting to imitate classical architecture, Venturi created a small house of ordinary construction, evoking the small, Mannerist pavilions of the seventeenth century.

In 1972, Robert Venturi, Denise Scott Brown, and Steven Izenour published *Learning from Las Vegas*, based on a studio course they had taught in 1968 at Yale University. Analyzing Las Vegas as a phenomenon of architectural communication, it served as a critique of the modern movement, which had ignored popular taste, and called attention to the "messy vitality" of the strip. Classical parallels and contrasts are found in the use of statuary and decorative neon signs. The relevance to the earlier work of Venturi and to later urban planning projects reinforced the dialectic; sign and symbol became the underlying theme of the office of Venturi, Rauch, and Scott Brown.

Responding to early criticism of his architecture by architects Philip Johnson and Gordon Bunshaft as being "ugly and ordinary," Venturi, rather than ignoring the reference, adopted the phrase to refer to some aspects of his work.[22] He used "ugly and ordinary" (U&O) and, in contrast, introduced the term "heroic and original" (H&O), to apply to modernist design. Contrasting the Central Fire Station in New Haven, Connecticut (1959–62) with his own recently completed fire station in Columbus, Indiana (1968), Venturi wrote:

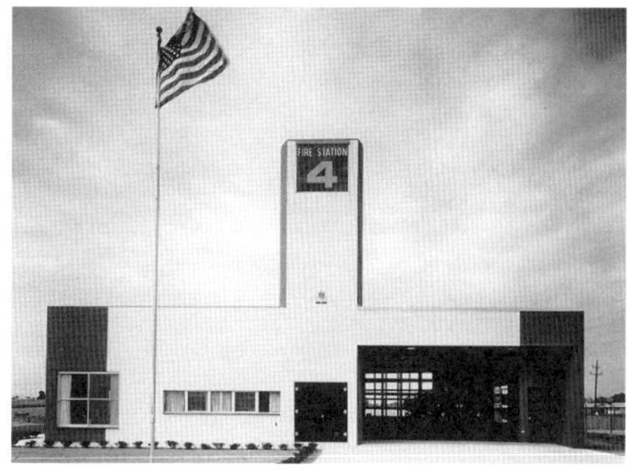

Venturi, Scott Brown and Associates, Inc., Fire Station #4, Columbus, Indiana, 1968.

> We have shown how heroic and original (H&O) architecture derives dramatic expression from the connotative meanings of its "original" elements: It gives off abstract meanings—or rather, expressions—recognizable in the physiognomic character of the architectural elements. Ugly and ordinary (U&O) architecture, on the other hand, includes denotative meanings as well, derived from its familiar elements; that is, it suggests more or less concrete meanings via association and past experience. The "brutalism" of an H&O fire station comes from its rough texture; its civic monumentality comes from its big scale; the expression of structure and program and "truth to materials" comes from the particular articulations of its forms. Its total image derives from these purely architectural qualities transmitted through abstract forms, textures, and colors, carefully composed. The total image of our U&O fire house—an image implying civic character as well as specific use—comes from the conventions of roadside architecture that it follows; from

> the decorated false facade, from the banality through familiarity of the standard aluminum sash and roll-up doors, and from the flagpole in front—not to mention the conspicuous sign that identifies it through spelling, the most denotative of symbols: FIRE STATION NO. 4. These elements act as symbols as well as expressive architectural abstractions. They are not merely ordinary but represent ordinariness symbolically and stylistically; they are enriching as well, because they add a layer of literary meaning.[23]

Venturi applied this analysis to his later works. He referred to the Wislocki House (1970) as "ordinary and ugly" and to the larger Trubeck House (1970) as "complex and contradictory." These two small houses on Nantucket Island, Massachusetts, designed in the shingle style of the nineteenth century but adapted to more current life-styles, enforced the idea that choices of style can be made. Venturi's dwelling style prototypes (a concept not unlike illustrations found in J. C. Loudin's *Encyclopedia* of 1834)[24] led to his proposal, "A Garden Party of Styles: Eclectic House Facades" (1977). Venturi's proposal, as opposed to Graham's "Homes for America," suggests a noncorrupted point of view. In "Homes for America," the architect is denied "his former 'unique' role,"[25] and the consumer and the developer are the sole arbiters of taste. However, in the case of Loudin and Venturi, the choice of style is selected by the user but the architectural design is controlled by the architect.

In his essay "Art in Relation to Architecture: Architecture in Relation to Art," Graham summarizes the interaction between artist (Pop and Conceptual) and architecture (Bauhaus and Postmodernist) in the current social structure. Graham observes the multifaceted aspects of Venturi's work:

> By displaying its rhetoric and (social) function openly, and by using contradictory conventional codes in the same building, Venturi opts for a realist (conventional) and multivalent architecture, one whose structure is conventional (semiotic) rather than abstract or materialistic, and whose aim is basically communicative.[26]

Graham concludes with a sympathetic summary of Venturi's point of view:

> The task of the work of art or architecture is not the resolution of social or ideological conflict in a beautiful artwork, and not the construction of a new ideological counter-content; instead the artwork directs attention to the seams in various ideological representations (revealing the conflicting variety of ideological readings). To do this the work uses a hybrid form, one which partakes of both the popular code of mass media and the "high" code of art/architecture, of both the popular code of entertainment and a theoretically based political analysis of form, and of both the code of information and of the esthetically formal.[27]

The earliest pavilion/sculptures produced by Graham are more related to Bauhaus architecture (reflective glass, steel, etc.) and Conceptual Art (minimal construction, abstraction, etc.) than to the architecture inspired by Venturi (decorated sheds, signs, etc.). Since transparency allows for multiple, yet clear, meanings, Graham's pavilion/sculptures share the idea in common with Venturi's architecture that a building's exterior (sign) represents the interior (content). One project which codifies Venturi's theories and relates to Graham's "'high' code of art/architecture" is Venturi and Rauch's Franklin Court (1976) in Philadelphia. The architects were commissioned to restore Ben Franklin's house but instead proposed and built a "ghost" of the once-existing house based on information from archaeological excavations. The museum was built underground and a small urban park was placed above the museum along with "a 'ghost-house,' a work of Conceptual art: A schematic, painted-steel framework whose linear outline approximates the form that the earlier house took, two open-framed cubic forms topped by a schematic chimney."[28]

Graham identifies the underlying significance of Venturi and Rauch's Franklin Court in "Not Post-Modernism: History as Against Historicism, European Archetypal Vernacular in Relation to American Commercial Vernacular, and the City as Opposed to the Individual Building":

As a signifier of eighteenth-century Philadelphia and the "complete" form of the rebuilt eighteenth-century apartment, the use of an obviously twentieth-century grid section to represent the former existence of the house is more than merely ironic. It alludes to the invisible, neutral, and conventionally atemporal space-grid utilized in compositions of Bauhaus architecture and city planners, a grid assumed to run throughout the city.[29]

This text also brings into focus the urban, political, and utopian inferences that are to be found in Graham's work. Beginning with the European architectural historian Manfredo Tafuri's socialist view of "urban design during the capitalist epoch as a series of individual and symbolic statements about society,"[30] Graham introduces the theories of European architect Leon Krier, who sees individual Postmodern buildings as simply useless attempts at creating a better society. Instead, Krier proposes a reconstruction of the European city to revitalize its environment. This is to be accomplished by introducing enormous structures into negative or public spaces between buildings, unifying the city's fabric and creating social centers, "open 24 hours,"[31] which would replace churches, schools, and municipal social functions. Krier sees the city as an integrated whole bounded by "natural or artificial elements, rivers, valleys, hills...also parks, canals, railroads, motorways, avenues, boulevards."[32] The theories of Laugier relating to the design of parks and cities are used as a point of reference by both Tafuri and Krier. They consider Laugier's primitive hut to be a pivotal work that signifies the human condition, the state of architectural philosophy, and the relationship of man to the landscape in the Age of

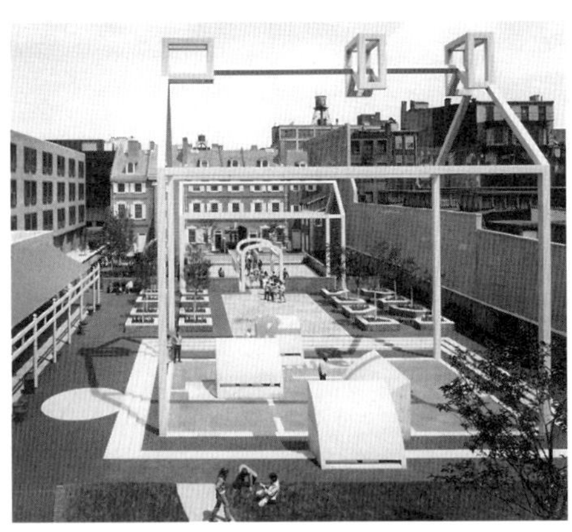

Venturi, Scott Brown and Associates, Franklin Court, Independence National Historical Park, Philadelphia, 1976.

Enlightenment. Graham's pavilion/sculptures are rooted in the social phenomena of the present age through his use of structure in its relationship to its environment.

Arcadian Utopias

A late video work, *Video View of Suburbia in an Urban Atrium* (1979–80), marks the transition from Graham's video installations to his pavilion/sculptures. In this work, viewers sitting in a coffee concession in the Citicorp building atrium in New York City are able to view the outside of a suburban house on monitors. The interior "vest pocket" urban park is thereby contrasted with the suburban environment. Graham states: "If the atrium's design represents an urban fantasy of the picturesque brought to the city center, the image on the monitors represents the actual suburb on the edge of the city."[33]

This juxtaposition of fantasy and reality by way of reference to isolated natural settings recalls Graham's interest in nineteenth-century industrial construction. Usually built of cast iron and glass, those structures were conceived as controlled environments to house and study vegetation and "to capture nature and thus preserve the memory of a natural utopian world."[34] London's Crystal Palace, for example, built in 1851 for the first International Fair, was the first building to bring together industrial products, technological inventions, art, and botanical gardens in a single, enclosed structure in the midst of a metropolis.

Pergola/Conservatory (1987), exhibited at the Marian Goodman Gallery in New York, is a longitudinal, open-ended arched walkway with two-way-mirrored glass ceiling and sides. Covered with greenery, *Pergola/ Conservatory* is a "hybrid" symbolizing the arcadian aspects of

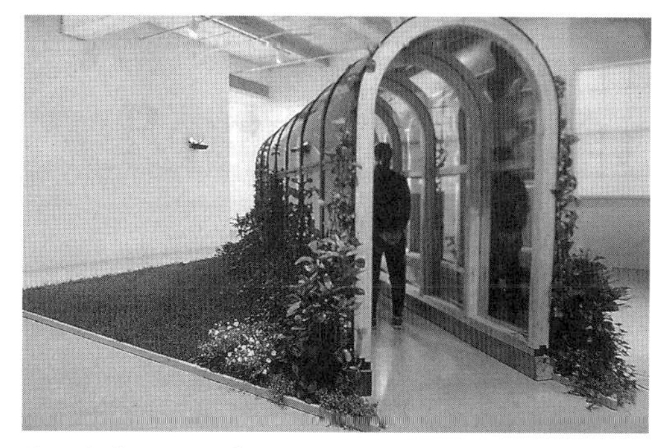

Dan Graham, *Pergola/Conservatory*, 1987.

nineteenth-century greenhouses and interior "public spaces" isolated within contemporary urban structures. As curator Anne Rorimer astutely observed:

> The work, as a result, does not function as a conventionally self-contained sculpture isolated in space but instead is activated by the viewers in their awareness of themselves as part of it. Graham compares the spectators' view of themselves on the mirrored vault to the experience of Baroque ceiling frescoes, while he supplants such painted visions of saints and angels in heaven with the viewers' own "vision" of themselves, here set against the real, and not an illusory, sky. Anamorphic distortions of the viewer's image relative to the spherical mirror do not rely on artistic sleight of hand but pertain to optical fact. In *Pergola/Conservatory* natural phenomena in conjunction with man-made, industrial materials replace human artifice. It is the rays of the sun that are responsible for creating a sense of ongoing visual variation within the work and that contribute to the effect of chiaroscuro and movement produced by the shadows of the leafy vines.[35]

Fantasy, operating in conjunction with representation, reinforces the impact of this and other works of this period. In *Octagon for Münster* (1987), an octagonal pavilion is supported in the center of its pyramidal roof by a wooden pole. Its sliding door allows the viewers to completely enclose themselves in the two-way mirrored interior. This pavilion was placed at the end of an allée of trees, a remnant of a former eighteenth-century garden that once contained classical octagonal pavilions. Graham states:

> While the octagonal form, its siting in the allée and the use of mirrored surfaces related it to the classical baroque period, the use of wood, the "primitive" wood pole and its compact scale alternatively related the pavilion to the simple "rustic hut" associated with romantic, antiurban ideology of the post-Enlightenment garden. The music pavilion, [an existing structure] which is opened on five of its sides, is something like a

gazebo. My pavilion has a similar relation to a nineteenth-century gazebo, but contradicts this traditional form. Instead of the sides of my "Octagon" being open so that those inside might have the prospect of the natural setting and be better seen by those outside the pavilion, the use of the two-way mirror turns both inside and outside views into self-reflections.[36]

In "Corporate Arcadias," Dan Graham and Robin Hurst codify these observations. Using the Age of Enlightenment and Laugier's rustic hut as points of reference, they analyze the skylighted atriums of modern buildings with respect to their inflection or rejection of the outer environment. Graham and Hurst cite structures such as Frank Lloyd Wright's Larkin Building (1904–06, now demolished) in Buffalo, New York, which contained skylighted atriums isolated from the streetscape with its adjacent railroad lines and industrial traffic, and Disneyland's "Tomorrowland," which seeks to promote an idyllic, technological life-style. These buildings contained utopian concepts that promised idealized conditions for working and living detached from the real world. Graham and Hurst observed:

> During the '60s, the American city's core came to be dominated by high-rise office buildings. Metaphorically, these corporate showcases use the social openness and transparency of window glass to merge the image of technology implicit in the buildings' construction with that of efficient business practice, for the passerby can observe, through the glass, the workings of the company. At the same time, the building seems to open to the environment, incorporating into itself the light and sky reflected in the glass or, sometimes, visible through the glass on the structure's other side.[37]

Specifically, owners of buildings such as the Ford Foundation, New York (1968) by Roche and Dinkaloo, and Hyatt Regency hotels by architect/developer John Portman, took advantage of this concept, creating interior atriums which, privately owned, maintained, and controlled, eliminated the threat of crime and drugs usually associated with urban living. Not only were these utopian settings considered "public amenities," but their developers took advantage of incentives such as additional square footage of rentable office space in exchange for providing public access to them. The atrium (with other similar corporate endeavors) signified "an attempt to smooth over contradictions between environmental decay and technological progress. As miniutopian retreats from the stresses of city life, it reevokes the notion of 'garden' as idealized landscape (the return to a preurban Eden), attempting to reconnect it to the idea of technology as an aid to man."[38]

The long-term *Rooftop Urban Park Project* (1991) at Dia Center for the Arts may be compared to several early works. According to Graham:

> ...the solution came out of wanting to go back to that period when I was doing films and video. The first film that I made, *From Sunrise to Sunset*, actually was concerned with the horizon line making a gradual spiral to map the entire length, and so you were at the very top of the sky at sunset and at sunrise ....And for the last film that I did, *Body Press*, I built a mirrorized cylinder, and I had a man and a woman, each naked, holding a camera against their bodies and making a spiral, mapping their bodies....Also, because it was clearly handled, held in people's hands, it had that subjective sense of being identified with the performer, so the spectator identified with the performer....It also picked up all sorts of issues from Godard to Jacques Lacan about the other and the mirror stage.[39]

Besides its affinity to Graham's videos and to film, the pavilion/sculpture *Two-Way Mirror Cylinder Inside Cube* (1981/1991), perched on a platform on the roof of Dia Center for the Arts, and the related *Video Salon* can be traced to an earlier unrealized work, *Cylinder Inside Cube*, created in model form in 1986 and in 1988 as a detailed drawing. In the drawing, an open-ceilinged, square room of lightly reflective glass, twelve by twelve feet, housed a six-foot-diameter cylinder of glass with a clear glass ceiling; the viewer could enter the square room and observe the viewers inside the cylinder or vice versa. Panoramic reflections of the surroundings would be activated by the movement of the viewer and by changes in light, atmosphere, sun, and clouds. The Dia work combined these attributes while relating the work more specifically to its surroundings. Dia's brochure for the work summarizes the project:

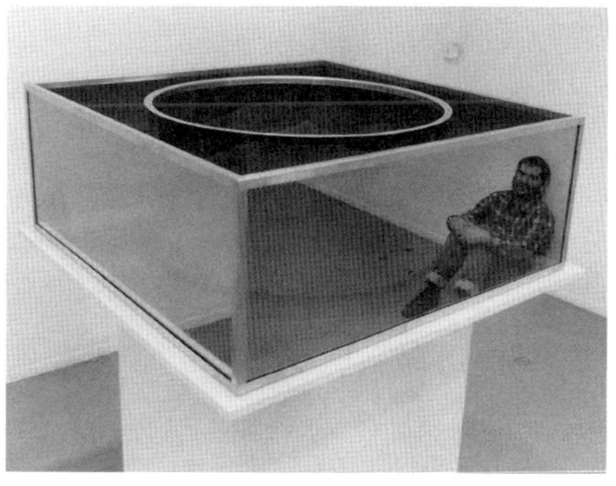

Dan Graham, model of *Cylinder Inside Cube*, 1981.

> The inner cylinder takes its form metaphorically from the bodies of the viewers, as well as, more literally, from the adjacent water tower, a ubiquitous feature of the Manhattan skyline. Graham is keenly aware, too, of the proximity to Battery Park City, also on the Hudson River, whose public art projects were devised for functional as much as decorative ends. But the location has, for him, an additional linkage, namely to certain "cutting edge" alternative venues like The Kitchen, for like them, his structure is intended to be used also for dance, music, and other types of performance events. Consequently, he argues, "My two-way mirror pavilions can be seen as microcosms of the city environment as a whole." Yet, significantly, he brings these ideas together in an abstract and generalized way, one which permits him to incorporate the process of viewing as an integral aspect of the thematic content.[40]

The Dia pavilion/sculpture is Graham's largest work to date. Taking sculpture, performance, and video into account, it enabled Graham to clarify his role as a sculptor. Working with Baratloo/Balch architects, the construction and design of details such as the raised platform, staircase, revolving curved panel of glass, and mullions with domed nut-and-bolt fasteners, raise issues of the aesthetics initiated by the architect, which can confuse authorship of the total work. In the case of *Cylinder Inside Cube*, Graham's intentions are clearly identified. Due to the overwhelming size of the pavilion/sculpture, however, the details introduced by the architect are a secondary concern that distracts from the essential form of the initial design. The Farnsworth House of Mies van der Rohe, also on a raised platform, with its perfectly proportioned facades and the integrated design of its asymmetrical staircase, is clearly the work of one person; in *Cylinder Inside Cube*, however, two separate disciplines, that of the architect and that of the sculptor, are at work in opposition to one another.

The concept and the reality of the work, once it has been executed, introduce an intriguing element of contrast. One is reminded of the Statue of Liberty (1886), designed by Frédéric-Auguste Bartholdi, engineered by Alexandre-Gustave Eiffel, which stands on a base (now mostly obliterated by a surrounding additional platform) designed by architect Richard Morris Hunt. In this case, the respective roles of architect, engineer, and sculptor remain clearly separate, yet equal in terms of the work as a whole. Graham's pavilion/sculptures, unlike traditional composites of architecture and sculpture, introduce a new dimension into the relationship insofar as they give priority to their concept over their execution. *Cylinder Inside Cube*, therefore, is able to assume new form and meaning depending on the variable secondary elements (i.e., its material, construction details, and, necessarily, its site conditions).

The reflective surface, so crucial to Graham's sculpture, has precedence in both contemporary art and earlier architecture. For example, Larry Bell's pristine Plexiglas cubes, sometimes as small as ten by ten inches or as large as forty by forty inches, made an impression on Graham when they were exhibited in the late 1960s because of their sleek, reflective surfaces and architectonic framework. The vitreous surfaces in such structures as the Amalienburg *Spiegelsaal* by François de Cuvillies (1695–1768) on the grounds of the Nymphenburg Palace in Munich also inspired Graham to incorporate mirrors into his earliest architectural works. An explicit description written by Graham in relation to *Two Adjacent Pavilions* illustrates the metaphoric potential of pavilion/sculptures:

> My pavilions are placed in an analogous relation to the large Fridericianum palace, as similar, small pavilions were placed in

> relation to the bureaucratic main palace in the seventeenth century. One example of such siting would be Munich's Amalienburg Pavilion.…It contained a ten-sided *Spiegalsaal* or hall of mirrors, with open corridors at two ends. The formal aesthetic of this *Spiegalsaal* connected the king to the mythology of artificial nature upon which the plan of Nymphenburg's formal garden, as well as the alchemical principle of the pavilion was based. The mirror room related the exterior to the interior, sunlight to the material qualities of mirrors and windows, and daylight to the artificial light of night-time. Each of the four windows was oriented to a cardinal direction. Pedestrian pathways radiated from each window, continuing into the woods toward north, south, east, and west nodes.…The sun's light turned the silvered mirrors and hence the entire room (including its intricate silverwork of artificial nature "imitating" the arranged "real foliage" of the exterior park) gold.[41]

Other parallels between existing architectural projects and the sculpture of Graham come to mind. The pavilion/sculpture *Altered Two-Way Mirror Revolving Door and Chamber with Sliding Door (for Loïe Fuller exhibition)*, 1987, was designed for exhibitions in Lyon and Dijon as a passageway to a performance space wherein the films of the dancer Loïe Fuller were projected and re-creations of her dances were presented. The entry, with its mirrored revolving doors and sliding panels, reflected the viewer and created movement, alluding to the dancer. The plan concept (a circle bisected by an octagon) suggested the schematic plans of nineteenth-century buildings, such as William Strickland's Merchants Exchange (1832) in Philadelphia. Plan abstractions

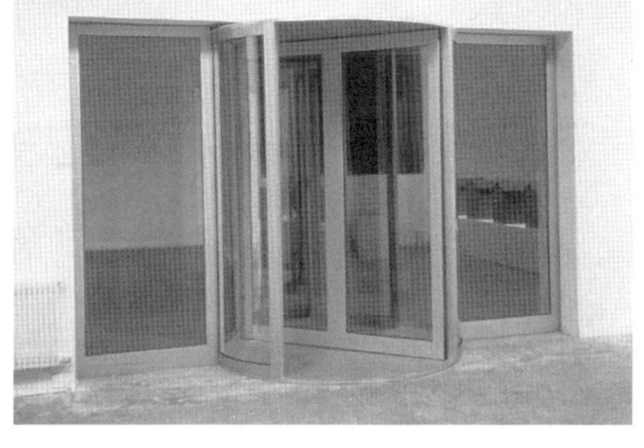

Dan Graham, *Altered Two-Way Mirror Revolving Door and Chamber with Sliding Door (for Loïe Fuller exhibition)*, 1987.

from other buildings, such as Henry Walter's Capitol building (1846) in Columbus, Ohio, with its classical drum placed on a rectangular plan, can also be projected onto Graham's work of this period.

Later pavilion/sculptures, such as the *Heart Pavilion*, made for the "Carnegie International 1991," took on a symbolic dimension. Placed at the entrance of the museum, adjacent to a wall with a large Warhol painting of Elvis Presley, reflective glass walls created a heart-shaped enclosure. Based on an earlier maquette, the pavilion/sculpture related to Graham's interest in rock music and his admiration for popular culture. Another recent pavilion, the *Gate of Hope* (1990–91), built in Stuttgart in 1993 for the "International Garden Year" (an ecological world's fair occurring every ten years), takes the form of a three-sided pyramid composed entirely of equilateral triangles, open on one side, with a truncated corner creating a triangular archway at the opposite end that suggests eternal life and thus hope for society and its environment.

Graham's use of architecture as a basis for his pavilion/sculptures has expanded the scope of his earliest works and has prompted an entirely new reading of the relationship between work and site. The "architecture" of Graham's work, in a sense, is constructed not only of glass and framework, but also incorporates other factors such as reflection, sociopsychological interaction, and historical references including the rustic hut, nineteenth-century conservatories, and corporate atriums. These elements are metaphors for broader implications of social interaction. Graham's works are conceptual manifestations realized by an intermediate figure such as the model maker, the architect, and/or the structural engineer. They are predicated on the ability of the viewer/user to experience the work. Graham's pavilion/sculptures are an innovative contribution to the meaning of sculpture and its relationship to architecture in an interactive environment.

November 12, 1992

Notes

1. Dan Graham, "Homes for America," *Arts Magazine* 41, no. 2/3 (December 1966–January 1967), pp. 21–22.

2. Ibid., p. 22.

3. Dan Graham, "Present Continuous Past(s)," in *Video-Architecture-Television*, ed. B.H.D. Buchloh (Halifax: The Press of the Nova Scotia College of Art & Design and New York University Press, New York, 1979), p. 7.

4. Dan Graham, "'Picture Window' Piece," in ibid., p. 35.

5. Dan Graham, "Conventions of the Glass Window," in ibid., p. 66.

6. Dan Graham, *Dan Graham: Buildings and Signs*, ed. Anne Rorimer (Chicago: The Renaissance Society at the University of Chicago, 1981), p. 24.

7. Dan Graham, "Glass Used in Shop Windows/Commodities in Shop Windows," in *Video-Architecture-Television*, p. 72.

8. Dan Graham, "Glass Buildings: Corporate 'Showcases,'" in ibid., p. 74.

9. Ibid., p. 76.

10. Graham, *Dan Graham: Buildings and Signs*, p. 29.

11. Dan Graham and Robin Hurst, "Corporate Arcadias," *Artforum* 26, no. 4 (December 1987), p. 68.

12. The model for these pavilions was built in 1978, and a version with an aluminum frame was constructed in 1982 for Documenta 7 in Kassel, Germany.

13. Dan Graham, "Two Adjacent Pavilions," in *Dan Graham*, ed. Gary Dufour (Perth: Art Gallery of Western Australia), p. 46.

14. Jeff Wall, "Dan Graham's *Kammerspiel*," in ibid., p. 14. See also the revised version of this essay, *Dan Graham's Kammerspiel* (Toronto: Art Metropole, 1991).

15. Ibid., p. 29.

16. As quoted by Professor Alfred Caldwell in relation to Mies's work. Caldwell lectured at Illinois Institute of Technology during Mies's tenure. His lectures on Mies and other figures of the nineteenth and twentieth centuries, such as Louis Sullivan and Frank Lloyd Wright, have inspired thousands of students to the present day.

17. Wall, "Dan Graham's *Kammerspiel*," p. 38. Here Wall is citing Kenneth Frampton, *The Glass House Revisited* (New York: Institute for Architecture and Urban Studies, 1978), p. 51.

18. Robert Venturi, *Complexity and Contradiction in Architecture* (New York: Museum of Modern Art, 1966), p. 16.

19. Ibid., p. 23.

20. Ibid., p. 103.

21. Ibid., p. 118. Illustration pp. 112–113.

22. Robert Venturi, Denise Scott Brown, and Steven Izenour, *Learning from Las Vegas* (rev. ed.; Cambridge, Mass.: The MIT Press, 1977), pp. 128–129.

23. Ibid., pp. 129–130.

24. Interestingly enough, these illustrations were incorporated in the original *Learning from Las Vegas* (1972).

25. Graham, "Homes for America," p. 22.

26. Dan Graham, "Art in Relation to Architecture: Architecture in Relation to Art," *Artforum* 17, no. 6 (February 1979), p. 25.

27. Ibid., p. 29.

28. Dan Graham, "Not Post-Modernism: History as Against Historicism, European Archetypal Vernacular in Relation to American Commercial Vernacular, and the City as Opposed to the Individual Building," *Artforum* 20, no. 4 (December 1981), p. 54.

29. Ibid.

30. Ibid., p. 50.

31. Ibid., citing Leon Krier, "The New *Rione* Centers," in *Roma interotta* (Rome: Incontri Internazionale d'Arte, 1978), pp. 195–204.

32. Ibid., p. 52, citing Leon Krier, "A City Within the City," *A + U*, no. 84 (November 1977), pp. 69–152.

33. Graham, *Dan Graham: Buildings and Signs*, p. 43.

34. Anne Rorimer, *Dan Graham: Pergola/Conservatory* (New York: Marian Goodman Gallery, 1987), n.p.

35. Ibid.

36. Dan Graham, "Pavilions, Stagesets, and Exhibition Designs, 1983–1988," in *Dan Graham—Pavillons*, ed. Zdenek Feliz (Munich: Kunstverein Munchen, 1988), p. 46.

37. Graham and Hurst, "Corporate Arcadias," p. 70.

38. Ibid., p. 71.

39. Dan Graham, in Lynne Cooke, *Rooftop Urban Park Project* (New York: Dia Center for the Arts, 1991), n.p.

40. Ibid.

41. Graham, "Two Adjacent Pavilions," p. 48.

Decoy: Displacements of Loss and Hope

MAUREEN P. SHERLOCK

> The light in the prison, that late in the day, reminded Farragut of some forest he had skied through on a winter afternoon. The perfect diagonal of the light was cut by bars as trees would cut the light in some wood, and the largeness and mysteriousness of the place was like the largeness of some forest—some tapestry of knights and unicorns—where a succinct message was promised but where nothing was spoken but the vastness. The slanting and broken light, swimming with dust, was also the dolorous light of churches where a bereft woman with a hidden face stood grieving.... The last light of that sweaty day was whitish, the white afterglow you see in the windows of Tuscan paintings, an ending light but one that seems to bring the optical nerve, the powers of discernment, to a climax.
>
> —John Cheever, *Falconer* (1977)

The severing of art's poetic capacity to measure meaning in our lives was an unintended consequence of the critique of representation. Our energetic deconstruction of Nature as the primary edifice of the real has often degenerated into a formalist exercise that displaces the actuality of history. Seduced by a brilliant but nonetheless neo-Kantian rhetoric, we allowed theory to ossify into a politically correct doxy for the already privileged. The inadequacies of this progressively academic Poststructuralism become more apparent each moment. Would that economic oppression be merely a production of the Lacanian Imaginary, and death but a rhetorical conceit of a mannerist Postmodernism? What theory first disclosed with rigor has now settled into a rigor mortis of shadow categories that will forever haunt the possibility of direct experience. The project we face is reconnecting these abstract moments to the concrete specificity of a social life that is felt as well as thought.

Among the most important sites of contested meaning, we must include the ideological mapping of the body, the construction of gender, the intellectual colonization of race, and the ubiquity of capital's forms of consumption, labor, and social relations. The linchpin of these debates has been the critical deconstruction of a Nature no longer simply there or fully present. It has initiated an ever more complicated dialectic between the various codes of representation and the legitimacy of political action. This new nature is calibrated by history, by economics, and by politics for an individual subject who must still negotiate a life of both community and intimacy in the face of his or her institutional definitions. Though understanding one's ideological determinations seems necessary for change, it does not necessitate any real political practice. After all, how does one displace the dominant day-to-day narrative of the "real," in all its presumed legitimacy, with an opposing subtext produced by people who reject the very subject positions implied by this "real"? How can we produce other frames of intelligibility with which to understand those parts of our lives not sanctioned by forms of ideological subjectivity?

Our great difficulty today is to ascertain how we can represent what has been lost, or what we long for in our social relations, without the romanticism we have so carefully critiqued. Not wanting to return to a naïve position of immediacy, how do we acknowledge a sense of personal loss free of nostalgia? How indeed do we ever restore a space for hope in an age of cynical reason without merely returning to an imaginary homesite warmed by an illusion of unity and identity?

On multiple levels, Robert Gober's installation at Dia Center for the Arts salvages the possibility of a future out of a society of calculated despair. His is an art where the operation of repetition and transformation brings us ever closer, but never quite there, to a site that acknowledges both the real conditions of history, which subvert our aspirations, and the maneuvers necessary to begin to reconcile, at least partially, memory and hope. His method is as wily, as perspicacious, and as determined as the entrenched forces he struggles against. From our first entry into the darkened space, bracketed within the confines of the building, the artist lures us to a false door surrounded by unreadable piles of newspaper. Even as we reach for the doorknob, we fear setting off an alarm system as we apprehend a red emergency light above. We *know* what it means; museums, after all, house precious property. The door, however, is a decoy set for the viewer, unnerving our sense of art even while drawing us to the lair of the camoufleur who waits for his prey. Disguised and protected by an artificial terrain, a mask in the heart of nature, in a structure called a "blind," he waits to see—such is the art of hunting. We are all unprepared, novice and aficionada alike, for Gober's room in the center of the city, filled with heat and light and the sounds of the waterfall the *Étant donnés* only represented. Duchamp's Diana laid bare may be missing, along with her unfortunate hunter, Acteon, but seeing is still dangerous!

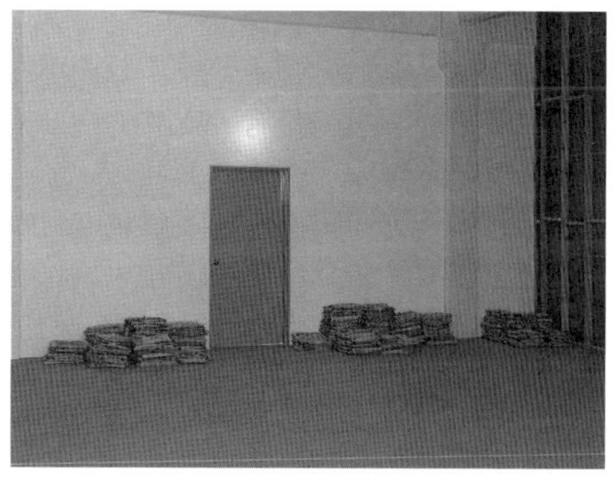

Robert Gober, installation at Dia Center for the Arts, 1992.

In that other manly art called war, a Dazzle is a peculiar kind of camouflage invented by Norman Wilkinson of the British army. He calculated that speed and direction cannot be accurately determined when ships are covered with the brilliant abstract forms of modern art. Less than one percent of the ships so painted in the First World

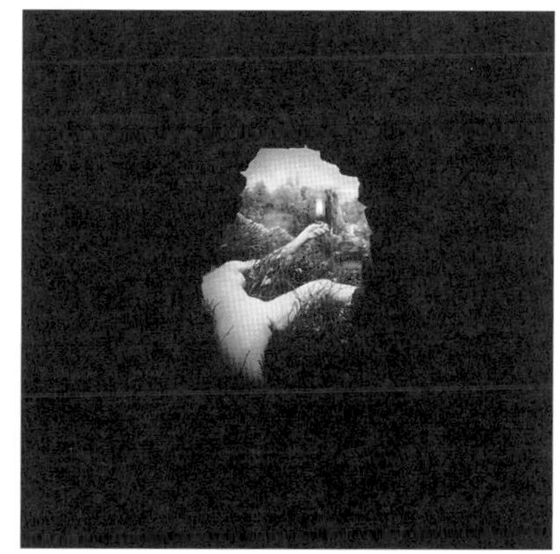

Marcel Duchamp, *Étant donnés*, 1946–68.

War were destroyed. Here camouflage protects both the hunter and the hunted; they reverse the roles as fast as you can say Kandinsky. Later, radar rendered the Dazzle obsolete and in the Second World War both the Allies and the Germans returned to the even older art of trompe l'oeil, camouflaging airport complexes, runways, hangars, even the surrounding countryside on the ground, not picked up by the radar. The Germans disguised a huge hangar as an already-bombed French château that was not uncovered by the Allies until after the war ended. Disney created whole "fake" suburbs, undreamed by Baudrillard, to disguise a military production plant in California. Dive bombers regularly attacked the painted shadows of cardboard boxes in every theater of war.

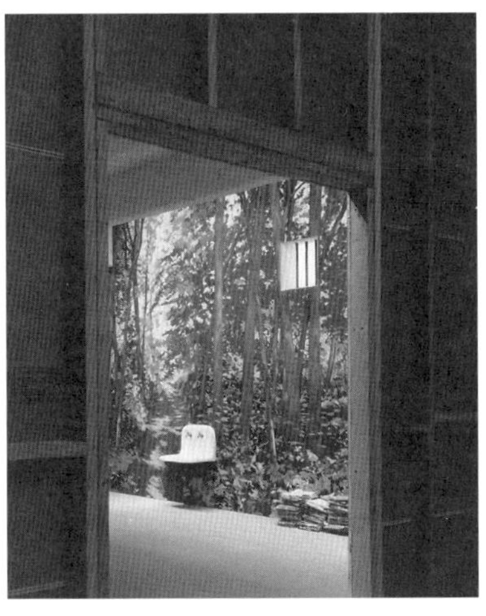

Robert Gober, installation at Dia Center for the Arts, 1992.

Lured by the sound of waterfalls and an uncanny sunlight *in* the museum, we are ourselves dazzled by entering a constructed, artificial grotto. It is opened on two ends—one by which we enter, while the other, presumed to be an exit, takes us up a blind alley. Behind the outside of an inside of an outside double wall, disguising the falseness of simulated rat poison boxes to the "outside" world of four prison windows in forest walls, we find there is no back to the decoy door we first encountered in this endless round. In a dark corner are more newspaper images of a very strange, unnerving bride in a Saks advertisement. To continue, we are forced to retrace our steps to the inside outside of the bright room.

The trompe l'oeil forest painted on the brilliantly lighted walls looks more like army camouflage; in any case, it is more theatrical and artificial than realist and representational. It does not really help to know that the forest was painted by set designers from professional photographs taken of woods the artist frequents to look for mushrooms, or that in several places the images are mirror reflections or reversals of other sections. Gober's hand-built sinks with their strange, enigmatic presence are already a familiar part of his vocabulary, signs of ritual cleansing and shared intimate public spaces. Here, the six sinks, three on each side, sing to each other with running water like choirboys across the apse. Each is guarded by a silent sentinel: "Enforcer Rat Bait, Kills Rats and Mice, Ready to Use." More baits and traps: where is the cat and its litter now, who's the bait, who dies here, who will dispose of the dead bodies? In a double take, we remember that Gober's earlier sinks did not have running water—though we half-remember some of them that way. No hope to be read into that though; a news clipping from one of the bundles of newspaper nearby alerts us to the fact that New York City's water is contaminated by lead—clear flowing water disguises danger.

The heat generated by the light seems almost suffocating, but still the sound of the water draws us into an imaginary, sonorous space. The longer we stay, the more the sound dominates, and the less we care about having been tricked—that, of course, is the final decoy. In this space, we hover between compiled news and fantasies of the "real" outside world fabricated by a solitary editor with an odd sense of humor; a site where there is a confusion between utopian and dystopian cues, like some strange intertwining of Thoreau and B. F. Skinner. There is, of course, an easy read of the failure of romantic representation, and a clawing phenomenological feeling that something more is going on. That something more is something missing; the pillars seem like those other trees of stone that once shaped the center of the earth—those kivas of everyone's past where the world was filled with symmetry, where one went for healing to make right one's life. Unable to integrate this magical space before self-consciousness, we turn to read the news clippings or leave not knowing what to say. No one can seriously be raising the question of Walden or romantic retreats to nature in the face of deconstructive critiques. Or can they?

It is these questions of loss and hope which have permeated Gober's work. Each of the contested sites of meaning is addressed in his work from two sides: the ideological constructions of the social order run parallel to his attempts to renegotiate his and others' lives in the borders of that order. Refusing to simply abandon the sites left in ruins by criticism, he rebuilds slyly and with great care the concerns of love and intimacy as forms of social practice. Whether as a nature camouflaged, an alternate documentation of history, or a representation of gender that insists that there are as many sexes as there are people, his work refuses to capitulate to the cynicism of late capital. He reinscribes and renegotiates as he lures us into a series of camouflaged spaces where, if as careful as he, we are free to think for a future.

Legitimate society only represents the world from the side of political economy and accumulation; it never represents the side of what Antonio Negri calls "self-valorization." The social order disguises its forms of domination by naturalizing those interpersonal relations that serve its vested interests and modes of production while suppressing and reviling other forms as perverse, threatening, or unnatural. Much of the 1980s critical apparatus was directed at the exposure of *how*, but rarely *why*, representation promoted repressive ideologies. Precious little was done to articulate the other side of the analysis, that is, the concrete forms of resistance and alternative social forms being developed by those who assert their collective needs to be greater than those of capital and its system of abstract labor.

Commenting on Marx's *Grundrisse*, Negri takes both sides into account as adversarial, as the origin of the perpetual series of crises inherent in capital:

> *Simultaneity and parallelism distinguish the independence of the worker-subject, its own self-valorization face to face with capitalist valorization.* Modern economists outline this relationship…as a *double spiral* or a double windmill of parallel convergences…[1]

Thus, Negri sees individuals and groups as struggling on a day-to-day basis in order to prevent rigid institutions from having control over every moment of their lives. He asserts our parallel autonomy even in the controlling context of a hegemonic culture, and he calculates an endless and ever-present series of tactical moves against the strategies of the state.

How can this conflict be represented? How can we establish a beachhead against an overwhelming sea of propaganda? How can we define the terrain as a zone of combat without slipping into romantic theory? Mas'ud Zavarzadeh suggests that we tell another narrative on the very site of the tales woven by propaganda. Each site offers at least two tales: the one we are expected to believe and the tale of the combat that established it, the story of "*WHY it means what it is taken to mean...*"[2] This *renarration* contests the official story and undermines its natural or determinate force. By inserting "a tale of counter-intelligibility"[3] at the center of the regulative discourse, that discourse can be revealed as a contested territory with an independent history.

Often what we think of as the subversive merely confirms the dominant narrative. As Judith Butler points out in her analysis of Jennie Livingston's film *Paris Is Burning* (1991), miming and cross-dressing—first taken as a critique of white, heterosexual standards—end up confirming those standards. Yet, in what Hegel once called "the cunning of history," the film *does* subvert accepted notions of "home" and "family," "mothers" and "children" with a substitute kinship system of people with whom you like to "walk." Butler clarifies the miming as pastiche of gender:

> ...becoming gendered involves impersonating an ideal that nobody actually inhabits, and that's where I have a certain sympathy with Lacanian discourse. Because symbolic positions—"man," "woman"—are never inhabited by anyone, and that's what defines

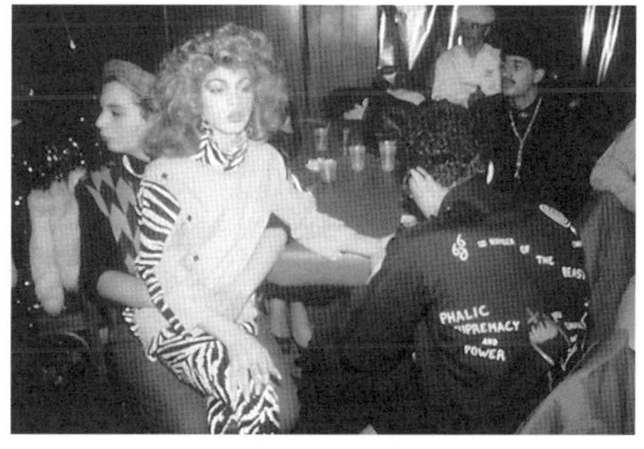

Film still from *Paris Is Burning*, directed by Jennie Livingston, 1991.

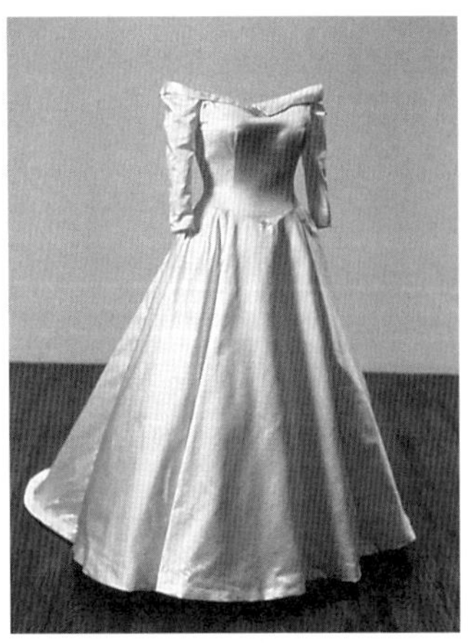

Robert Gober, *Wedding Gown,* 1989.

them as symbolic: they're radically uninhabitable.[4]

The question is one of *choosing* partial inhabitation—of wanting to *choose* some but not all of both positions. Would this really change uninhabitable ideals? To what extent are private and public negotiations of gender still fundamentally subversive?

Gober's work reveals a history camouflaged as the naturalized—an alternate representation of gender that insists that there are as many sexes as there are people. He reinscribes and renegotiates the fetishism of heterosexuality, rethinking the other side of sexuality. His hand-sewn *Wedding Gown* (1989), for example—first freestanding in a gallery installation and later appearing in ads in the newspaper piles of the Dia installation—might serve as a point of departure. When the gown was shown at the Paula Cooper Gallery, the walls were covered with Gober's wallpaper design of simple, repeated drawings of a black man hanging from a tree and a white gay man sleeping in bed.[5] Invoking Billie Holiday's lynching metaphor of "Strange fruit hanging from Southern trees,"[6] the piece paired these euphemistic "fruits" and provoked the issue of violence against these two groups of men, as well as their frequent tolerance of the exploitation of the other. The wallpaper also clarifies earlier works by Gober, such as the flannel dog bed, the chair covered with hand-painted flowers, or the series of sinks, cribs, and beds.

But something quite dramatic happened when the images were paired with the homely wedding gown. Objects as heavily charged as these are always overdetermined, and Gober's repetitions are double-edged: they offer both a moment of critique and a quiet longing. The repeated gestures of *Slides of a Changing Painting,* first shown at the Paula Cooper Gallery in 1984, documents the changing image of a painting as it was repainted over and over during the period of one year between 1982 and 1983. In the face of the grandiose Neoexpressionist paintings from Germany and the United States, which dominated contemporary art at the time, the use of repetition here attempted to diminish painting's claim to permanence. It also undermined the nongestural quality of emerging work of other artists in New York at the time.

There has always been a wonderfully perverse dumbness about Gober's work, which rarely shows up in reproduction. It is a directness that separates the quality of his work from the fetish quality of much commodity- and media-based work. It is, however, the presence of these discrete works, the obstinacy of their repetition both as solitary objects and their use in multiple installations, that betrays a more tangled web. There is a subtext in the work that dwarfs the others.

"When I first came to New York I looked around very carefully to see what was missing," Gober said in 1988. What *was* present in the art world was a certain romantic fatalism about the nature of capital and an equally romantic image of Neoexpressionist painting. Clearly for Gober, there was no possibility of returning to a precapitalist mode of production or craft. But neither were there sites for dealing with the *affect*—only the *effect*—of institutions

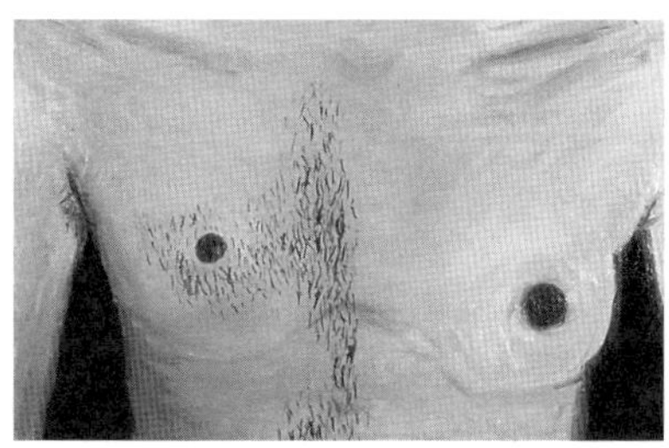

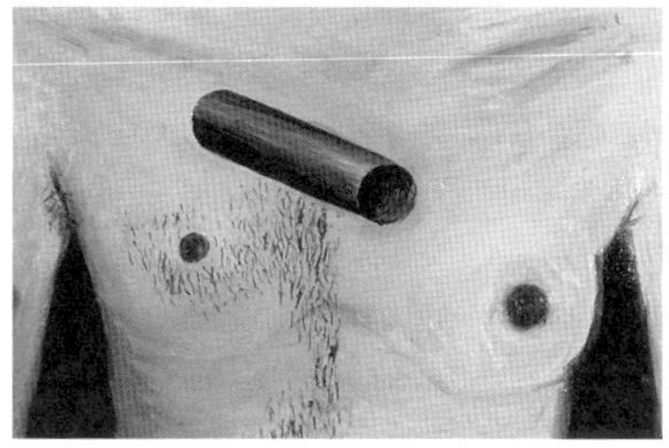

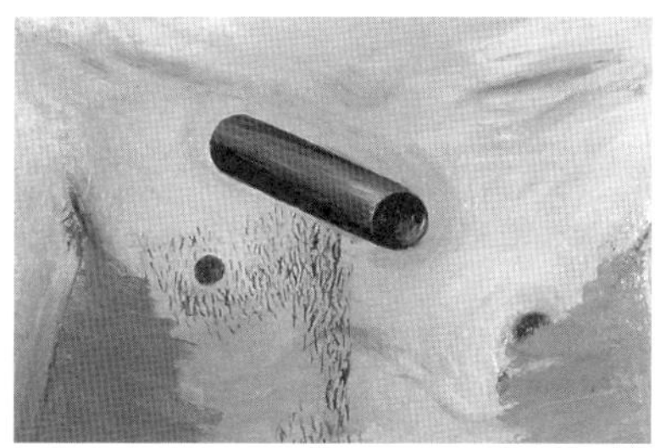

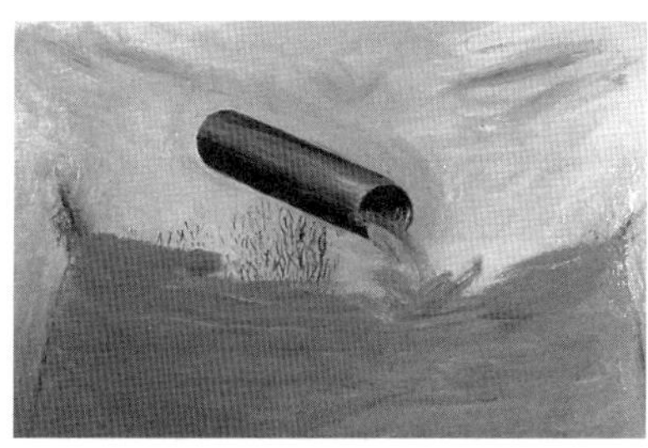

Robert Gober, *Slides of a Changing Painting*,

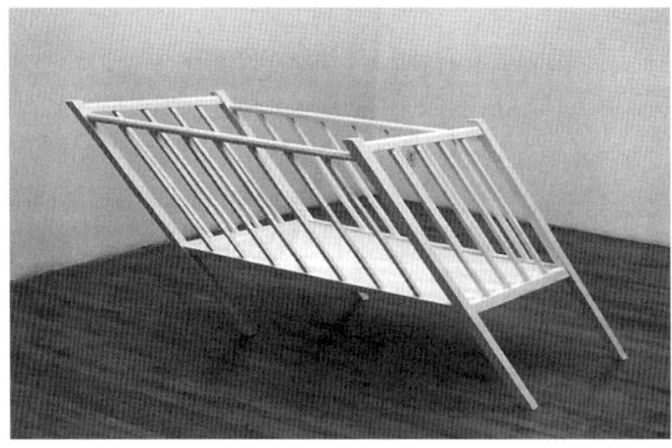
Robert Gober, *Pitched Crib*, 1987.

on individuals. There were lots of criticisms of the nuclear family, but Gober's *Pitched Crib* (1987) or *X Playpen* (1987) directly challenged the constraints of that familial space that "normalizes" us all in the eyes of the society.

The site where one contests the social order might also be either the site of an "uninhabitable ideal" or the place where we harbor our anticipatory hopes, those utopian longings that sustain us affectively. These transitional objects may indeed mark an "endless memorial search for something in the future that resides in the past...[and where each] aesthetic frame promises to metamorphose the self."[7] Christopher Bollas calls it "the shadow of the object," which appears and disappears, promising wholeness and transformation but ultimately delivering only a mute absence. Life is negotiated through these objects, which are the intrapsychic essence of Marx's analysis of the commodity fetish in the first chapter of *Capital*. Though the wholeness is an illusion, it is also our cache for utopia, an imaginary landscape free for the future beyond alienation. Utopia may be a fiction, but one necessary for life. "Illusion," says Ernst Bloch in *The Utopian Function of Art and Literature*, "is moved through anticipatory illumination to a realizable future that is reachable no matter how far away."[8]

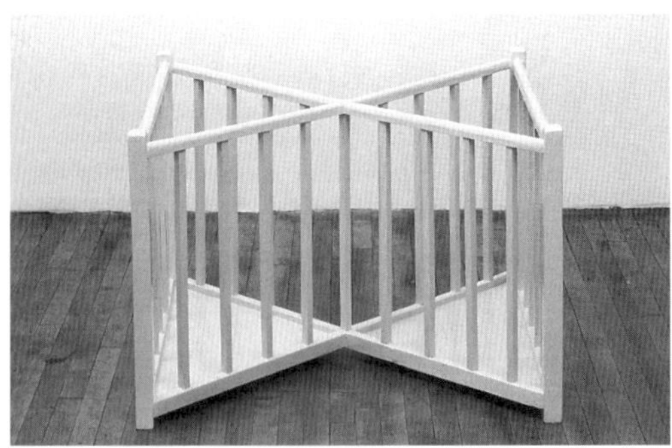
Robert Gober, *X Playpen*, 1987.

Standing autonomously without a visible armature in several different installations, Gober's *Wedding Gown* has prompted a variety of plausible readings from cross-dressing and gender issues to an inversion of Duchamp's *Bride Stripped Bare.* If we only ask who is absent from the dress, we fail to observe what is present. The commercial imaging of the dress in the series of reconstructed Saks Fifth Avenue ads began to appear among Gober's faux montage pages of the *New York Times.* Posing himself as the bride in commercial photo shoots, Gober seemed to have a more simple and direct issue camouflaged beneath a critique of gender roles. Above one image was the manipulated headline "Vatican Condones Discrimination Against Homosexuals: Concern that Gay Rights Threaten Marriage." The obvious critique of gender roles is itself another decoy of the hunter-bride: Gober's persona of Duchamp.

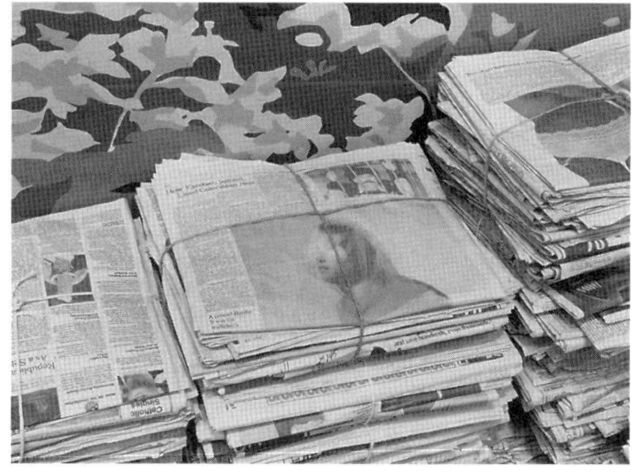

Robert Gober, installation at Dia Center for the Arts, 1992.

For most people, there are a host of interpersonal values at stake in marriage, irrespective of its institutional and regulatory functions. In the Catholic theology of marriage, for example, the officiating priest is only a witness; the actual sacrament is performed by the couple who give public witness in their vows of mutual commitment. For lesbians and gay men, marriage is a celebration of a shared life not sanctioned by church or state, since official spaces do not permit these relationships to be recognized. Even obituaries cannot bear their witness: "longtime companion" is just another euphemism for a love that is socially denied.

A society without meaningful marks of identity and intimacy for gay men requires an adversarial collective action to invent new forms of social life that can claim in concrete poetry the truth of those relationships. Men, who by the uninhabitable ideal are not nurturers, nurture, care for, and nurse one another. They are, in the words of Michel de Certeau:

> unrecognized producers, poets of their own acts, silent discoverers of their own paths in the jungle of functionalist rationality....Their trajectories form unforeseeable sentences, partly unreadable paths across a space...composed with the vocabularies of established languages (those of television, newspapers, supermarkets, or museum sequences) and although they remain subordinated to the prescribed syntactical forms...the trajectories trace out the ruses of other interests and desires that are neither determined nor captured by the systems in which they develop.[9]

What is missing is that which is yet to be culturally constituted, a new grammar of gender and sexuality continuously reinvented by the artists and poets of everyday life.

There is also a shadow of silence in the very heart of Gober's work. As Pierre Macherey puts it:

> Theory begins from that incompleteness which is so radical that it cannot be located....The silence...is not a lack to be remedied....In its every particle, the work *manifests*, uncovers, what it cannot say. This silence gives it life.[10]

This absence is not created by some mysticism that could deliver us from loss, but by the real incoherences and omissions in our social lives—as well as in our representations. This vacancy can only be vanquished by our collective operations, for it is only revealed through the competing discourses of race, sex, and class in the lived world. Both art and criticism have no immanent meanings to be disclosed according to some preexisting or eternal code, no matter how much the canon may claim this privilege. This radical lack of self-sufficiency is not a fault to be overcome; without its absence, there would be no reason for us to speak, write, or make art.

In what Nathalie Sarraute once called "the age of suspicion," there are two fundamental forms of silence: first, Freud's unconscious, which consigns the unspoken to another place in order to regulate it; and second, ideological formations, which hide the truth of the dominant economic and political system. The current entrenchment of power, therefore, remains stable through repression and silencing. It is at this twin fork that Gober's textual reinscriptions of headlines found in discarded issues of the *New York Times* and the *New York Post* come to bear. Fabricated of actual and fictional articles and ads, his "reproductions" of the news tell another tale. Gober weaves an unofficial narrative of an America where stock quotes command more space than the sexual exploitation of children by priests. Macherey's book *A Theory of Literary Production* examines the classical realist text as a narrative snare that promises clarity at the conclusion. Its determinate quality—its center—falls apart, however, under the pressure of the reeling contradictions and deficiencies of the world. Gober's realist text—a facsimile newspaper—operates in an inverted fashion. At first glance, the world appears to be in collision: two-thirds of a page is taken up by a double ad of women's lacy underwear, provocatively displayed on the model; above it are two items, one headlined "Teen-Ager Sentenced in Love-Triangle Killing," the other, "Insurers Sue Diocese Over Molestation Case." Over time, these conflicting montage elements become necessarily connected *in the world.*

Solicitations for a singles club for Catholic "professionals" sits next to an ad showing three women in white bras. A polyphony of male and female beefcake ads, often sadomasochistic, run parallel to images of "real" men—presumably heterosexual jocks—shot from sexually explicit angles. The endless images of women as fetishized bodies are coupled with "news" of their actual political struggles with the state over control of their own bodies. There are articles on the Republican myth of the nuclear family and a picture of President George Bush, presented as "Champion of Family Values," holding up a doll of his wife. We are even treated to law-school graduation pictures of Dan and Marilyn Quayle. Straightening her phallic tie, this self-sacrificing mother-lawyer never thinks of using her privileges to offer free legal services to the Children's Defense Fund, clearly stating in the accompanying article that she has "nothing in common with Mrs. Clinton."

In Gober's photomontage titled "A Photographic Turnabout," artist David Salle is posed in his favorite female position, his hands placed demurely over his genitals. The piece is set in the lower left-hand corner of a page of art and auction ads, under the "For Children" section, which announces a puppet exhibition, oddly titled "Breaking Boundaries," and a Nintendo-like video disk offering sound bites from *The Magic Flute*. In the "Art in Review" section, there are two more references to the intertwining of sexual and monetary economies, with headlines that seem to be alternate titles for the Salle image: "Royal Treasures" and "On Top of the Auction World."

Compulsory heterosexuality pervades the death notices of men and women, many of them artists, in Gober's newspapers. Often listed as survived only by parents and siblings, these dead are portrayed as if they had no adult personal lives: "'He died of AIDS,' said Jonathan Sheffer, a friend." Gay men and women are returned in death to the regulative normalcy of the family they were denied in birth. The normative nature of gender reappears elsewhere, in the endless announcements of "straight love"—engagements and weddings. Here, "real" love is for sale; natural, god-blessed love, free of artifice or convention, sealed by an Eternal Bliss ring from Tiffany. In his creative reediting, Gober exposes a "natural" sexuality filled with dangerous props, "dangerous supplements," as Derrida once called them. America's obsession with softness and cleanliness is underscored by endless ads for Tide, Bounce, Downy, Cascade, and Dawn. What are we trying to wash out with designer antiseptics for every occasion? What makes us unable to confront the exigencies of a global epidemic? An image of a sock is headlined: "Ten Years Into the AIDS Epidemic and This Is the Closest Our Government Has Gotten to Showing a Condom."

On one pile of newspapers to the right side of the entry, there is a devastating amalgam of life in the United States. A book review of a biography of Margaret Sanger is juxtaposed with headlines reading "Protestor Thrusts Fetus at Clinton as He Goes Out for a Jog" and "Student Killed After Objecting To Racial Slur." An ad for *Christopher Columbus: The Discovery* is adjacent to the headline "Case Dropped Against Men Holding Hands in Cincinnati." Here, conflicting discourses battle for space and attention—the censor that once guarded consciousness breaks down, revealing the political unconscious.

It is, however, an obituary for David Wojnarowicz, an artist who died from AIDS at age thirty-eight, that restructures the axis of the room:

> He would talk now and then about suicide, but as death came closer, he didn't talk about it anymore. He'd always understood we each have to figure out what to do with the darkness.[11]

All formalist analyses are rendered impotent in the specificity of this one death. It ruptures the rhetorical construction of nature to a degree of zero, to a space beyond speech in the overwhelming silence of a voice lost forever. In *Memories That Smell Like Gasoline*, Wojnarowicz proclaimed,

> I'm a xerox of my former self. I can't abstract my own dying any longer. I am a stranger to others and to myself and I refuse to pretend that I am familiar or that I have history attached to my heels. I am glass, clear empty glass....I am a stranger and I am moving. I am no longer animal, vegetable, or mineral. I am no longer made of circuits or disks. I am no longer coded and deciphered. I am all emptiness and futility....I can't speak your language any longer. See the signs I try to make with my hands and fingers. See the vague movements of my lips among the sheets. I am a blank spot in a hectic civilization. I am a dark smudge in the air that dissipates without notice....I am a glass human disappearing in the rain. I am standing among all of you waving my invisible arms and hands. I am shouting my invisible words. I am getting so weary. I am growing tired. I am waving to you from here. I am crawling around looking for the aperture of complete and final emptiness. I am vibrating in isolation among you. I am screaming but it comes out like pieces of clear ice. I am signaling that the volume of all this is too high. I am waving my hands. I am disappearing. I am disappearing but not fast enough.[12]

Suddenly another reading to this room.

Gober's installation dissembles itself like a series of Chinese boxes, with baffles invented only to protect a place to recollect and heal. It is like Walden, where Thoreau went to grieve the death of his brother, his closest confrere whom he loved and nursed through his terrible death from lockjaw. Like Walden, where he was cramped by all sides of society, constantly interrupted by the sounds of the train across the lake, with news and notes left by people from town. There must be someplace like Walden, where survivors can open themselves to the future again, where one can assert, however tenuously, the continuity of life.

Not since the nineteenth century, with America's Civil War and the epidemics of influenza, diphtheria, and consumption, has the fragility and vulnerability of the body been so present to our lives. Walt Whitman, calling himself the "wound dresser," nursed lovers, friends, and even stranger-soldiers from another battle. He wrote in "To One Shortly to Die":

> Softly I lay my right hand upon you, you just feel it,
> I do not argue, I bend my head close and half envelop it,
> I sit quietly by, I remain faithful,
> I am more than nurse, more than parent or neighbor,
> I absolve you from all except yourself spiritual bodily, that is eternal, you yourself will surely escape
> The corpse you will leave will be but excrementitious.
>
> The sun bursts through in unlooked-for directions,
> Strong thoughts fill you and confidence, you smile,
> You forget you are sick, as I forget you are sick,
> You do not see the medicines, you do not mind the weeping friends, I am with you…[13]

We read bodies very differently now: illness and death appear in the everyday—a small sore on the face of a student, baseball caps over balding heads, a certain pallor and tonality. These all make us tentative and fearful and sad. The specter of AIDS transposes all images of the body. Gober himself has remarked how ordinary death now seems in New York:

> There is nothing extraordinary about it at all. If people aren't themselves sick, they know someone who is, or they are struggling to assimilate the loss of someone who was. For me, death has temporarily overtaken life in New York City. And most of the artists I know are fumbling for ways to express it.[14]

To *know* someone is dead is not the same as *feeling* someone is dead, not the same as letting them go.

Psychoanalysis teaches us that children may acknowledge the death of a parent intellectually while sustaining their existence on an imaginary level, unable to let a loved parent leave the house. Grieving is a long process, according to Freud, one that is never really completed by a preadolescent child, for we first learn to grieve when we abandon our infantile relationship with our parents in favor of adult sexual relations. The child acknowledges the death of a parent conceptually, but secretly keeps them alive as fantasy. We all repeat this pattern as we come to grips with loss. Magritte is the artist most strongly associated with this double stance of knowing and feeling. As a young boy, he watched his mother's body being dragged from the Seine with her white chemise pulled up over her head. A suicide, she appears and reappears throughout his paintings; she is the source of the animism that pervades his work, where feet grow into trees and bottles into bodies.

While Magritte may have been unable to complete his grieving process for unconscious reasons, Gober is prevented from doing so by the real demographic politics of a disease. The dynamic between these two artists is not a formal or historic one, much less some conveniently read abstraction of style. Both use decoys and camouflage for similar ends. Gober always cues back to the real, for the imaginary never delivers in the context of history. His spaces are always only temporary respites, while Magritte was always trying to get to the other side of the painting.

Gober's earlier haunting series of body fragments are transitional pieces to the Dia installation. They are markers on the way to our surrendering to memory the longed-for presence of lost comrades. The deployment of these fractured legs and torsos in fragmented

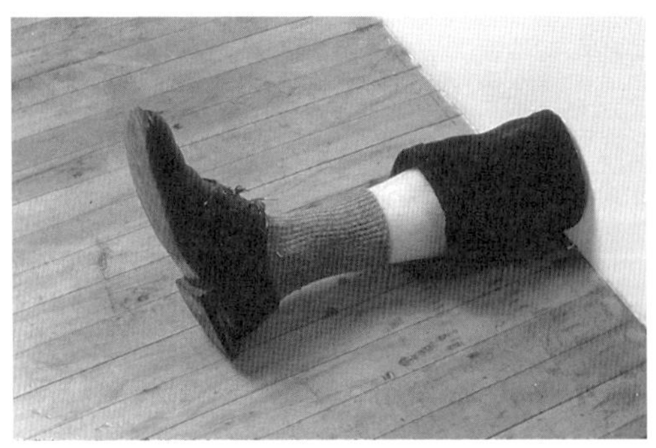

Robert Gober, *Untitled Leg*, 1989.

and "unnatural" positions and places announces a bracketing from "actual" space to a reflective image of departure. These imaginary bodies are frequently ruptured and pushed back into the real by the presence of those votive candles so familiar to all of us raised in "the one true religion." They are a Catholic kaddish, a prayer for safe journeys through Charon's crossing. Some of the figures are marked with drains, partly as sores, but also as sites of transformation in Gober's vocabulary of repetition and difference.

The convention of hyperrealism is always connected to an uncanny double of those missing from the actual. It is also why there is such a wide range of reactions to Gober's fragmented wax cast bodies, particularly the amputated legs. For some, they are horrifying, but the horror comes precisely because these sculptures confuse the borders erected by a binary culture between the dead and the undead. For others, dealing with their own acts of mourning, they may be reassuring, even a humorous memorializing of the vulnerability and poignancy of the body of another as it begins its journey into the past.

Not all these sculptures come from mourning; some have already made their way to memory. There are also torso bodies, androgynous bodies, and bodies with perfect little behinds. Each of us brings to them the bodies we too have loved. They are, for me, the celebratory sexual bodies that populate the pages of Walt Whitman, who, like Gober, is a consummately American poet. They exceed in humor and affirmations the constrictions of a strictly gendered body politic. There are those autoerotic bodies of "Song of Myself":

> Cushion me soft, rock me in billowy drowse,
> Dash me with amorous wet, I can repay you…[15]

There are also joyful body images, filled with the pleasure taken in that young ass Socrates tells us in the *Symposium* is the beginning of all love of beauty and wisdom. Joyous bodies, heavenly asses inscribed with music to which Whitman wrote the lyrics in *Calamus*:

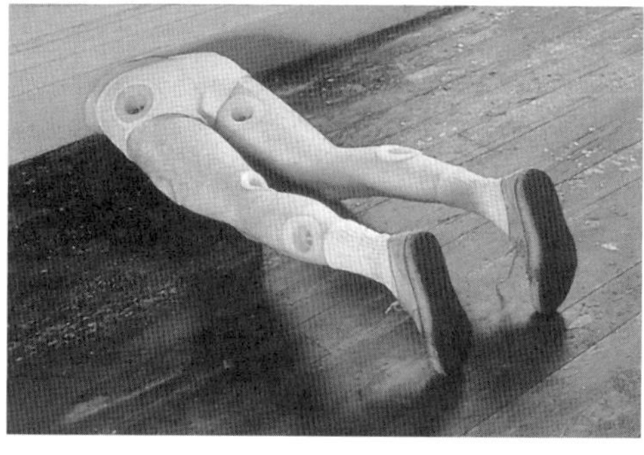

Robert Gober, *Untitled*, 1991.

> We two boys together clinging,
> One the other never leaving...[16]

Some representations of the body hover near the border, not quite ready to bid adieu, alien yet familiar.

Now, in the Dia installation—this "wish-landscape," as Bloch might have called it—there are no bodies, just the water rushing, baptismal founts where we are bathed and restored for a few moments. I like to think that as David went to his elemental night, gushing old Greybeard met him and his friends with these leaves of grass:

> Good-bye my Fancy!
> Farewell dear mate, dear love!...
> Long have we lived, joy'd, carress'd together;
> Delightful!—now separation—Goodbye my Fancy.
>
> Yet let me not be too hasty,
> Long indeed have we lived, slept, filter'd, become really blended into one;
> Then if we die together, (yes, we'll remain one,)
> If we go anywhere we'll go together to meet what happens,
> May-be we'll be better off and blither, and learn something,
> May-be it is yourself now really ushering me to the true songs, (who knows?)
> May-be it is you the moral knob really undoing, turning—so

now finally,
Good-bye—and hail! my Fancy.[17]

January 14, 1993

Notes

1. Antonio Negri, *Marx Beyond Marx* (Brooklyn: Autonomedia, 1991), p. 136.
2. Mas'ud Zavarzadeh, *Seeing Films Politically* (Albany: State University of New York Press, 1991), p. 8.
3. Ibid., p. 29.
4. Liz Kotz, "The Body You Want: Liz Kotz Interviews Judith Butler," *Artforum* 31, no. 3 (November 1992), pp. 84–85.
5. This same wallpaper offended Hirshhorn Museum guards who were mostly African Americans. Gober maintained the work was not racist, as he wanted to indicate both the complicity of a silent white society and to create a parallel reference to the treatment of gay men.
6. This was first noted in my essay "Arcadian Elegy: The Work of Robert Gober," *Arts Magazine* 64, no. 1 (September 1989), pp. 44–49. Jerry Salz later added his own reflections on this parallel in his essay "Strange Fruit: Robert Gober's *Untitled*, 1988," *Arts Magazine* 65, no. 1 (September 1990), pp. 25–26.
7. Christopher Bollas, *The Shadow of the Object: Psychoanalysis of the Unthought Known* (London: Free Association Books, 1987), p. 40.
8. Ernst Bloch, cited in Jack Zipes, introduction to Ernst Bloch, *The Utopian Function of Art and Literature* (Cambridge, Mass.: MIT Press, 1988), p. xxxv.
9. Michel de Certeau, *The Practice of Everyday Life*, trans. Stephen F. Rendall (Berkeley: University of California Press, 1984), p. xviii.
10. Pierre Macherey, *A Theory of Literary Production*, trans. Geoffrey Wall (London: Routledge, 1978), p. 84.
11. C. Carr, "Obituary," *Village Voice* (4 August 1992), p. 23.
12. David Wojnarowicz, *Memories That Smell Like Gasoline* (San Francisco: Artspace Books, 1991), pp. 60–61.

13. Walt Whitman, "To One Shortly to Die," in *The Complete Poems*, ed. Francis Murphy (Harmondsworth: Penguin Education, 1975), p. 464.

14. Robert Gober, quoted in Joan Simon, "Robert Gober and the Extra Ordinary," in *Robert Gober* (Paris: Galerie Nationale du Jeu de Paume, 1991), p. 79.

15. Walt Whitman, "Song of Myself," in *The Complete Poems*, p. 84.

16. Walt Whitman, "We Two Boys Together Clinging," in *The Complete Poems*, p. 162.

17. Walt Whitman, "Good-bye My Fancy," in *The Complete Poems*, p. 568.

Low Fidelity: Notes on the Work of Katharina Fritsch

STEPHAN SCHMIDT-WULFFEN

Katharina Fritsch often confronts us with lots of things that are simple to name—a chimney, a mill, flowers in vases, boxes, pots, cars and trucks, tables and chairs, madonnas, and brains. There is a cat, an elephant, and, now, a rat. Ironically, the simplicity of naming Fritsch's objects hints at the complexity in her work. What does constitute the meaning in her objects? You could say that the rat invokes danger or disgust. Or, it might be seen as a metaphor for chaos or a symbol of decline; as a New Yorker, you could be offended by the suggestion that the rat symbolizes New York. Or, the rat could even be seen as the alter ego of the artist. Perhaps it is easy to create metaphorical connections like these, but the meanings of the artworks become more and more dubious once these connections are made. For there is no clearly defined connection between the object and a verbal formula called its *meaning*; artworks are mute, works of art don't "stand for" things, and only for that reason is art's theoretical discourse possible.

What is it that a work of art gives to us in this historical moment? How should we behave in relation to it? How can art in a time of a constant flux of imagery and semantic consumerism make an important statement? How can artists today develop images that resist a simple, cursory glance and a quick commentary, and remain in our minds as a presence, forcing us again and again to look for new interpretations? How can these images be so stalwart that they compel us to produce a series of ideas, not just a single one? Fritsch's work formulates answers to such questions and is guided by a set of rules. Here I would like to discuss the secret rules of her game.

Fritsch's small chimney, *Schornstein* (*Chimney*), 1979, resembles an industrially produced toy, cast in one piece and formed in plastic.

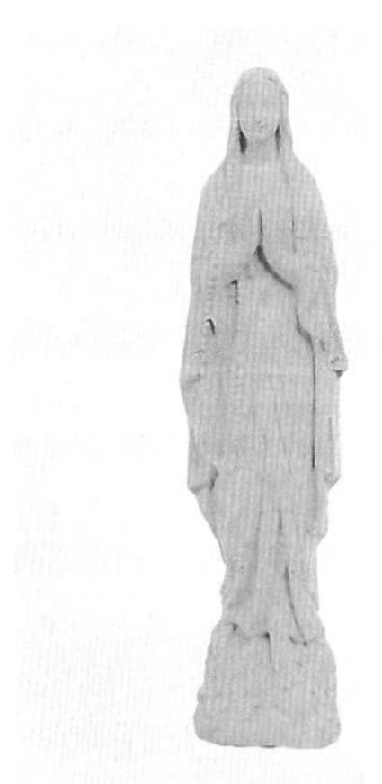

Katharina Fritsch, *Madonnenfigur* (*Figure of Madonna*), 1982.

There are some subtle yet significant differences in its construction. For example, the artist built it as a bricklayer would a real, functional chimney, brick by brick, using mortar. When she produced *Madonnenfigur* (*Figure of Madonna*) in 1982 (which reappeared in a life-size version on a public square in Münster in 1987), Fritsch colored the object with bright yellow; it otherwise remained the same as an original, mass-produced devotional figure from Lourdes. In 1985, she produced *Schwarzer Tisch mit Geschirr* (*Black Table with Tableware*); the dimensions of the table and chairs were only slightly bigger than its utilitarian counterpart. And, in 1986, she produced a bookshelf with two hundred copies of the same empty book. Repetition, one of her devices to remove the everyday object from the conventional topology of language, returns in the symmetrically regulated *Tischgesellschaft* (*Company at Table*), 1988, exhibited at the Museum für Moderne Kunst in Frankfurt.

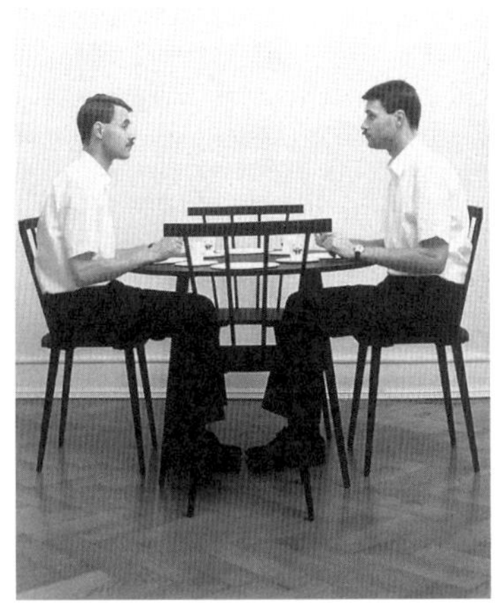

Katharina Fritsch, *Schwarzer Tisch mit Geschirr* (*Black Table with Tableware*), 1985.

Fritsch's objects are never readymade, like those of her American contemporaries, and this form of production is semantically important. Her method doesn't really suit the product: form doesn't follow function. Her minimal deviations from the "real-life objects" are slowly recognized and contribute to the strange aura of her objects. An object that is so common is nonetheless taken out of ordinary experience. Fritsch's subtle alterations place her objects out of reach of the signifying process. Her rules might be compared to those of a game of chess, where the chessmen are clearly placed upon the individual squares. To transform the object of the game, she remains on the playing board working between the squares, inventing new rules to cope with the loss of predictable positions.

The relationship between the social and the subjective has become crucial to recent artistic debates. While subjectivity was the secret source of artistic ideas during the times of the heroic avant-garde, the structure of language and its social institution has replaced the paradigm of the inventive individual. In the relation between a mental image of an object and the object itself, that object's aesthetic is encoded with certain philosophical standards and cultural attitudes. Fritsch's mode of production represents the externalization of her internalized mental images. This externalization is a way for her to objectify and visualize the imagination.

Fritsch begins her process with a common image, which she then transforms through a complex procedure carried out by numerous producers. (In the case of *Elefant* [*Elephant*], 1987, these producers included a natural scientist, a taxidermist, a moldmaker, and casters, among others.) The method of production is the first interpretation of the internalized image, informing one of its many meanings. The procedure is a fight *against* chance, *against* the mistakes and deviations of her own psychology. Finally, with the help of her collaborators, the image is reformulated in terms of its social and organizational structure. The production itself becomes a social form. Translating the image into a product of divided labor, Fritsch distances herself from subjectivity.

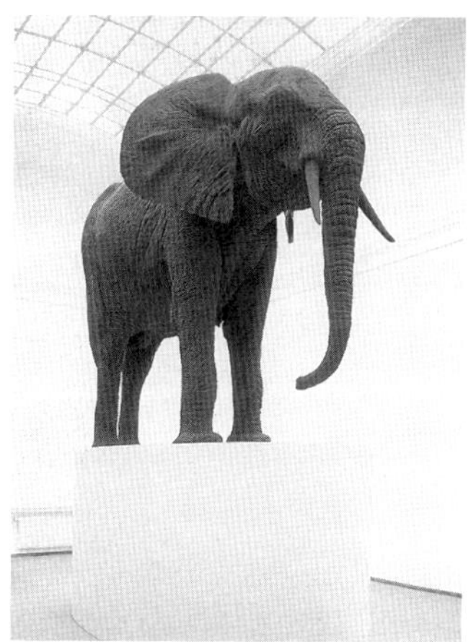

Katharina Fritsch, *Elefant* (*Elephant*), 1987.

Fritsch's process of production might be compared to that of another German artist from Düsseldorf, Reinhard Mucha. Influenced by architecture, a topic of great interest in Düsseldorf, as well as the theoretical lectures of art historian Benjamin Buchloh and the aesthetic habits of Joseph Beuys, Mucha manipulates combinations of

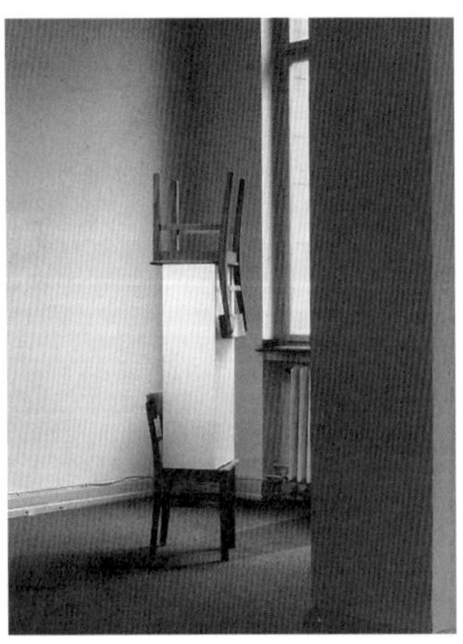

Reinhard Mucha, *Untitled (Chair)*, 1982.

everyday materials, objectifying his internalized, private image of the objects. The form and the function of the objects are misused to create a new, though related, image, in order to question certain behavioral, intellectual structures. Mucha might use tables, for example, because they have flat surfaces, to signify floors. In contrast, Fritsch breaks up our knowledge of the object, deconstructing it by altering its production. Mucha speaks by manipulating existing objects; Fritsch's object *is* a proposition.

We encounter in Fritsch's imagination the common items of everyday life—cheese, a car, a chimney, a flower, things we can buy—but certainly no objects from the unique, visionary realm of Rimbaud's "salon on the bottom of the sea." Since the Independent Group and Andy Warhol, the commodity, a prescription for the crisis of autonomy, is the rhetorical content of contemporary art, abbreviating the role of the visual arts in our societies. Ideas, so to speak, are coined by everyday life, and imagination is not a genuine experience but is formulated by social structures themselves. The language of things formulates our thinking.

Thus, the commodity performs a practical critique of autonomous art. When artists were looking for the way out of modernism's ivory tower, the commodity seemed to be the golden bridge. If the idea of genuinely individual and original thinking is out of order, how does the artist defend her practice, and be of use to society? The signifying character of a work of art is supported by its presence in the museum. To question the propositional character of the artwork, artists left the museum and introduced their work to the realm of established behavior with the notion that familiar objects might provide a new kind of access to art. The loss of an artwork's purely aesthetic character and its metamorphosis into a functional object provides its meaning—we understand the content of a chair by Scott Burton, for example, by sitting in it. Fritsch also produces objects that at first seem as if they could be appropriated for use. In 1981, she offered works available for order: a coat, a book, and a sweater. But these objects could not be used conventionally, and though they retained their position as signs, they were also distinctly propositional. Our comprehension is intensely provoked by the "signifying" character of Fritsch's artwork over the "functional." For example, Fritsch developed schemes for public spaces; she conceived of *Tennisplatz* (*Tennis Court*), 1987, a tennis court that would have a fence around it so high that it would lose its function as a tennis court. Recently, many artists have concluded that functional proposals operate primarily as commentaries on the role of art, and that the autonomy of a work of art is ultimately necessary. Without the background of the museum, Burton's chairs or Mucha's objects lose their symbolic significance. This ambivalence toward the traditional context is also a working space for Fritsch's art.

As Fritsch's subjective images dissolve into the socially structured narrative, they have formed an obsessional, private language, the repertoire of which includes just a few indelible images repeating themselves. Nearly all of the images she has worked with once appeared on a merchandising rack she exhibited in 1984. The rack is like a catalogue raisonné. Two male twin figures sat at the *Black Table* during the opening of an exhibition in 1985. One reappeared as the guest who attended the dinner party of *Company at Table* three years later. He returns again in *Mann und Maus* (*Man and Mouse*), 1992, lying in bed under the terrifying gaze of a large looming figure of a mouse. There are also numerical relations between the pieces: the dinner party united two rows of sixteen men each, who mirror one another in an eyeless, artificial alter ego. *Rattenkönig* (*Rat King*), 1993, is also comprised

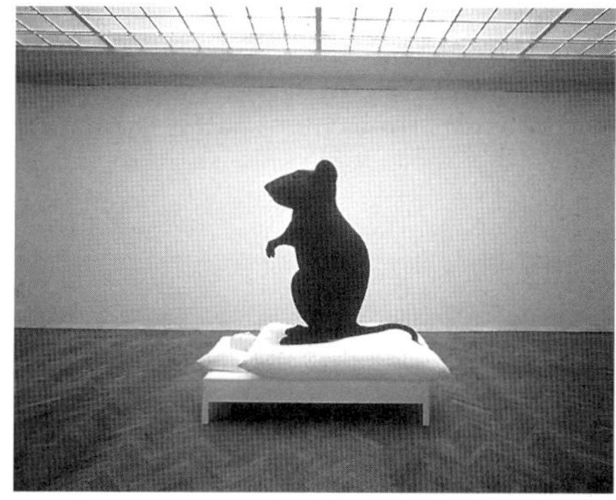

Katharina Fritsch, *Mann und Maus* (*Man and Mouse*), 1992.

of sixteen rats—is there a parallel in the communities of rats and men? Repetition serializes individuality; mass reproduction leads us to question subjectivity. The artist Thomas Schütte once reminded me that obsessive repetition by an artist of autobiographical experiences are often images about self-longing for security and protection.

As Fritsch attempts to move between the squares and the rules of the chessboard—between public and private, between artwork and commodity, and between the social and the subjective—she seems to pull away from language and denotation. Fritsch avoids territories that can be described by language, thought, or theory. Using very precise means, she circumscribes a realm recombining ideas and images, leaving us with a less clear image of the everyday world. Today the idea of subjectivity is being reshaped—the issue is more complex than the "death of the subject." There is something emotional and troubling, nearly existential in Fritsch's *Rat King.* The semantic effect of her work might be a kind of epiphany. Remember James Joyce, who wanted to open the very soul of objects, and Thomas Aquinas, who believed the essence of objects could be grasped only by apparition, not by reflection. By depriving the thing of its simple name, Fritsch aims for a language of the object which lays bare its substance. Color, dimensions, and symmetry function by turning the object into an apparition—singular, overwhelming, unforgettable. The speechless aura, the sublimity, of her works establish their presence. And, thus, pure participation with the work would be shattered by commentary.

April 29, 1993

Monochrome and Photojournalism in On Kawara's Today Paintings

JEFF WALL

We can begin to study On Kawara's paintings with the observation that he has written something on a monochrome. This is different from writing or lettering something on a blank surface or an empty piece of paper. For us, a new piece of canvas is not blank, though a new piece of paper or a new piece of foamcore might be. A new piece of canvas is already a monochrome; that is, it is already a certain kind of painting. I'm sure I don't have to rehearse here all the reasons why this is so, except maybe I should say that it is the historical identity and character of what we call "avant-gardism" that compels us to experience an empty canvas this way. Perhaps I should also say that the aesthetic categories created or revolutionized by the avant-garde have become objectivities for us, inescapable and necessary structures, transcendental conditions for the experience of works of art.

More than any other single type of painting, the monochrome marks a threshold. The moment the figure-ground relationship is suppressed or transcended is the moment we break with the whole tradition of figuration, of art as essentially figuration. When Rodchenko produced his "tri-monochrome" *Pure Red-Yellow-Blue Color* (1921), he proclaimed that with this gesture a new artistic and cultural model had come into being. The new art form leaves behind the introversions of representation and illusionism, the world of craft, wizardry, and isolation, a neurotic world of substitution. It breaks away from "bourgeois art," which it interprets as the art of all ruling groups isolated from humanity as a whole. It recognizes everything that nineteenth-century art had inherited from the aristocratic cultures of the past, all the political cynicism in the manipulation and metamorphosis of power symbols that once had been the prerogative of kings but that had fallen into the hands of ordinary citizens in the new democracies of modern times. Rodchenko's model of painting was a critique of bourgeois aestheticism and was based on a radical critique of bourgeois democracy.

For the avant-garde of the 1920s, the revolution created the conditions (or the "preconditions") for new cultural models, new models of creation, production, and literacy. The existing models, the bourgeois forms of art, were redefined as "obsolete." They correspond to what Marx called "the prehistory of humanity." The "death knell" for painting was sounded by the new kinds of sovereignty established in modern constitutional states, and the new technologies produced by capitalist inventiveness. By the 1920s, whatever historical, social, and spiritual projects associated with the skilled practice of figuration had been completed. The monochrome is the last glance, the last moment of the great figurative, musical, poetic art of painting.

Had Rodchenko's social revolution not been unsuccessful, the whole generic structure of art would have been radically transformed, presumably in the direction of a more complete, more symphonic, more synaesthetic productivism, an emancipated play-structure of environmental aesthetics. But because this did not happen, and because bourgeois art continues, the monochrome remains the boundary-marker of a point we have not been able to reach, a reminder of the culture we have not been able to create. As such, the monochrome stands outside painting, outside all genres and all aims of painting. It stands as a reflection of the historically completed character of all genres, all projects undertaken as figuration.

The special status of the monochrome implies that the incomplete social transformation of art is now the transcendental ground for the continuation of all actually existing genres of painting. The continuation of the genres is a mark of the arrested state of historical transformation and progress. From this viewpoint, all the genres now continue through the act of putting something on top of a monochrome—by effacing, supplementing, or disfiguring a monochrome. Thus, all painting is by definition a return to painting, a revival or restoration of it.

The act of putting something on top of a monochrome is, then, the act of resuming the development of the traditional generic structure of modern painting. What is specifically resumed in any individual case depends on what is added to the monochrome. In Kawara's case, it is the date on which the painting has purportedly been made. The presence of the date compels us to redefine Kawara's work in relation to a particular genre: history painting. This is to say that Kawara's work is not history painting in any direct sense, but its identity has been constructed in a negative relation to that genre, a negative relation established specifically by the orders of avant-gardist discourse.

Why should the writing or lettering of a date on a monochrome compel us to bring Kawara's Today series into contact with history painting rather than with some other genre? Traditionally, history painting has been defined as an imaginative depiction of an event that is considered significant, usually in the context of dynastic or national formations. Generally, the event has already been depicted or recounted in some way before the painter begins to work. That is, it has already been configured as the problematic entity, "the historical event." The historical event, in being real, is presumed to have taken place at some particular time; that is, it has come into conjunction with the calendar and has been given a date. The essential thing about a historical event is this fact of its occurrence in measured time, so the subject of a history painting is distinguished from the subject of any other genre by the necessity of its bearing a date.

In history painting, the floating and subjective character of the art of painting is disciplined by the ineradicable validity of the known occurrence, an occurrence that can be named just by the citation of a date for example, July 14, 1789, Bastille Day, a day

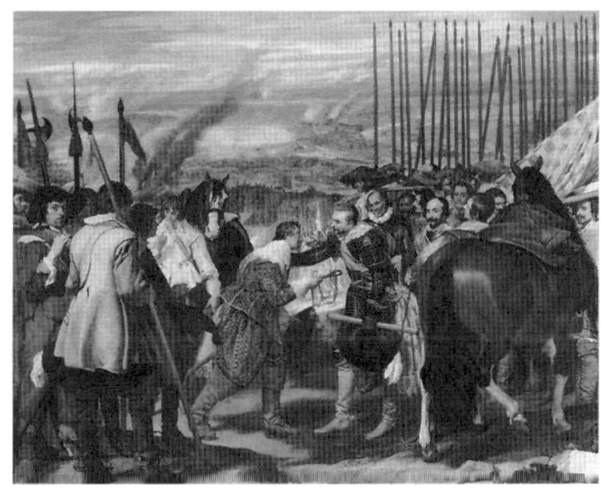

Diego Velázquez, *Surrender at Breda*, 1634–35.

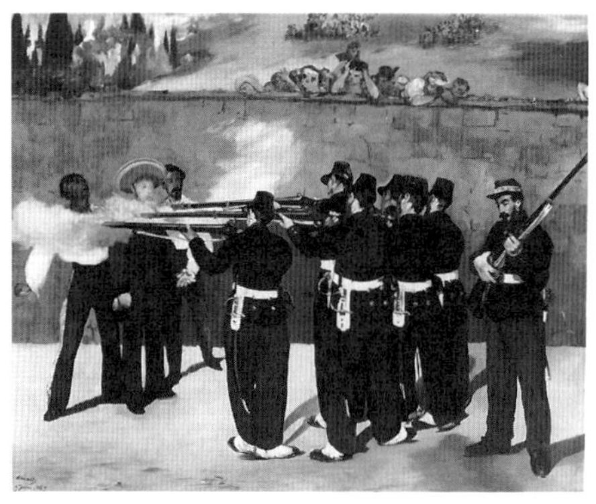

Édouard Manet, *The Execution of the Emperor Maximilian*, ca. 1867.

that becomes a festival, a public holiday and is singled out as such on calendars. Great history paintings, like Velázquez's *Surrender at Breda* (1634–35), to choose among the traditional ones, or Manet's *The Execution of the Emperor Maximilian* (ca. 1867), to choose maybe the first modernist one, are obviously rhetorical, ideological, conforming, or dissenting poetic expressions, subjective "readings" of the same sources other people were reading at the time. This kind of painting was thrown into crisis by photography—or, more specifically, by photojournalism. The historical period as well as the character of this transformation can itself almost be delimited in terms of paintings and their dates. During the sixty-nine years that elapsed between the making of Manet's *Execution* in 1867 and Picasso's *Guernica* in 1937, photojournalism as such came into existence and began to dominate historical discourse. Photojournalism, in the form of both motion and still pictures, can be said to have canceled the social bases for history painting, and even for all the attendant and "lesser" genres, like the "painting of modern life." But, even though the social bases have changed, the structure of the genre of history painting remains in our consciousness, at least as a memory within the realm of painting, the "body politic" of the "society of painters."

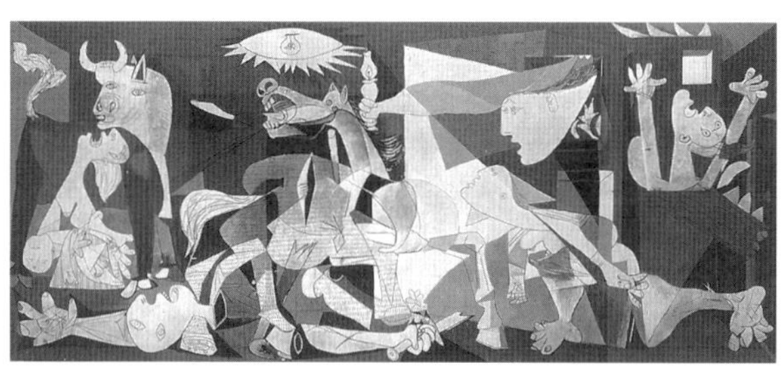

Pablo Picasso, *Guernica*, 1937.

Maybe it is time to think about the death of the death of painting. Once types of painting are revealed as "obsolete," they begin to appear to us as relics of a former age. I believe this to be a sociological illusion, a part of the avant-garde rhetoric that gambled everything on the concepts of discontinuity and the "epistemological break." The historical condition of painting and the vanguard's radical experiments in it are determined not by the fact that the older genres have died but by the fact that they haven't, even though vanguardists think they should have.

The radically analytical, "molecular" investigations of avant-garde painting beginning around 1900 developed by means of the interrogation and dismemberment of specific pictorial types. Picasso and Braque made Analytical Cubism in still lifes, portraits, and a few landscapes. Mondrian worked out from landscapes, too. Malevich developed Suprematism from a Cubo-Futurist version of *la peinture de la vie moderne*, and he also "refunctioned" traditional icon painting. The discourse of radical painting claims that these artists and those who followed them into abstraction and further experimentation revolutionized painting as such, that they transformed what could be termed the "ontology of painting," or maybe the "social ontology of painting." But, the truth of this claim needs to be mediated by an awareness that access to the "Being" of painting as such is possible only by experiments made on and within specific types of paintings. In the process of making these experiments, painters invented the new types of abstract art and the monochrome, and at the same time they placed the old genres in a new, negative condition.

It has been argued that the "lower genres," like still life, were reworked by Cézanne, Picasso, or Mondrian because they were the freest spaces for experimentation within the traditional institutions of painting. The Goncourt brothers had earlier traced this idea of the potential radicality of the lower genres back to the eighteenth century, connecting it to the modernism of "light" Rococo art and opposing it to the old-fashionedness of the more carefully controlled and loftier types like history painting and state allegory. The revolutionization of painting was said to have been carried out in the lower genres, and it has been considered adequate therefore to think that the lower genres stood for "painting as such," painting comprehended historically as an art and an object of an aesthetics.

This is an interesting model, one that is most interesting for its boundaries, especially since it is itself a model of a search for boundaries. From the beginning, modernist painting saw itself as a speculative project aimed at making visible the transcendental conditions that permit a picture to be seen as a picture. Traditional painting was an art of picturing. The break with the making of pictures, stimulated as it was by new technologies of imaging like photography led to two distinct yet interdependent directions. The first was that of nonrepresentational painting: the opening of new visual realms, the creation of spaces and experiences not bounded by pictorial laws and precedents. The second, of course, was the analysis of those laws as the invisible laws of the visual and of the relation of the visual to the pictorial. This was the content of the critique of illusion and illusionism. But it was the obsolescence of traditional types that formed the basis for this reflexivity. If modernist painting developed by reflecting on its own conditions and criteria, the obsolete genres are the mirror in which these conditions become visible. Analytical painting comes to know itself in this mirror, comes to know itself in the knowledge it discovers or produces regarding the internal relations of the pictures that preceded it and made it possible and necessary. Analytical modernist painting inherited academic knowledge about genre, but developed that knowledge into something new by making works that were models of both their own internal relations and those of the genres out of which they themselves emerged in a revolutionary process.

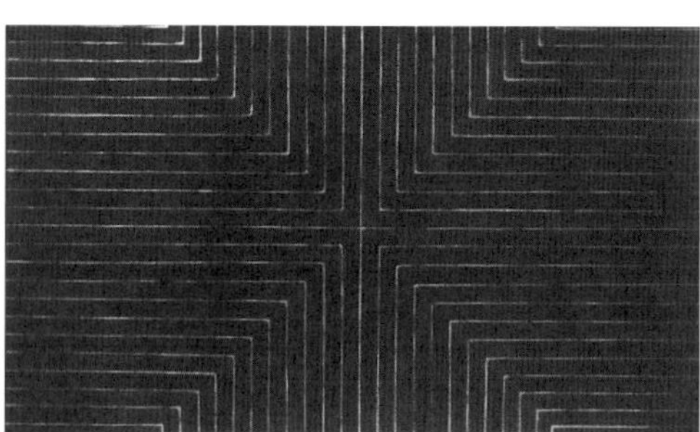

Frank Stella, *Die Fahne Hoch!*, 1959.

But what has happened to the higher genres? In particular, what has happened to history painting which, along with religious works and allegories of the state, was once the highest? One of the most suggestive studies of this question was made by Frank Stella in his

Harvard lectures, published as *Working Space* in 1986. Stella's analysis is also relevant for the light it throws on forms of thinking that to a certain extent can be identified with the New York School idea of art. Stella argues that important formal and structural aspects of Baroque dramatic painting were taken up by abstract art, then rejected by it, and need to be taken up again. He claims that his own work, especially that of the past fifteen years, is a model for such an engagement.

Stella shows that the forms of High Baroque dramatic painting, as exemplified by Caravaggio in the South and Rubens in the North, were developed as a structure of action, composition, and atmosphere for the higher genres. So, the presence of a Baroque structure in a work is a trace or sign of that work's relation to those genres. This is not to say that such formal structures do not appear in lower genres; they obviously do, but their rhetoric of turbulence and massiveness is less at home in depictions of relatively undramatic motifs. The complexity of Caravaggio's work is in part the result of his unprecedented combination of high-genre formal rhetoric with low-genre stagecraft. This combination helped to ignite the whole idea of a modern painting, and has had an influence on the aesthetics of the cinema as well. Stella suggests that dramatic relationships can be expressed by nonrepresentational forms, the way a composer of pure music could evoke epic or dramatic moods without having the means to represent them. We can take this analogy seriously because of our experience with symphonic or art music, and our familiarity with the traditional analogy of art to music in post-Romantic art theory. The idea that an "abstract Baroque" could do what the higher genres of traditional art did is not necessarily an impressive one, because it rests on a metaphor for, not a concept of, representation. It does suggest, however, that visual drama has a Baroque structure, and that moving away from that structure has deep implications for abstract art.

Stella is attempting to preserve an idea of painting as an art of high imagination and advanced technique in an era that sees itself as having crossed the threshold of representation. The abstract Baroque intends to preserve and develop the idea of painting as a

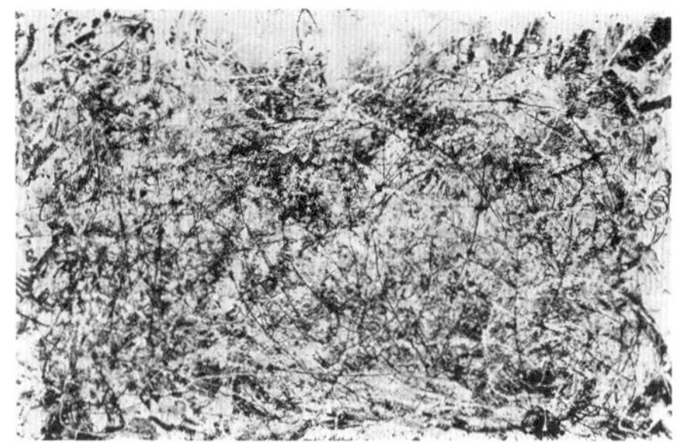

Jackson Pollock, *No. 1, 1948*, 1948. The Museum of Modern Art, New York. Purchase. Photograph © 1996 The Museum of Modern Art, New York.

profound and poetic expression of a significant theme and to defend this idea against both academic versions of representational art and the reduction of abstract art to banality. Stella sees artists like Franz Kline, Jackson Pollock, Barnett Newman, or Mark Rothko as having accepted the inner codifications of the higher genres but having rejected the identification of those structures with the institutions that had been their home for centuries—the church and the aristocratic state. This rejection was couched as a refusal to conform to any conventional iconographic program. In the 1940s, the radical cause of abstract art fused with needs for the expression of new moods of persecution, guilt, and anxiety. The result was the startling and innovative reconfiguration of the higher genres in Abstract Expressionism, a reconfiguration that brought things to a state of crisis.

Because this reconfiguration was done in the experimental spirit of radical abstract art, the New York School painters also carried on the program of reflexive analysis that had, as we have seen, developed in the deconstruction of the lower genres. The consequence of this fusion of high and low was a new epic-lyric art, rooted not in conventional symbols but in a self-critical, reflexive approach to form. The New York School painters combined a symphonic massiveness of affect with a reductivist interrogation of paint-

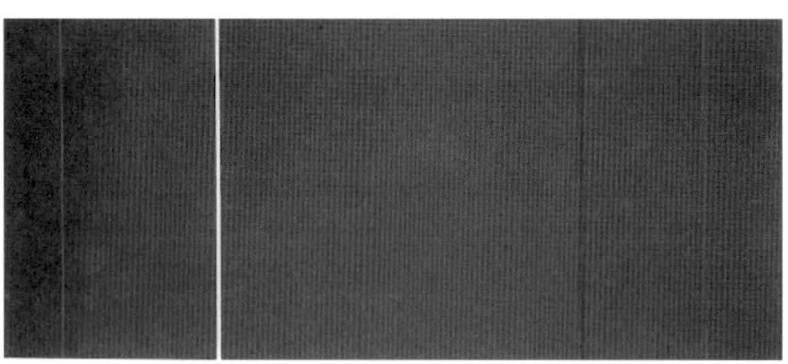

Barnett Newman, *Vir Heroicus Sublimus*, 1950–51. The Museum of Modern Art, New York. Gift of Mr. and Mrs. Ben Heller. Photograph © 1996 The Museum of Modern Art, New York.

ing's capacities. At times, paintings by Newman or Rothko hint at the postulation of an epic monochrome, a work that would simultaneously transcend the categories of traditional art and go beyond a spirit of critique into a new realm, a new form of culture. These artists shook the structure of painting and gave a whole new mood—a loftier, more tragic mood—to reductivism.

This new mood has less to do with investigating the ontology of the art object than with casting a lyrical but penetrating glance at the essentials of the obsolete high genres, and thereby making a definitive statement about their obsolescence. A comparison of, for example, Kline's *Siegfried* (1958) with Picasso's *Massacre in Korea* (1951), done within a few years of each other, gives a sense of how Kline's type of painting continues the impulse toward the higher genres, and how it reveals the limitations of any direct attempt within modern art to continue them as such. Kline's painting excerpts the dynamic elements, those that can express a sense of high drama, and suggests that the codes of pictorial art can no longer approach these essentials. *Massacre in Korea* is lost in musings on conventionalism, in being obsolete, not in inventing the conditions of visibility for the state of obsolescence of the high genres.

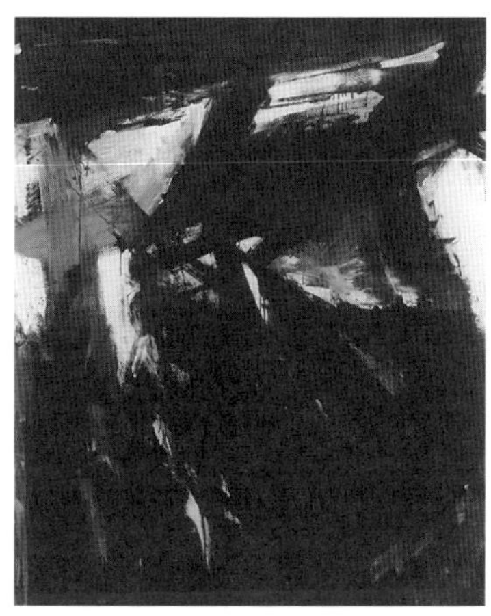

Franz Kline, *Siegfried*, 1958. Courtesy Carnegie Museum of Art, Pittsburgh; Gift of the Friends of the Museum.

In important aspects of Abstract Expressionism, the higher genres remain present, though radically mutated. They are reconstituted in a paradoxical state of absolute subjectivism, an anticonventionalism that is so different from what the higher genres were traditionally about that it is surprising that there is any indisputable connection at all. But the continuity of this generic identity takes place negatively. It can be thought of as that which survives a radical reduction to essentials and which, while it cannot appear directly, can nevertheless be experienced in the work. Abstract Expressionism fails as history painting, maybe it fails as high allegory, too. But the logic of Abstract Expressionism is that its failure allows the essentials of the older and collapsed genres to make an indirect appearance again, as "the New," as that element of the archaic which, in unexpectedly recurring at the site of its negation, permits the complex and almost inexplicable sense of revolutionary innovation.

This dialectic of negativity, this image of painting's achievement taking the form of revelatory failures, is one of modernism's most significant inventions. The earliest rationale for abstract painting was that it would reform the whole domain of the visual and create a new universal visual language, one whose horizons would be more vast and open than anything pictorial art could create. Slowly, the legitimacy of this attitude has weakened, as it has been recognized that the transcendence of the pictorial and the breakaway from bourgeois art would not take place in the way the radical avant-garde had theorized. At this moment, which we can speculate represents an end moment for avant-gardism, there emerges the doctrine that the legitimacy of the new forms of painting is based not on their actual transcendental force but on their failure to be this force (a force they could have imagined themselves to be but did not actually succeed in becoming). At this moment, painting enters a new relationship with its own history and with the notion of obsolescence upon which it had posited its own legitimacy. This new negativism, which was epitomized philosophically by Theodor Adorno's *Aesthetic Theory* (1969), has its roots in the debates of the 1920s but does not become a dominant factor in the definition of modernist painting until a younger generation began to reflect critically on the idea of avant-gardism, from a distanced position, in the 1950s.

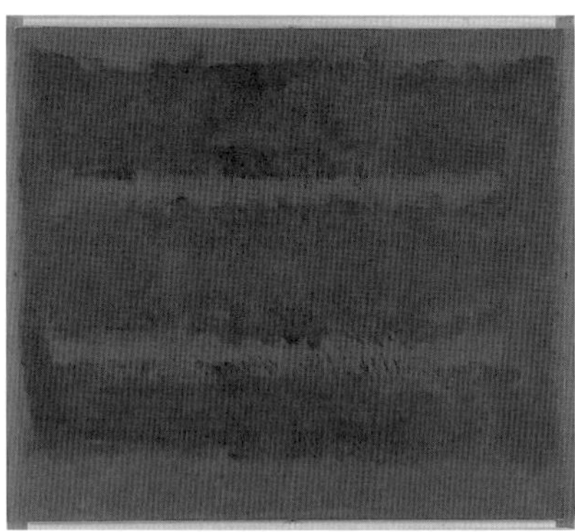

Mark Rothko, *Black on Maroon*, 1958. Tate Gallery/Art Resource, New York. Copyright © ARS, NY.

What Peter Bürger calls the "neo–avant-garde" began with an

expression of the disappointments felt by younger, postwar artists at the unfulfilled claims of the radical movements of the 1920s and '30s. In this atmosphere of reevaluation, the subjectivism of Abstract Expressionism and *l'art informel* was subjected to the sharpest criticism. Younger painters—Stella prominent among them—recognized that the aims of painting in the higher genres were both achieved and not achieved by figures like Newman, Rothko, or Clyfford Still. It was achieved in that these artists managed to imbue the formal and technical procedures of experimental abstract painting with the sort of moral imperative enjoyed by the epic works of the past. It was not achieved because, in the process of formal revolutionization, a logic of reductivism set in and artists began to valorize the rejection of capacities in painting, the divestiture of means, and an aesthetics of silence and failure (in place of an aesthetics of conflict and transformation). This was the authentic expression of those artists who had "made works" instead of "refunctioning institutions," as Brecht defined it, who had abandoned and betrayed the revolution. The guilt was theirs, and they claimed it.

The younger painters of the 1960s were obliged to begin at an intersection in the logic of reductivism. From there, they recognized that although Abstract Expressionism had provided many of the terms for a continuation of the structural and generic redefinition of painting and a redefinition of its obsolescence, its grandiose lyricism was an obstacle to the elaboration of a new analytical approach. These artists were struck by the routinization of subjectivist painting, the sense that the "spontaneous" had exhausted itself or had hidden itself from what New York School painting had been. The first strong statements of Jasper Johns, for example, were

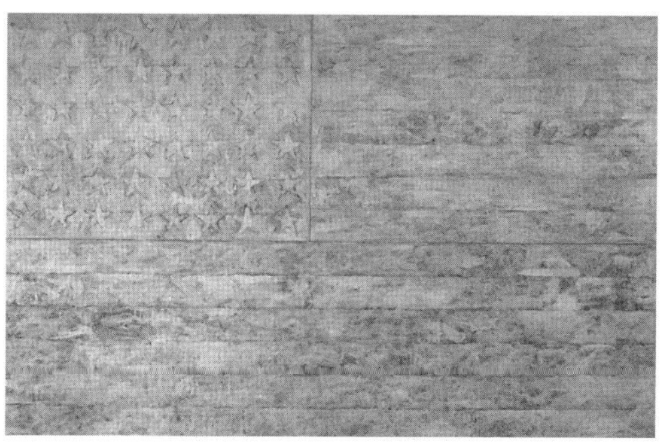

Jasper Johns, *White Flag*, 1955. Copyright © 1996 Jasper Johns/VAGA. Courtesy Leo Castelli.

recognitions of the departure of spontaneity from painting and its unexpected reappearance in prosaic signs and symbols.

It is at this point—in the mid-1950s—that Stella sees the eclipse of the idea of an abstract baroque. No doubt he sees his own paintings of the late 1950s and early 1960s implicated in the new prosaic, investigative attitudes, the rejection of drama and complexity, the argument that further knowledge of the nature of painting as such could not be gained directly in terms of the higher genres. Those forms seemed to be too literary, too full of extraneous moral feeling, too pretentious to be able to focus on the conditions of their own construction. The reductivist painting of the 1960s was a return to the domain of the lower genres and to the attitudes characteristic of Cubism and Constructivism. So it is not surprising that the monochrome reappeared as a central issue at exactly that moment.

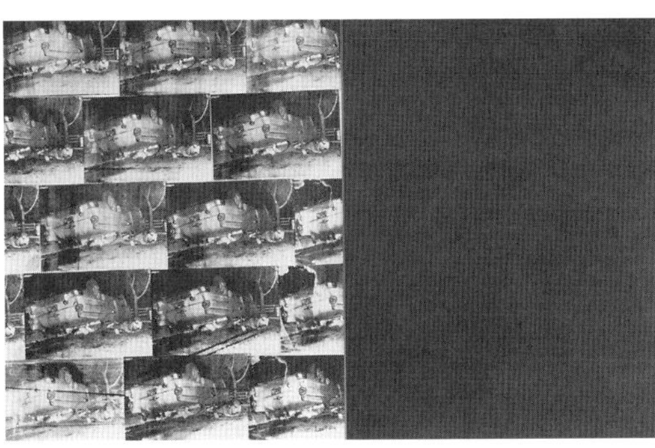

Andy Warhol, *Five Deaths Seventeen Times in Black and White*, 1963. Öffentliche Kunstsammlung Basel Kunstmuseum.

The revival of interest in the experimentalism of the 1920s meant not only a new concern with monochrome painting but also a renewed attention to the functions of photography, specifically photojournalism. Andy Warhol's *Five Deaths Seventeen Times in Black and White* (1963) explicitly demonstrates the polarity, or relationship, between these two constructs. The panel with the images is a zone in which the already-read, already-seen, already-forgotten images of photojournalism are reiterated. The other panel provides only the ground for a possible, or imaginary, repetition, one which does not take place. Warhol has formulated as precisely as possible the two levels at which the art of painting is compelled to renounce the kinds of projects and capacities that had been identified with it historically up to that point. First, on the image side, the painting announces that what it has to express or formulate is the historical and technological fact that photojournalism has taken over the normative agency for the depiction of events and for the construction of historical images. It suggests that what is left for painting to do is to reflect on the conditions of its own displacement and on the resulting irony that paintings can be made under these negative terms. Secondly, the monochrome side casts doubt on the image side. It further suggests that even the reflection of photojournalism is unnecessary, or, at least, that it is not certain that it is a ground-condition for the continuation of self-critical painting. The monochrome panel in *Five Deaths Seventeen Times* tells us that, in the context of the domination of photojournalism, painting's essential practice may be to prepare a surface for a reflection of its own relation to photojournalism. But this surface is one in which a *specific* reflection does not take place. This "does not" is really a "should not."

The image of the car crash is an instance of photojournalism and of the system of reproduction of images as a whole. The problem is that in being an instance of photojournalism it is also necessarily the instance of the appearance of a specific subject matter. Any specific subject, by requiring an emotional and associative response from the spectator, tends to create an atmosphere of legitimization for the representation of that subject. That is, once the artist permits the spectator to become involved with a specific subject, he or she is postulating that the means by which that subject is made visible is therefore a viable means for involvement with the subject. But with Warhol, of course, this validity is just what is questionable. His repetition of the photograph tends to emphasize the questionable nature of any involvement with representations constructed by either photojournalism or by painting. Thus, legitimacy is withdrawn from a representation in the act of re-presenting, or reiterating it, as the case may be here. This is what was—and remains—so striking about these works.

So, the monochrome panel takes the process of ironic delegitimation a step further than does the one with the images on it, and both parts of the process are presented simultaneously, side by side.

This suggests that since the presentation of representation constitutes an expression of the lack of validity of what is being represented and the act of presenting it, then the logical conclusion of the process is the presentation of the absence of representation (and of a specific absence of a specific representation in this case). A monochrome is once again the logical and conclusive form of painting within the logic of reductivism and the predominance of photojournalism.

The monochrome now comes to signify the erasure of the legitimation of the whole complex made up of painting as figuration and photojournalism as social norm. It reiterates the claims made by the radicals of the 1920s, but this time without the same horizon of social change. What was "positively negative" for Rodchenko becomes something else here. This logic was an important part of the experimental art of the 1960s and '70s. What we might call the tropes of Conceptual Art are bound to certain structural hints in Warhol's picture. The idea of a monochrome surface bearing a questionable mark or image recurs constantly in the work of Joseph Kosuth, John Baldessari, Art & Language, Ed Ruscha, Lawrence Weiner, Daniel Buren, and Kawara himself. Painting tends toward sign painting. At the same time, the whole problem of photojournalism enters art again in the many new experiments with "photo-documentation."

In a monochrome, by definition, no event can make an appearance. The appearance of events in art is what is negated by the monochrome, and this negation is its aim. Photojournalism, on the other hand, aims at nothing but making events visible as pictures. But photojournalism as such does not function as art—or, at least, not as modernist art. There is a moment, around 1930, when a new phenomenon emerges. This is the state of mutual imitativeness in which photojournalism begins to appear as art and art as photojournalism. Two important early formulations of this were Walter Benjamin's essay "The Author as Producer" (1934) and Walker Evans's exhibition and book *American Photographs* (1938). What was created in these and other works was what I would call the "art-concept of photojournalism." This innovation was based not on the achievements of photojournalism but on its boundaries, its inadequacies, even. The journalistic photograph is made viable as art by concentrating attention on its limitations. This closely resembles (and even imitates) the frame of mind in which painting recognizes itself in the concept of its obsolescence.

Both Evans and Benjamin were influenced by Parisian Surrealism, and I think we can go back to 1928, to André Breton's *Nadja*, his novel or prose-poem illustrated with photographs, to find the first expression of an art-concept of photojournalism. What Breton did in *Nadja* was to make it evident that the dualism between text and photograph (or, in Benjamin's terms, the relation between photograph and caption) was grounded not on the prose of written journalism but on poetry, on a poetic concept of both prose writing and picture making. Breton's concept of poetics was deeply implicated in the idea, first emphasized by French Symbolism, that poetry did not define itself in a dualism with prose as such, prose as a whole, but specifically with journalism. Mallarmé had made this issue absolutely explicit for Symbolism. The realm of the poetic was established by a conscious and even militant secession from the logos of property, the state, and the laws of identity, which are framed as language above all in journalism. The aim or task of poetry was to realize the negation of the instrumentalization of language. Symbolist poetry, like abstract art, wanted to open doors to new dimensions of being, realms that had been closed off by progressivism and rationalism in what Martin Heidegger in 1938 called "the age of the world picture," the age of high capitalism, cinema, and the press.

In the first historical phase of the critical definition of photography, the dominant note was sounded by those who emphasized the likeness of photography to machine products, to the factual and the prosaic. It was a great poet, Charles Baudelaire, who launched this mode of discussion with his denunciation of photography in 1859. "Poetry and progress," he said, "are like two ambitious men who hate one another with an instinctive hatred, and when they meet on the same road, one of them has to give place." This, written by maybe the greatest connoisseur of hatred in the history of poetry, indicates the bond he sensed between poetry and photography. And it was this bond that became the issue with Breton and with the second critical phase in the attempt to theorize photography as art. *Nadja* revealed that the identification of prose journalism with photography was an illusion, albeit a socially necessary one; that is, it was—and is—an ideology. The striking effect of this revelation on theories of representation was the sense that photography is not structured like prose.

The experience of a photograph is one of immediacy and simultaneity. Any occurrence recorded photographically is seized in the process of its unfolding and condensed into a single image in which all the inconclusible energies of movement and interaction are arrested as a pattern. This patterning is the means by which photography resembles earlier forms of pictorial art, in which the illusion of an event was constructed through a process of rendering and composition, a slow process, one which takes time. As a synchronic phenomenon, as an arrested image, the photograph has a dialectical relation to the event, to the narrative, to the account, to the chronicle. A photograph cannot, fundamentally, be an account. It can only be interpreted as having a relationship to an account by means of an analysis of its technical incapacity to encompass such a structure. This analysis could be called a "narratology" of photography. The experience of a photograph is associative and simultaneous, and in this respect it resembles our experience of poetry. In poetic writing, meaning is not achieved by means of a consistent structure of controlled movements along lines made up of sentences. Rather, the poem is made of lines that may resemble sentences typographically but which abrogate the requirement to be read the way sentences are read. So there is a break with any necessary relation to the chronicle.

This sense of the unlikeness of photography to prose established the foundation for the antagonisms that have characterized the history of the photojournalist's path to self-recognition as an artist. These antagonisms derive from the inner conflicts of photojournalism as an institution. The new form of artist who emerged in this process was the photographer-employee who, for various reasons, abandons his employee status, strikes out on his own, and confronts the market for pictures directly, as a free agent. Walker Evans's career is exemplary here. He and others like him identified the open situation of the speculative picture maker with the poetic condition of photography as art and, working across the hazy boundary between employee and independent creator, found themselves once again in a narrative of modern art. At the beginning of the modern period, the traditional fine artist also passed through this development, breaking from the state academic system out into the uncertain world of capitalist culture, ruled by public opinion, fashion, and anxiety—that is, ruled by the press.

So, ironically, the photojournalist, having discovered that he (or his forebears) was instrumental in bringing into existence the modern art world and shaping the lives and characters of its occupants, must himself pass through this same development, but, historically speaking, for the second time. Here, we recognize that the photojournalist is in a mimetic relation to the modern artist and must experience the passage from employee to speculative producer at second hand, that is, dramatically. He follows a path trodden once before. Photojournalism's path to artistic self-consciousness involves its mimesis of the idea of the artist as it was constituted by the aesthetic thought of the nineteenth century and later brought under intense critical scrutiny by the avant-garde of the 1920s and 1930s. By 1930, the art-concept of photojournalism had come into being, and it was a concept quite different from photojournalism itself. It was a way for photojournalism to imitate art and thereby to arrive at the need to define itself in terms of its limitations, rather than in a celebration of its seemingly infinite capacities. In this way, the art-concept of photojournalism came to see itself as if it were the modernist painting it had helped to engender, that is, to see itself as delegitimated and obsolete *avant la lettre.* In establishing photography as art by being poetry and by being obsolescent—that is, as being inadequate as an image of its subject matter—the art-concept of photojournalism participates in the avant-garde's interrogation of art by its own means and simultaneously opens the door to a third critical phase in theorization. This began with the parodic redeployment of the idea of photo-documentation in Conceptual

Art, performance, and Land Art around 1966, and was later codified in the new critiques of art-as-photography articulated by writers of the late 1970s and early '80s who were decisively influenced by Conceptualism and Poststructuralism.

The monochrome as the transgeneric or postgeneric moment of painting, photojournalism as the mimesis of avant-garde auto-critique: these two big conceptual "knots" are brought together repeatedly in On Kawara's paintings. Kawara's gesture of repetition is the road on which Baudelaire's two ambitious antagonists confront one another. But, here, neither gives way. The confrontation is repeated ad infinitum, becomes permanent, and the dilemma becomes the foundation for a production. There will not be a resolution of this dilemma, partly because it has become a ritual, a necessary staging of a metaphysical crisis. And partly because the staging takes place on the stage of the last theater built by the avant-garde—the stage of art in its negative state of being, a state of lament for itself which has been defined as the negative form of its validity.

I need now to return once more to the framework of history painting. The confrontation in Kawara's painting is marked as such by the only point of agreement between the antagonists: the dates. These dates can be read both on the paintings and on the pages of newspapers usually included in the boxes containing the paintings. Both painting and photojournalism have been brought to a point of historical self-consciousness, whose content is the insistence that neither of them can produce any valid rendering of any subject. Painting has arrived at this state by reflecting back into itself a self-image it thought it saw in photographs. Photojournalism made it by imitating the reaction of the painter. This confrontation can be thought of as a double mimesis, a sort of comedy of misrecognitions. Be that as it may, the product of the confrontation is that no result can be derived from either of these arts which resembles claims made by any genre of representation or any type of figuration, painted or photographic. Kawara's painting since 1966 is one of the most consistent expressions of the project of realizing painting by a renunciation of all its means—and this includes photojournalism as a means of renunciation, not a cause for renunciation.

Only Warhol and Gerhard Richter have come to similar conclusions and have developed them as rigorously. Both Warhol and Richter became involved with photojournalism as part of a re-creation of a sort of *peinture de la vie moderne*, to use another of Baudelaire's famous phrases. In "The Painter of Modern Life," Baudelaire wrote the scenario for the definitive transformation of the noble genres, what he called "Philosophical Painting," into the low genres. The painting of modern life took over all the qualities of high imagination from allegory and history painting and reconfigured those art forms explicitly in terms of journalism. Constantin Guys was the model of the artist as journalist and, what is more, as free-lancer. Baudelaire set the stage for the emergence of modernist painting as the dissolution of the higher genres into the low and, at the same time, as the search for the specter of the high genres in the low. In the same manner, History, the phantom and *éminence grise* of the nineteenth century, was sought in the Now. The work of Richter and Warhol in the 1960s was a kind of continuation of the idea of the painting of modern life as much as it was Pop Art.

We could speculate that the whole world of the high genres has vanished, like Proust's childhood, and exists now only in their always-present, constantly disappearing reflection in the low, in scenes of everyday life, in the Now. As low-genre art, history painting becomes a painting of Now, of "history in the making." It also, however, becomes part of an analytical project in which it observes its own disappearance into the lens which regards it. Kawara's painting project is permanently fixated on Today. It seems as if every structural aspect of the historical movement of the forms of art I've tried to describe here comes to constitute a part of his painting's physical makeup, as if each part of his work—container, canvas, newspaper—were an emblem of the forces that have caused it to come into existence. In perfect modernist fashion, the content of the work is the experience of its forms and its materiality. But the forms are also the outcome of a speculative movement of artistic intelligence that observes not only history itself but also what it regards as necessary and binding limitations on the possibility of anything historical appearing as an image in art, any art.

Each Today painting is a marker of a moment that the painter feels obliged to let pass without making any image of it. The painter recognizes that a historical moment, the Now, has arrived, and has found him in front of his empty canvas. At this moment, the painter recognizes the canvas as a monochrome, as already a painting, and this recognition commits him. It commits him to affirm that any mark he adds to the existing painting will return it to the apparently ceaseless and futile play of genres, to the play of disappearance and restoration that seems to be painting's comedy. This opportunity, the invitation to participate in this comedy, is presented each day, and each day the painter declines it. Instead of painting, he letters the date of his refusal to paint. This refusal, of course, mars the monochrome on which it is marked as much as would, for example, the face of a dead young woman (as in *Tote* from Richter's series 18 Oktober 1977 of 1988). But it mars it differently.

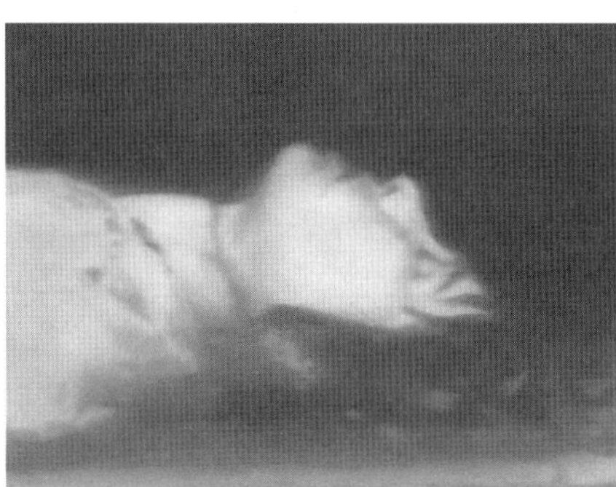
Gerhard Richter, *Tote*, 1988.

Richter's *Tote*, and the series to which it belongs, attempts to actualize the chimera of high history painting glimmering within the problematic of painting and photojournalism. It hypothesizes that painting might still have the means to do this, if the times, the mood, and the subject all come together just right. 18 Oktober 1977 seems to be an attempt to redeem history painting from the double negatives in which it has been placed. Its ambivalence at even seeming to base itself on a concept of the possibility rather than on the prohibition of representation can be felt in the tendency toward effacement of the image which can be seen in, for example, *The Arrest, 1*. It is as if Richter is expressing a wish that these pictures could have remained the monochromes they began as, and not become the disfigured monochromes they are.

Kawara's disfiguration is less dramatic to be sure. In fact, it is not dramatic at all, since there is no image on the canvas. The day's image is expelled to the selection from the newspaper that accompanies the painting. These photographs, whose captions used to give the painting what the artist calls a "subtitle," are instances of photojournalism unredeemed by not having been transformed into paintings. But they are not, by that token, unredeemed photojournalism, because photojournalism is present in Kawara's work only in the state of having been transformed by its mimetic relation to an artwork it cannot inflect. The photographs follow the path of renunciation broken by the paintings. Their presence poses a question about representation and, by implication, about whether art retains any figurative capacities at all. But the question is answered in the negative—and in advance.

Kawara disfigures his monochromes to make an elemental, lucid, gesture of support for the monochrome as the principle of judgment of art. This gesture renounces the figurative or form-creating capacities of his art. The moment of Now must pass unpainted but nevertheless must be acknowledged as that specific something which is not to be made visible. In declining to make a history painting, or a painting of the Now of history, Kawara's painting points to the orders of the world which have defeated it and which now escape it, or which he believes should escape it. Painting, for him, continues in a state of repetition; each day, its lack of viable means is announced afresh, and this announcement once again reminds us of the time elapsed since this condition began.

Old history painting related to the calendar as festivals do; it showed what happened to create a special date, even a sacred date. Great history paintings bring together two such dates, the one depicted and the one on which the painting was made. Traditional art subordinated the glory of the second date to that of the first: its festivals were public affairs. Modern art brought the second date into such prominence that the possibility of there even being a first date all but vanished. In the state to which modern art has brought us—that of the obsolescence of all the genres—painting's only festival is that of its own continuation. Painting is celebrated and mourned as such; that is how it is made today. Kawara's dates are what we might call the absolute expression of this situation. The painter has only his own act to memorialize. At this vanishing point of both painting and photography, infinite dilemmas arise. One of them is the disenchantment of time.

December 16, 1993

The starting point for this essay, the idea of discussing On Kawara's work in relation to photojournalism, was suggested in conversation by Ydessa Hendeles.

Ann Hamilton: *tropos*

SUSAN STEWART

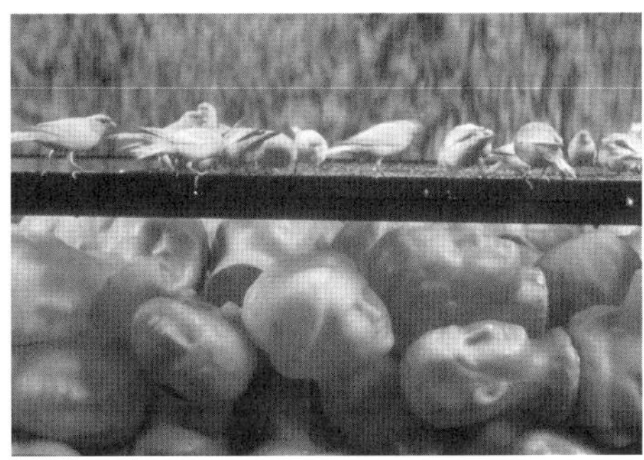

Ann Hamilton, *accountings*, 1992.

Since 1986, Ann Hamilton's installations have explored the relations between the senses, experience, and human work as the transformation and recognition of nature. These installations are the outcome of a monumental labor, yet their material existence is fleeting—for the works are always temporary. Therefore the way in which they are experienced—by those who make, attend, and observe them—is the key to their aesthetic. The stunning visual impact of her recent pieces is only the first of their remarkable qualities. *accountings* at the Henry Art Gallery in Seattle used handsmoked walls, wax heads in vitrines, and thousands of copper tags nailed to the floors and walls of four large rooms. Hamilton's recent collaboration with David Ireland at the Walker Art Center in Minneapolis used 40,000 pounds of flour, emptying and filling adjacent rooms. *aleph*, a recent piece at the MIT List Visual Arts Center, displayed enormous walls of books about outdated technologies and a stack of mirrors, each with the tain erased, accumulating to the height of a person. *indigo blue*, her 1991 exhibit at an abandoned garage in Charleston, South Carolina, featured 4,000 blue work uniforms folded and stacked.

Numbers here are a mere index to a vast sensation of time evoked within the relatively brief period during which the artist has created these works. The literal communities that have arisen

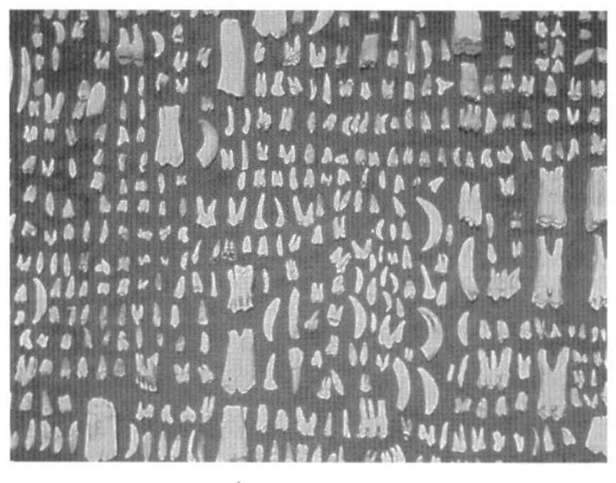

Ann Hamilton, *between taxonomy and communion*, 1990.

around their making across four continents stand in stark contrast to the intimate level of hand and eye within which they are apprehended. And yet, that sense of contrast belies the interconnectedness that is part of the political philosophy running through these projects. For Hamilton, the interrelation of local and global is not a vague aphorism but rather the concrete underpinning of each human act and each product of human labor.

As in all of Hamilton's work, *tropos* is specifically connected to its site; here, a factory building reinscribed by its connection to Dia and the avant-garde of the 1980s. In past works, the specificity of the site has prompted the artist to evoke invisible or forgotten pasts—as in her allusions to Native American materials in the piece called *between taxonomy and communion* at the San Diego Museum of Contemporary Art in 1990. At other times, her use of the site has meant allusions to continuing presences, such as trade beads, flower bulbs, and canal travel in Amsterdam or candles and local insect species in Brazil. In *tropos,* the site haunts the work in its recapitulation of industrial and handwork technologies. The industrial sounds and traffic of West Chelsea come to us intermittently through the now opaque glass of the building. The horsehair industries of nineteenth-century Philadelphia and New York are evoked by the pelt and by the history of the piece itself, which was made in those two cities. Two tons of imported horsehair were brought from China where it had already been collected from slaughterhouses, sorted and tied into bundles that uncannily resembled their source—the horses' tails. The work itself was replete with connections to the site, including the division of labor and transport of manufactured goods. Eight weeks of twelve-hour days were worked by at least six people at a time. Further, the physical transformation of the room evokes the space of a reverie to which we are *obligated.*

We enter it with dramatic immediacy. The skin of the room has been sealed against specific knowledge. We are drawn toward the signs of its abstract penetration by sound and light. Whereas many of Hamilton's works have explored the space and experience of daydream brought about by repetitive labor, the connection of *tropos* to factory labor and piecework gives us a sense of the near claustrophobia brought about by the sealed work environment, as well as the freedom offered by aesthetic cognition given such conditions of repetitive work.

In the past, Hamilton's installations have often alluded to the impossible tasks in fairy tales. Hamilton approaches work at the level of hand labor—what she calls "lap work," making a pun on both the lap as body space and the lap as measure of exertion. Yet linked to this hand labor are forms of small-scale manufacturing and industry. The cleaning and sorting of thousands of teeth, the knitting of several miles of thread, the washing and arrangement of 750,000 pennies on a skin of honey are previous large-scale hand tasks she has undertaken. By combining these two forms of work—lap work and industrial-scale production—Hamilton has reminded us of the human labor that underlies the smooth-talking images of commodity culture. She has emphasized experiences that characterize work itself: repetition, permutation, and accumulation. In this way, her installations avoid the sentimentality or nostalgia that might attach itself to the products of this labor alone or to the permanent display of them within a museum. After finishing her works, Hamilton often returns the materials to their sources or to other usable functions: thousands of wrestling dummies filled with sawdust were recycled as wood pulp; the 750,000 pennies were turned back into usable currency for a public art program; the books from *aleph* were

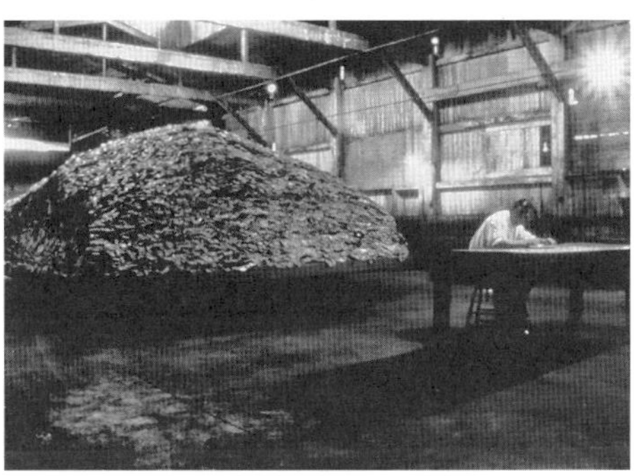

Ann Hamilton, *indigo blue*, 1991.

recycled as toilet paper; the flour from the Walker show was donated to a hog farmer to be used as feed.

Hamilton's installations often use most of their funding for materials; the work itself is generally done by a shared, artisanal community of volunteers—often family or friends with the artist in the role of nurturer and co-worker. However, *tropos* proceeded in a somewhat different way, shifting the balance between hand and industry toward the latter. Members of the Fabric Workshop of Philadelphia, workers with experience in industrial sewing, members of the Dia staff, and Hamilton herself all worked on the piece as paid laborers. When we consider the history of Hamilton's installations, *tropos* marks the passage from a communal to an industrial model of work. We could also say that it has produced a luxury good—the pelt on the floor. Although *tropos* is one of her most spare installations, it also investigates and confronts the relation of the aesthetic economy to excess. If Hamilton's earlier pieces were dependent on a larger economy that afforded the leisure of handcraft, *tropos* has produced art as a supplement, as what Georges Bataille would call a "sign of excess." This supplement is in rigorous concert with its place in industrial culture. As funding for art stands in relation to the general economy, so does *tropos* stand in relation to the conditions of its manufacture. The sewing of the horsehair is a synecdoche for animal death. The labor of assembling the horsehair begins in the agrarian world and includes the dark responsibility of slaughter—the killing, sorting, and collecting of remains—their transport, transformation, and use.

Of the four principle tropes of classical rhetoric—metaphor as carrying over; metonymy as the transformation of name; irony as the dissembling of speech; and synecdoche as the receiving together and reversal of part/whole relations—it is synecdoche that is most emphasized in *tropos.* The notion of synecdoche as "receiving together," the attachments that all phenomena carry and present, is signaled by the recovery of their histories. What is brought forward in Hamilton's *tropos* is the communal context of weaving and weaving's relation to early industrialism, for this enormous pelt has been sewn as lap work and glued and assembled by hand. The relative coarseness, silkiness, and strength of the hair is dependent on the breed of horse and the weather conditions under which it grew and lived. This hair is usually imported for use in brushes and the finest is used for the bows of stringed instruments. And like other weavings—that of the dumb struck Philomel, or the dueling tapestries of Athena and Arachne—what is constructed out of the fibers is a kind of voice, a phenomenon that *speaks* beyond its mere utility as an object.

The materiality of the work thus turns on its synecdochal relation to a transformed substance. The trope of metaphor is also employed here in carrying meaning from one context to another. But, like all of Hamilton's work, *tropos* resists both allegory and theatricality by emphasizing process and refusing any framing devices. Fixed reference and spectatorship are the antitheses of the turning, transforming processes of Hamilton's aesthetic. Consider, for example, some of the meanings carried over by this horsehair pelt. In her use of Baudelaire's well-known prose poem "A Hemisphere in Your Hair," the artist marks the convergence of hair, ocean imagery, and the erotic sublime in the Symbolist tradition:

> Your hair holds a whole dream of masts and sails; it holds seas whose monsoons waft me toward lovely climes where space is bluer and more profound, where fruits and leaves and human skin perfume the air. In the ocean of your hair I see a harbor teeming with melancholic songs, with lusty men of every nation, and ships of every shape, whose elegant and intricate structures stand out against the enormous sky, home of eternal heat....On the burning hearth of your hair I breathe in the fragrance of tobacco tinged with opium and sugar; in the night of your hair I see the sheen of the tropic's blue infinity; on the shores of your hair I get drunk with the smell of musk and tar and the oil of coconuts. Long, long, let me bite your black and heavy tresses. When I gnaw your elastic and rebellious hair I seem to be eating memories.[1]

The sea horse, the sea of horse-tails, mare's tales, nightmares, the mare/*mer* link in Romance languages. The Trojan horse, that other manufactured horse which played such an important turn in a war fought for beauty and trade. The white horse on the chalk down at Uffington, where the landscape is defined by outline or edge in contrast to here, where it is defined by skin as the lining of an interior. The memento mori of Victorian lockets, the hair wreath; the golden-haired Margaret and ashen-haired Shulamith of Paul Celan's "Totenfuge," Donne's "bright bracelet around the bone," Rapunzel, straw into gold, and three hairs from the head of the giant. The associations are not endless—but they are manifold and each carries over meaning, opening another sphere of associations and consequences. And this carrying over continually emphasizes the contamination and continuity between the animal, the human, and the god; between the material and spiritual, the senses and abstraction.

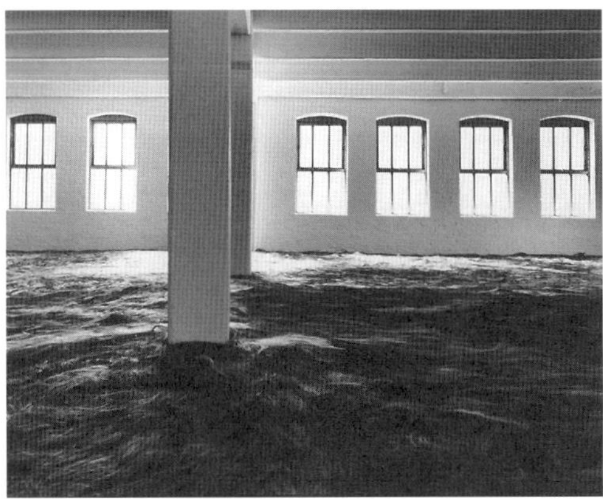

Ann Hamilton, *tropos*, 1993.

The animal pelt situates our feet, placing us immediately in the human world that is both contiguous with nature and built, through work, out of the wresting of form from nature. Meanwhile, the tropism of sound and light here pulls our attention toward language and spirit. The hair is *played* like a lyre, the voice outlines the body, the weaving narrates in silence. One *goes toward*, is *drawn toward* these phenomena with the two senses that, since antiquity, have been most elevated by philosophy—seeing and hearing. Yet, at the same time, we remain tangled in the material, sensual, and *made* reality of the floor. Like the organic forces mimed by Nathalie Sarraute's *Tropismes*, we are pulled and turned toward light and yet rooted and situated within human convention. It is the starkness of this juxtaposition that most affects our experience of it. Plunged into the interiority of this piece, we find that our traversal is both imperative and snagged. The subtle change in elevation, the physical rise of the floor as we approach the farthest point from the entrance, gives a sense of vastness. The spread, wave, and swirl of the pelt with its undulating palette close to that of human hair and its temporal changes; the surface textures of hair, cotton, flesh, steel, and plaster; the sound of a voice moving in and out of intelligibility; and the industrial and traffic sounds intermittently rising—all the senses are summoned, but only in a process of constant movement. Spectatorship is turned into *wandering*; visitors surf through the hair, moving like distracted daydreamers, intensely absorbed by the site. One cannot escape immersion; but the two cures for claustrophobia here are permeation by light and permeation by sound.

tropos is illuminated at its edges during the day and in this, too, it resists the pictorial. It is not defined by an outline or a frame, but rather by the shifting movement of the sun and the observer's circling and spiraling movement through the space. This use of light recalls the idea of blessedness, the outward sign of holiness or grace, as coming into a receiving of the light and a hearing of the voice. Hamilton thus presents a meditation on the ideas of illumination and crowning. The speakers for the taped voice are placed outside the windows and work on a disjunctive cycle. The visitor cannot continuously follow this voice, yet must constantly turn to it and, in doing so, turn toward the light. But spirit is not redemption here. Rather, it throws us back upon the material process by which interiority is constructed—the work of language and knowledge. If one imagines this enigmatic voice as something like an oracle, then one must make the message intelligible to one's self. The modeling of this process on the tropes of metonymy (or change in name) and irony (dissembling speech) occurs in the use of voice and figure. I want to consider Hamilton's uses of voice and reading figure here more specifically because I believe that a recovery of the artist's intention can deepen our experience of the work.

"Two, too, holy, known and likeness, carved pieces, old rose leaves, leaving wait melt but have." These are the words I wrote in the back of a book I was carrying during my first visit to *tropos.* They are the words I thought I heard coming from outside the windows. But on subsequent visits, the words were irrecoverable, as they were discontinuous and barely discernible from the beginning. I do not think it is an accident that the words I imagined—if one can imagine in a completely auditory way—arranged themselves into pentameter groups and proceeded by moving through the inventory of vowel sounds in English. Language is known as sound by the body before it is known as meaning by the mind. The continuum between the sensual and the rational is the site of making and perceiving in this aspect of the work, just as the sensual and rational are in tension in its visual and tactile aspects. Hamilton has emphasized hearing and the human voice in other installations as well. In her recent installation at the Walker, she had a tape running from the interior of a desk. On this tape, with what Hamilton has described as a "liquid and sensuous voice," an actress read in Latin from Linneaus's taxonomy of plant species. *aleph*, at MIT, used a visual and auditory image of stones being rolled in the interior of the mouth and the consequent sound of stones hitting stones and stones hitting teeth. And, more recently, in *malediction,* Hamilton's solo piece at the Louver Gallery, speakers buried in the wall projected the sound of a voice reading sections of Walt Whitman's "Song of Myself" and "I Sing the Body Electric."

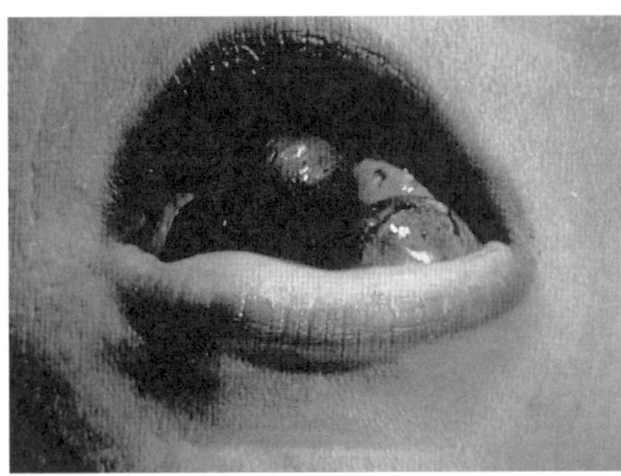

Ann Hamilton, *aleph*, 1992.

By emphasizing the grain or materiality of the voice, Hamilton is able to continue Whitman's project of linking the human body to organic and animal life, on the one hand, and to a politics of democratic and poetic expression, on the other. Such commonplaces of loss as "if only these stones could speak" or "these walls have a story to tell"—acknowledging the stubborn refusal of things to surrender their histories—are worked through as productive grounds for making meaning and speaking to others. In refusing the separation of body and mind, Hamilton's use of voice maintains the idea of singularity and signature in the concept of "one's own voice." At the same time, it accepts the listener's eagerness and anticipation as the necessary condition for the voice to serve as an agent of action. Whereas in earlier installations the use of voice was a kind of complement to a range of sensual effects, in *tropos*, with its more minimal elements, the voice is a key trajectory of the work. It defines a spatial limit as well as an auditory limit and is responsible for the centrifugal movement of the visitor toward the edges of the piece. Isaac Newton's concepts of *centrifugus* and *centripetus* can be used to describe the viewers' movements. Fleeing from the center and seeking the center—two movements that in biology describe the development of certain flower clusters—connect the reception of this piece to two directions of organic growth.

Voice is a force toward exteriority here. It moves from the interior to the exterior in such a way as to recapitulate the evolution from organic life to social meaning. Halting at the edge of intelligibility, voice in all of Hamilton's recent pieces emphasizes the process of that evolution more than its sources or ends. What she does is a kind of reversal of the role that voice conventionally performs, as in Ovid's *Metamorphoses.* In that poem's early narratives, Io, changed into a heifer by Jupiter, tries to complain and is "terrified by her own voice," a lowing sound from her lips; her gaping jaw and strange horns make her flee from herself. Phaeton's sisters are transformed into trees, able to move only their lips; they call to their mother until the bark closes over their last words. Juno turns Callisto into a bear and, "lest her prayers and imploring words should wake sympathy, deprives her of the power of speech." And Ocyrhoe, the daughter of the centaur Chiron and the nymph Chariclo, loses her sense of prophecy when she is changed completely into a horse: "Now I seem to see my human form stolen away; now meadow grass is my food, to gallop over the broad plain is my delight." Ovid continues: "Even as she spoke, the last part of her lament was barely intelligible, for her words became blurred. Then the sound seemed to be neither human speech, nor yet the neighing of a horse, but was like someone trying to imitate a horse. In a little while she gave vent to shrill whinnyings and drooped her arms toward the grass." The slow motion with which Ovid lets us hear the transformation of her voice is the aural equivalent of what happens in Hamilton's use of a voice on the edge of articulation. The voice in *tropos* moves from random noise to the expression of pain or sensation to purposeful sound such as that made in animal communication to human speech, fully given and received.[2]

What one "really" hears coming from the speakers outside the windows is the voice of the comic actor Thom Curley, who has suffered a stroke that has left him with aphasia. At the artist's request, he is reading from Ivan Illich's treatise on literacy, *ABC: The Alphabetization of the Popular Mind*, and from T. S. Eliot's "Burnt Norton," the first section of Eliot's *Four Quartets*. In order to read for this recording, Mr. Curley had to teach himself how to pronounce the words to read aloud. Although he *knows* the words, in an interior sense, articulation is severed from that knowledge and must be reintroduced as a separate skill. Aphasia is the loss of *functional* speech—that is, the loss of the facility to make meaning and practice cohere in the use of language. In this collaboration between Hamilton and Curley, aphasia becomes a way to interrupt the fluency with which we approach the meaning and use of words. For Hamilton, this means that difficulty is introduced at the level of the actor's articulation; this frees us from both theatricality and any quick fix on meaning. For Curley, this means that his work as an actor continues—in both the heightened focus on his performance of individual words and in the slow pauses in his speech that are as themselves locations of significance.

In his classic investigation of the phenomenology of perception, Maurice Merleau-Ponty discusses aphasia as a way of getting at the interrelations of language, perception, and action. The aphasic can experience a disorder of voluntary or purposeful movement, or a loss of the sense of the application of objects which one might otherwise be able to name or imagine using, or an inability to recognize the form and nature of persons and things. More recent work by Hanna and Antonio Damasio and Patricia Churchland has specifically outlined the ways aphasia can affect multiple aspects of language, including syntax, lexicon, morphology, and grammatical production and reception.[3] Interior thought can be fluent even as its application is halted—as it is in Thom Curley's case. Or verbal performance can be fluent but meaningless because of errors in the application.

In *tropos*, the introduction of aphasic speech is the introduction of a kind of productive *irony* or dissembling of the usual modes of speech processes. Curley's voice is at the edge of our consciousness. Its intention is irrecoverable for us unless we *strain* at listening and thereby mime his strained efforts at speech. There is a passage in *The Phenomenology of Perception* which is useful for understanding what has been interrupted here. Merleau-Ponty writes:

> The essence of normal language is that the intention to speak can reside only in an open experience. It makes its appearance like a boiling point of a liquid, when in the density of being, volumes of empty space are built up and move outward. As soon as [a person] uses language to establish a living relation with himself or with his fellow [persons], language is no longer an instrument, no longer a means—it is a manifestation, a revelation of intimate being and of the psychic link which unites us to the world and to our fellow [persons].[4]

In *tropos*, as we strain to perceive the voice, we become aware of not only the efficiency and utility of words, but also their materiality, their being as the ground on which our own subjectivity is born in the recognition of the other.

I have not mentioned the specific texts that Curley is reading in any detail, for they do not appear to viewers in that specificity. But they are vividly, exaggeratedly, specific for the reader. Illich records the processes by which a broadly social agenda of transformation can arise from reading, while Eliot considers the ways in which an intensely spiritual agenda can serve as a critique of the social. The voice is speaking but the speaker is reading—with great effort making the words arise from the body, giving auditory form to what before was silence and thereby moving toward a mutually intelligible sphere of meaning. This is, in fact, the description of the very nature of the aesthetic in *The Phenomenology of Perception*:

> Aesthetic expression confers on what it expresses an existence in itself, installs it in nature as a thing perceived and accessible to all, or conversely plucks the signs themselves—the person of the actor or the colors and canvas of the painter—from their empirical existence and bears them off into another world. No one will deny that here the process of expression brings the meaning into being and makes it effective and does not merely translate it. It is no different, despite what may appear to be the case, with the expression of thoughts in speech.[5]

Merleau-Ponty goes on to claim that:

> thought is no internal thing and does not exist independently of the world and of words. What misleads us in this connection and causes us to believe in thought which exists for itself prior to expression is thought already constituted and expressed, which we can silently recall to ourselves, and through which one acquires the illusion of an inner life. But in reality this supposed silence is alive with words, this inner life is an inner language.... What does language express if it does not express thoughts? It presents or rather it *is* the subject's taking up of a position in the world of his meanings.[6]

But Merleau-Ponty's description is a description of the after-the-fact efficiency and adequacy of so-called normal speech. In the aphasic's speech, we are confronted with the diremption of the relation between thought, language, and subjectivity. The straining here is about recovering those three terms in a condition of urgency. That condition makes problematic or puts into question the nature of aesthetic expression. Just as Hamilton's work has previously concerned itself with the mutual labor underlying the production of beauty and aesthetic closure, here she reminds us of the material effort by which language is used to create interiority and the recognition of such interiority—that recognition which in its mutuality allows us to take up our individuality and position as persons.

I come, now, to that aspect of *tropos* which most visitors seem to consider to be its enigmatic center: the human figure who sits at a rusted metal desk during the hours in which the installation is open to the public. It is by means of the relation between our bodies and this figure that we determine the enormous scale of the space. For, aside from the figure at the desk, we have no experiential referent for a sea of horsehair—it seems as unquantifiable as fire or light or an ocean itself. And this figure counters the centrifugal movement compelled by the voice, pulling us back in a kind of elliptical movement. Yet, if the voice reaches to us as expression, the figure distances himself or herself from us. Hamilton has for some time explored the use of a figure in her installations. This person, whether it is the artist herself or another, is always alone. He or she is a *tender* of the piece, someone engaged in making or unmaking an aspect of the work (knitting, wringing a cloth or hands, modeling dough in the mouth, erasing the tains of mirrors). The figure bears a direct relation to representation; he or she is not miming an action but is doing an action. The material consequence is evident, apparent to the perceiver, usually in an accumulation that is gathering as the piece gathers time. Gathering, as in the double meaning of "wool gathering," is actually a good term for many of these activities, which consist of the bringing together of what was previously scattered and inferring or assembling thoughts. The labor of the attendant is a public labor. Yet its repetitive nature evokes small permutations and increments that are self-transforming. Repeated action is augmented by new information and the participant or the viewer gains access to a sense of the *duration* of perception as in the poetry of Donne or in the Parthenon frieze of the battle between the lapiths and centaurs—this horsey bottom does tend to evoke images of centaurs!

In *tropos*, the attendant is engaged in an activity that at first—and, perhaps for many viewers, continually—seems like an abomination: he or she is slowly, letter by letter, word by word, line by line, paragraph by paragraph, page by page, and volume by volume, burning books. Using the kind of pyrograph tool employed in woodcut technology, the tender follows his or her reading the way a child does, with an index finger tracing the unfolding words. The tool is the servant of the eye's mastery of significance and meaning. The words disappear into curls of smoke evident in the light of the room, the smoke disappearing as inexorably as the voices of Ovid's poor mortals. As visitors come and go in the room they often seem to orbit around this figure. Although viewers are able to come very close to the figure physically, they find themselves unable to speak to or touch or otherwise engage his or her persona. I have several times seen visitors watch the figure reading as one would watch a person perform a forgotten handcraft in what are called "living history" museums. The figure, absorbed in the activity, remains impervious to movement and sound even when others are crowding about for a closer look. Soon the visitor moves away and circles outward again. Just as we might think of an aquarium show as a performance in which porpoises have taught human beings to clap on cue, so is the activity of *tropos* one of turns and modifications evoked and displayed in the receiver as dramatically as any evoked or represented within the work.

The reader in *tropos* calls to mind the general figure of a reader as a recurring subject in Western portraiture. In addition to the Cumaean sibyl, for example, we might consider Piero di Cosimo's portrait of Mary Magdalene in the Palazzo Barberini, Gerard Dou's portrait of Rembrandt's mother, or the many readers in nineteenth-century interiors, such as those of Berthe Morisot. In such paintings, the silence of painting and the silence of reading converge. And the relation between the gaze of the depicted figure and the gaze of the viewer is exaggerated by various means. When the figure faces us, it is all the more likely that the text will be hidden. Such frontal images emphasize that whereas speaking is done in the reciprocity of face-to-face communication, reading is a matter of an alignment of gazes, as when we read a letter over the shoulder of a character in a film. The side view, such as that used in Dou's portrait of Rembrandt's mother, gives us a sense of dramatic conflict between the two-dimensional effect of the profile or silhouette and the perpendicular axis of a text laid out as an object into the illusion of three dimensions. In *tropos,* as we circle around the figure of the reader, something of this tension between the flat world of the text and the orbiting world of the spectator is captured.

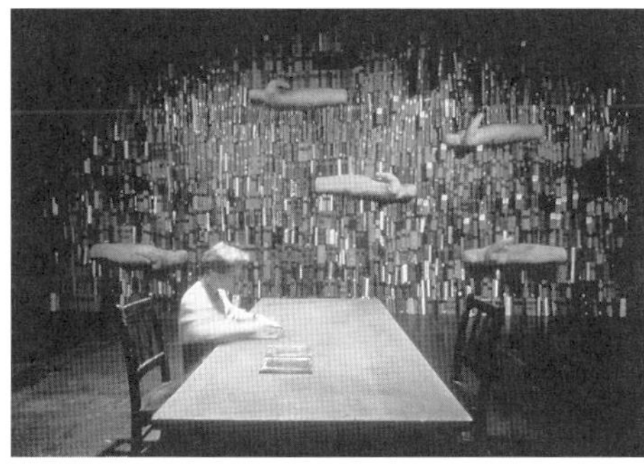
Ann Hamilton, *aleph,* 1992.

But even more specifically, a particular scene of reading is suggested here, one that holds a central place in the Western construction of subjectivity. That scene occurs in the famous passage in Book VI of Augustine's *Confessions* in which Augustine mentions that Saint Ambrose read silently. Addressing God, Augustine explains:

> But although my mind was full of questions and I was restless to argue out my problems, I did not pour out my sorrows to you, praying for your help. I even thought of Ambrose simply as a man who was fortunate, as the world appraises fortune, because he was held in such high esteem by important people. His celibacy seemed to me the only hardship which he had to bear. As for his secret hopes, his struggles against the temptations which must come to one so highly placed, the consolations he found in adversity, and the joy he knew in the depths of his heart when he fed upon your Bread, these were quite beyond my surmise for they lay outside my experience. For his part he did not know how I was tormented or how deeply I was engulfed in danger. I could not ask him the questions I wished to ask in the way that I wished to ask them, because so many people used to keep him busy with their problems that I was prevented from talking to him face to face. When he was not with them, which was never for very long at a time, he was reviving his body with the food that is needed or refreshing his mind with reading. When he read, his eyes scanned the page and his heart explored the meaning, but his voice was silent

> and his tongue was still. All could approach him freely and it was not usual for visitors to be announced, so that often, when we came to see him, we found him reading like this in silence, for he never read aloud. We would sit there quietly, for no one had the heart to disturb him when he was so engrossed in study. After a time we went away again, guessing that in the short time when he was free from the turmoil of other men's affairs and was able to refresh his own mind, he would not wish to be distracted.[7]

Augustine then goes on to guess why Ambrose might want to read to himself—to avoid questions brought about by obscure passages, for example, or to save his voice for his sermon-giving. He concludes that "whatever his reason, we may be sure it was a good one."

As visitors go toward and around the figure of the reader and then turn back into the room, they encounter a similar experience of another's interiority. Hamilton has suggested that all of her pieces with figures are intended to happen for the person within the piece—the tender. This person works between the position of subject and object and presents a way of using installation art to interrupt the conventional pictorial frames with which we approach the aesthetic scene. As we come to understand this person's situation, to recapitulate the intensity with which he or she is engaged in a process of work, it is we who are turned or changed. In *tropos*, as in a painting or film, one can read over the tender's shoulder. But the words will disappear according to the temporality of the tender—we must coordinate our perception to a time frame that is given by the other. This time frame becomes shared and hence social; yet, it is always known after the fact and, so, becomes a symptom of an unfathomable interiority. Like Thom Curley, we must struggle toward articulation and intelligibility. And like Augustine, we must have the good faith to overcome our objections to the burning of books and assume a "good reason" for the activity before us. In this dynamic of recognition, I believe, lies the politic of this piece, its power to make us consider our relation to nature and to other human beings. Private space is not enclosed within static spatial terms for either the speaker or listener, the reader or viewer. Rather, these positions are working toward a dynamic of recognition that will ultimately allow for a mutuality of tasks between artist and audience.

Because such mutuality always goes beyond the artist's intention, I have taken the liberty of bringing up a number of texts and allusions that may have significance to only a few people. Perhaps they will not even have much meaning for Hamilton herself. Ovid's trope of reversal between the human and the vegetable/animal world reminds us that the compensation for our mortality and perishable form is our voice—the ability to speak what we are. To my mind, the other great classical concept of turn is evoked here as well—the capacity for recognition and self-knowledge that Aristotle defined as "peripety," the change or turn that transforms our reading of a sequence of events. As *The Poetics* explains, peripety is always accompanied by discovery—a change from ignorance to knowledge is a turn to judgment and emotion. In Aristotle, the latter becomes the hyperbolic terms of love or hate.[8] The stakes in *tropos* are based on the possibilities of alienation, theatricality, and monumentality—all posed by the particular circumstances of the work itself. The reward is the recognition of one's self as another in a fleeting word that is heard or seen before it is gone.

February 10, 1994

Notes

1. Charles Baudelaire, "A Hemisphere in Your Hair," in *The Flowers of Evil*, trans. Jackson and Marthiel Mathews (New York: New Directions, 1989), p. 31.

2. Ovid [Publius Ovidius Naso], *Metamorphoses*, trans. Mary M. Innes (Harmondsworth: Penguin, 1955), pp. 45–68.

3. See Patricia Churchland, *Neurophilosophy: Toward a Unified Science of the Mind-Brain* (Cambridge, Mass.: MIT Press, 1986), and Antonio Damasio, Daniel Tranel, and Hanna Damasio, "Face Agnosia and the Neural Substrates of Memory," *Annual Review of Neuroscience*, no. 13 (1990), pp. 89–109.

4. Maurice Merleau-Ponty, *The Phenomenology of Perception*, trans. Colin Smith (New York: Routledge, 1962), p. 196.

5. Ibid., p. 183.

6. Ibid.

7. Augustine of Hippo, *Confessions*, trans. R. S. Pine-Coffin (Harmondsworth: Penguin, 1961), pp. 113–114.

8. Aristotle, "Poetics," in *The Basic Works of Aristotle*, ed. Richard McKeon (New York: Random House, 1941), pp. 1455–1487.

Blindness and Insight: The Act of Interrogating Vision in the Work of James Coleman

DOT TUER

Why does my heart beat so?
Did not a shadow pass?
It passed but a moment ago.
Who could have trod in the grass?
What rogue is night-wandering?
Have not old writers said
That dizzy dreams can spring
From the dry bones of the dead?

—W. B. Yeats, *The Dreaming of the Bones*

The universe (which others call the Library) is composed of an indefinite and perhaps infinite number of hexagonal galleries....In the hallway there is a mirror which faithfully duplicates all appearances. Men usually infer from this mirror that the Library is not infinite (if it really were, why this illusory duplication?)....The idealists argue that the hexagonal rooms are a necessary form of absolute space, or, at least, our intuition of space. They reason that a triangular or pentagonal room is inconceivable. (The mystics claim their ecstasy reveals to them a circular chamber containing a great circular book, whose spine is continuous and which follows the complete circle of the walls; but their testimony is suspect; their words obscure. This cyclical book is God.) Let it suffice now for me to repeat the classic dictum: *The Library is a sphere whose exact center is any one of its hexagons and whose circumference is inaccessible.*

—Jorge Luis Borges, *The Library of Babel*

In one of James Coleman's most enigmatic works, *La Tache Aveugle* (1978–90), the viewer enters an enclosed space to encounter a projected slide of a black-and-white film frame. Enveloped by the silence of the darkened room, watching not a cinematic narrative but its arrested image, the viewer becomes a witness to an almost imperceptible crack appearing in the image. A brown shadow, a faint stain, emerges from within the frame. The projected image suddenly seems off-kilter, slightly ajar, as if someone had opened a door for a moment to let a ghost inside a twentieth-century machine of mediation. A strange fleeting moment of panic, of the uncanny, ensues. It is as if something or someone has crept up upon the viewer unaware, as if one has become, in Lacanian terms, the object of the gaze, whereby

> in our relation of things, insofar as this relation is constituted by the way of vision, and ordered in figures of representation, something slips, passes, is transmitted from stage to stage and is always to some degree eluded by it.[1]

According to psychoanalyst Jacques Lacan, this gaze is at once omnipresent and elided, revealed in the liminality of dreams and eclipsed in the waking state of consciousness. Diffused through a pulsating play of light and opacity, it ensnares the subject in the realm of the visible through a paradoxical doubling of seeing and looking, whereby the conscious eye only sees from one point but is looked at from all sides. All that is visible is a trap for this gaze, and the subject produces images as masks to evade its lure. He or she shields him- or herself from this other, all-seeing eye through opaque screens of mediation. Camouflaging the split of the subject in the scopic field whereby "the gaze is outside, I am looked at, that is to say, I am a picture,"[2] the subject invests in the idealization of perception as a unified field of vision, in which the ordering of the visible world through representation shores up the illusion of an undivided conscious eye (I).

In the aesthetic and subjective realm of painting, Lacan goes on to posit, "something of the gaze is always manifested."[3] However, he argues, by also offering "something for the eye to feed on,"[4] the activity of painting functions to tame rather than to provoke the anxiety of this gaze. Simultaneously alluding to its lure and veiling its ubiquity, painting lays down the gaze at the foot of the conscious eye, holds up to the viewer a screen that soothes that uncanny sensation that one has been "caught" in the act of seeing. By contrast, James Coleman's *La Tache Aveugle* evokes the anxiety that painting serves to pacify. In this work, the gaze is no longer lulled into submission; the eye is no longer privileged as the focal point of perception and consciousness. Conjuring that which slips and slides along a registry of images, *La Tache Aveugle* exposes a disjuncture between the gaze and the eye that the ordering of representation disguises; it reveals the blind spot in a unified field of vision.

In so doing, *La Tache Aveugle* points to a central concern in Coleman's work: to cast the act of seeing into question. For it is ghosts and gaps, the looks slipping out of grasp catching the viewer off guard that haunt the visual fabric of Coleman's oeuvre. Deploying a number of representational strategies—from the displacement of sound and image to a play with the frozen gestures of cinema and masks of theater—Coleman unravels the threads that seamlessly bind perception and consciousness. His work becomes a reflection upon blindness and insight: destabilizing visual cognition to link what and how we see to what we can and cannot know. As such, his work does not concern itself with the spectacle of the image, with the surface authority of signs and their circulation within late capitalism, but rather with what lies in between the screens of representation. An interrogation of how conscious and unconscious structures of vision intertwine, Coleman's artistic practice leads to a questioning of how the subject is constituted and how culture is mediated, through a paradoxical doubling of looking and seeing.

Returning to that uneasy moment of the uncanny in *La Tache Aveugle*, for example, what the viewer cannot know, but sees, is the technical process that underlies Coleman's provocation of the gaze. Through a computer-controlled superimposition of thirteen separate film frames, Coleman's continuous slide projection gradually shifts a static image into motion. What the viewer also cannot know, but also does not see, is the presence of an "invisible" figure of representation hidden within the image itself. For the cinematic fragment that Coleman has chosen to isolate is culled from a scene near the end of James Whale's 1933 film adaptation of H. G. Wells's *The Invisible Man.* In this scene, the camera has followed the invisible man into a barn where he is seeking refuge from the angry posse that has been pursuing him across the countryside. This image of a seemingly empty barn interior, with dust-laden streaks of sunlight illuminating piles of hay, harbors a fugitive from the field of vision.

Through his choice of image, Coleman's play with the lure of the gaze slips beyond the sanctuary of a darkened room to entangle the viewer in a cinematic narrative that lies beyond its confines. Bringing cinema to a momentary place of respite, just as the invisible man has found a temporary refuge in the barn, Coleman's unraveling of the act of seeing in *La Tache Aveugle* becomes a mirror inversion of the hunt for the quarry of visual certainty in Whale's film. In *La Tache Aveugle*, the conscious seeing I is dispossessed as the locus of perception; the eye and the gaze are temporarily disoriented by the fracturing of a unified field of vision. Paradoxically, it is the uncanny sensation produced by the crack of image that alerts the viewer to a blind spot of representation, to the "look" of an undetectable cinematic ghost.

In *The Invisible Man*, on the other hand, the conscious seeing eye relentlessly chases its invisible quarry, seeking to quell the disorder that the invisible man has wrought by his capacity to look and not be seen. In the barn where the invisible man is hiding, a poke of a farmer's pitchfork detects a body slithering through the hay, and alerts the posse to the presence of their invisible adversary. Surrounding the barn, the posse flush him out into an open field, tracking and killing him by following his footsteps in the snow. Exposed in an open field, the invisible man comes within the firing range of vision, forfeiting his life in a deadly stalking game of the eye and the gaze. For it is only in death that his body becomes visible again: a screen that restores order to representation, and deflects that uncanny sensation of being looked at without being seen.

It is this enigmatic relationship between death and the ordering of representation through vision, this compulsion to hunt down what cannot be seen, that Coleman pursues in *Charon (MIT Project)*, 1989. A series of projected images with synchronized audio narration, *Charon (MIT Project)* presents thirteen parables about the paradoxes implicit in the production and reception of photography. Each image is projected in a darkened, enclosed space, accompanied by an authorial, masculine voice, "explaining" the stories that lie behind the image, that are not visible to the viewer in the frame. Serving as a counterpoint to the crack in representation that *La Tache Aveugle* unveils, *Charon (MIT Project)* examines the processes by which such a gap is papered over through mediation. In *La Tache Aveugle*, we, as viewers, cannot "see" the invisible man hiding in the straw of the barn; we can only sense the blind spot of representation through the uncanny sensation produced by the slightly askew image. By contrast, in *Charon (MIT Project)*, the disjuncture between the eye and the gaze, between what we see and what looks back, is located in the discomfort that arises between the image and what is described.

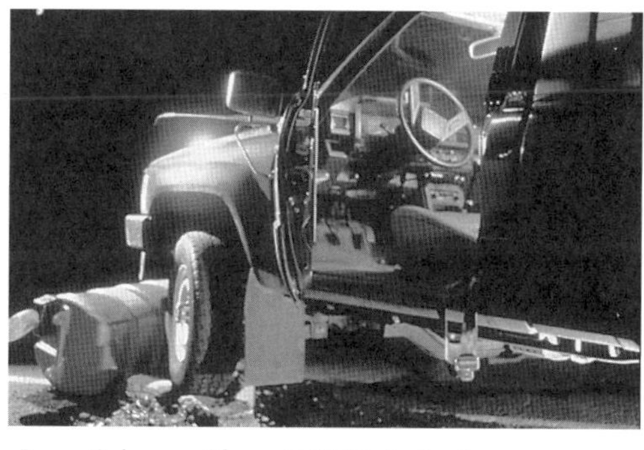

James Coleman, *Charon (MIT Project)*, 1989.

In one vignette, we "see" a man standing with his arms folded and wearing a blindfold. Listening to the voice over, we learn the man is posing for an advertisement for a new color film, and asked to be blindfolded when he read the copy that was to accompany the ad. The ad tells the story of a photographer, who, in trying to photograph the leader of a "revolutionary" group, was captured and subjected to interrogation by the group about who the photograph was for and how it would be used. He was then allowed to take the photograph and released. In another, we "see" an image of a television playing by an empty bed. The authorial and disembodied voice tells us the story of a woman who believes the photograph "constitutes living proof that there is no death." She has reasoned that since one's life flashes before one in the moment before death, death is evaded by an endless remembering of images, by an eternal return in the form of flashbacks. Thus, she sets about photographing herself in anticipation of the death she will never reach.

Apparently quite different, each parable suggests that vision is as much about blindness as seeing. There is a regression here, a slip from image to image that never reaches its destination. In *Charon (MIT Project)*, a cultural faith in the infallibility of the camera's all-seeing eye leads to a representational labyrinth. Self-deception and narcissism lie waiting in the twisted passageways, attendants to a belief in the reproducibility of visible certainty. The image is revealed as a decoy, an abstraction: entangling the subject in a deadly encounter with that which cannot be photographed. Caught in a culture of looking, blinded by the imposition of the invisible apparatus of the camera's gaze, the subjects of Coleman's parables are elided from the very field of vision they seek to objectify. Like the photographer of another parable who is commissioned to produce an advertisement for seatbelts, and "by projecting his vision through the eye of the camera," finds himself "a cadaver viewed by his own spirit, forced to ferry images of his absence and presence," they find themselves suspended in a visual purgatory.

In *Charon (MIT Project)* and *La Tache Aveugle*, the order of representation that requires the embodiment of the eye as a guarantor of visual certainty comes unraveled at the seams. Instead, the viewer witnesses the disappearance of the conscious seeing I within the picture plane. In *La Tache Aveugle*, the disembodied eye of the invisible man lurks within the projected image. In *Charon (MIT Project)*, the subjects of representation vanish into a maze of screens. Rather than serving to camouflage the division of the subject in the scopic field, in which "the gaze is outside, I am looked at, that is to say, I am a picture," Coleman's work exposes the viewer to a split between the eye and the body. The viewer, caught between the authority of the photographic image and the process of its undermining, becomes an uneasy accomplice to the unraveling of visual certainty. Occupying the position of an embodied eye within a fractured field of vision, the viewer stands in for the split subject that the order of representation disguises. His or her presence marks the absence of the embodied eye within a unified field of vision.

As an uneasy accomplice to the unraveling of visual certainty, the viewer is pivotal to the conceptual framework of Coleman's interrogation of the unconscious and conscious structures of vision. For Coleman's play with screens of representation explores not only that which eludes vision but also the ways in which the idealization of knowledge through sight is constructed through the apparatus of the camera. By enclosing the viewer in a darkened room, with the projected image as the only light source, Coleman's spatial containment of the viewer alludes to the role of the observer in two specific models of representation: the fixed space of the camera obscura and the spatial relativity of cinema. On one hand, the enclosure of the viewer as a lone spectator in a darkened room approximates the model of the camera obscura, in which the act of seeing is individuated and vision is anchored to the certainty of the natural world. On the other hand, the projection of the image in the darkened room evokes the dreamlike space of cinema, in which the act of seeing is collectivized and vision is anchored to a mass exercise in reception. Displaced between two models of representational knowledge, the viewer perceives neither a faithful representation of the external world, albeit upside down, nor its mimetic abstraction, but rather the gaps in between images that call into question the veracity of the embodied eye of the observer.

Coleman's positioning of the viewer as a witness to the cracks in representation and as an observer caught in between optical models of perception finds an interesting counterpoint in the arguments forwarded by art historian Jonathan Crary in his *Techniques of the Observer: On Vision and Modernity in the Nineteenth Century.* Tracing the shift in the observer's relationship to external reality and the body through a comparison of the camera obscura and early stereoscopic devices, Crary posits that the guarantee of visual certainty in modernity was sundered from the objectivity of the optical apparatus and transposed upon "the empirical immediacy of the observer's body."[5] Locating in the camera obscura a mechanical apparatus that redefined the relationship between knowledge, the body, and the eye, he argues that the positioning of the body of the observer within the body of the camera constructed "a spatial and temporal simultaneity of human subjectivity and objective apparatus."[6] The physical presence of the viewer as the embodied eye of the camera was separated from the external world he or she was observing. At the same time, a reality external to the apparatus guaranteed that what the viewer saw was an objective representation of a transcendent natural world.

With the invention of early photographic devices, however, the split between the observer and the world observed collapsed. Modernity, in Crary's estimation, deterritorialized vision, transposing a structure of knowledge anchored in the natural world onto the embodied eye of the observer. With the observer no longer isolated within the body of the camera obscura, the veracity of the image was no longer dependent on a physical relationship between the viewer and external reality. Instead, Crary argues, the "empirical immediacy of the observer's body" became the site of both subjectivity and objectivity in the ordering representation. And, he continues, once vision "became located in the empirical immediacy of the observer's body, it belonged to time, to flux, to death. The guarantees of authority, identity, and universality supplied by the camera obscura are of another epoch."[7] What guaranteed visual certainty in modernity, then, was no longer a static and transcendent representation but the conflation of the invisible apparatus of the camera's gaze and the objectifying eye of the observer.

Crary's arguments suggest that Coleman's choice to suspend the viewer in a darkened room with the image as the only light source—that is, between the fixed location of a camera obscura and the spatial relativity of photographic representation—links the act of seeing to the act of knowing. For, just as *La Tache Aveugle* reveals the gap in representation through a slight and imperceptible movement of the camera (like a slightly disjointed binocular hallucination) and disrupts a unified field of vision, so the displacement of the viewer between two models of visual cognition calls into question the authority, identity, and universality of the observer's role in perception. In so doing, Coleman's play with the screens of representation politicizes the relationship of the eye and the gaze and questions the ways in which vision is mediated through culturally and historically specific models of representation.

His work becomes an implicit critique of a formalist modernism that sought to isolate the art object and the observer from an ideological and social context of reception. For it is not the immanence of the object that the viewer confronts in Coleman's work but its ephemerality as an image, whereby the split between the eye, the gaze, and the body draws the viewer into a fractured field of vision and reception. In *La Tache Aveugle*, the cinematic narrative of *The Invisible Man* is exterior to the visual confrontation of the viewer with the image, yet it is central to the visual effect of producing a sensation of anxiety, of something or someone looking back. In *Charon (MIT Project)*, the ideological role of photography as a commercial and mass-produced medium constructs part of the representational labyrinth that envelops the desire of the conscious eye to map the body onto a unified field of vision. Like Crary, Coleman constructs an interrogation of the act of seeing in which vision is no longer conceptualized as an ahistorical a priori, but locates in the observer what Crary calls a "field on which vision in history can be said to materialize, to become visible."[8] For, as Crary has so cogently argued, "vision and effects are always inseparable from the possibilities of an observing subject who is both an historical product and the site of certain practices, techniques, institutions, and procedures of subjectification."[9]

In Coleman's 1987–88 *Seeing For Oneself*, this construction of an "observing subject" is explicitly addressed by exploring the ways in which the act of seeing and the gendered body are intertwined. Unlike *La Tache Aveugle* and *Charon (MIT Project)*, in which the field of vision is fractured by the slips and cracks in between images, *Seeing For Oneself* fractures a field of vision by embedding the competing points of view of the characters within a traditional narrative genre. Constructing multiple frameworks of subjectivity through the relativity of each of the characters' perspectives, Coleman interrogates the implications for an act of seeing in which visual certainty

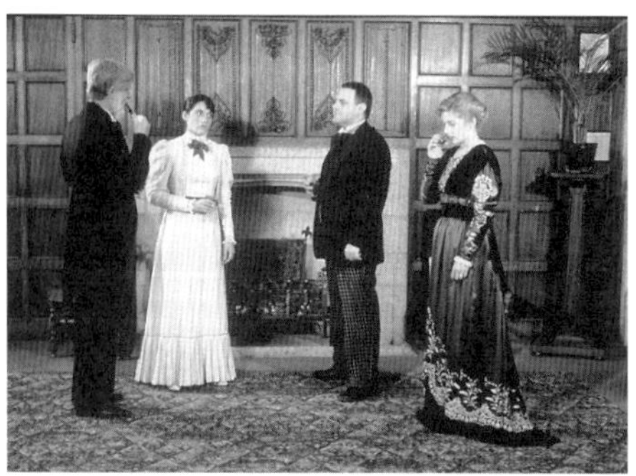

James Coleman, *Seeing For Oneself*, 1987–88.

has been transposed from a classical apprehension of nature to the "empirical immediacy of the observer's body."

Set in a château high in the Canadian Rockies that offers panoramic views of majestic valleys, *Seeing For Oneself* is a parody of a photo-novella, or soap opera. Simultaneously a love story and a murder mystery, it is structured in two parts. The first, a prologue, weaves the webs of representation that entangle the various characters. The second, the story, unfolds after Tamara, the female heroine, learns to see for herself by understanding how her body has been mapped onto a nineteenth-century order of representation. The twists and turns of the plot are narrated by the voice of Polly, the family servant. Occupying a position both inside and outside the familial drama, Polly offers the viewer another eye from which to "see" the power relations that underlie a cartography of vision.

The prologue begins with the arrival of Tamara, the heroine, to visit Neville, her father, at the château. Her father, the viewer learns from Polly, has designed the entire château based on "the divine proportions and image of a remarkable geometrician." From the vantage point of his laboratory, located deep in the bowels of the château amid the heating system, Neville maps the objects of the château into place much like one would sketch the circulatory system of the body. From this interior perspective, an inversion of the camera obscura, it is not a transcendent nature but a transcendent body that orders a representational model of knowledge. The château becomes an extension of the father's embodied eye: a site of authority, identity, and universality, a spatial location that fixes objects into view from a singular position of power.

Not content to construct an architectural structure that mirrors his familial position of dominance, Neville has also dabbled in alchemy, extracting a formula, an elixir, from his studies of the body and its relationship to seeing. This elixir has the power, when taken in small doses, to induce a deathly trance. In large doses, it is lethal. Like the scientist in *The Invisible Man* who imagines himself omnipotent because he has discovered the secret of invisibility, Neville wants to stretch the power of vision from life into death. But just as the invisible man's capacity to look and not be seen is foiled by a mob that hunts down the one who has disturbed the order of representation, Neville is foiled by human hands. Clarisa, Neville's wife and the stepmother of Tamara, who wishes to inherit the château—and, by implication the power of representation—poisons Neville with his own formula. As it turns out, however, she also has been foiled in her quest to position herself as the all-seeing eye of the castle. For the lawyer in possession of the will, played by Coleman, informs Clarisa that it is Tamara who is designated in the will to inherit the château. The only impediment to the inheritance, the lawyer notes, is a clause that voids the will if a "perfidious spirit" should appear.

A young doctor named Blake, who has befriended Tamara, warns her of his suspicions that her father has been poisoned. He also informs her that Neville's body has vanished, and that in its place have been found notes and drawings from his laboratory. With the disappearance of the embodied eye of the father from the château, the order of representation begins to unravel. Clarisa, like the archetypal stepmother in a classical fairy tale, decides to circumvent the will by poisoning Tamara with the elixir. Fed the formula, Tamara grows weaker and weaker, to the point that the family servant, Polly, believes her to be dead. Under the spell of the formula, Tamara cannot move, she cannot feel her body. The stepmother enters the room with a mirror, holding it up to Tamara's face to catch her reflection. The viewer hears Tamara whisper her interior thoughts: "My eyes are open but I cannot see. I cannot speak." Blinded by her stepmother's will to power and caught by the trap of her father's inheritance, Tamara becomes cognizant of her own disembodiment within an order of representation.

In Tamara's immobilizing trance, an inversion of the gaze, the gaze that sets a lure in *La Tache Aveugle*, has taken place. There is a regression here to a pre-Oedipal, preconscious place of visual cognition. For, according to Lacanian theory, the split between the gaze and the conscious seeing eye occurs before the acquisition of language in an infant's development, during what Lacan terms the Mirror Stage.[10] Held up to a mirror by the mother, the child no longer sees himself or herself as one with the mother, and an initial split between the self and the other occurs. Simultaneously, the act of self-recognition is accompanied by a false or mis-recognition, for what the child "sees" in the mirror is an Ideal I, pushing back into the unconscious the disordered fragments of a body that can never be whole. Following the Mirror Stage, the child passes through the Oedipal complex and into language, securing the specular illusion of an Ideal I through the encoding of sexual difference within language and within vision. The split between the eye and the gaze, between the child and the mother, is masked by designating Woman as the lack that underlies an unconscious desire for wholeness. Woman becomes the Other within a symbolic order of representation: that which upholds the fiction of the unified self, and the act of seeing with an undivided conscious eye (I).

In *Seeing For Oneself*, however, a disordering of representation unravels this process of misrecognition and thwarts the positioning of Woman as a lack within the familial drama. For it is not a mother who holds up the child to the mirror, but a stepmother who holds up a mirror to a grown woman. Tamara, the Sleeping Beauty of the château, who has been poisoned by the fairy-tale stepmother, is not awakened by a prince's kiss to ensure her reentry into the certainty of the external world. The prince who bends over to kiss Tamara in her deathly trance is not a prince but a young doctor, whose clinical eye gazes on the body with a deadly scientificity. Deciding to "operate on the body as if it were still alive," Blake prepares to cut up Tamara's body into parts, to return the body to its pre-Oedipal, specular state. Tamara must prevent her own death by autopsy through a will to representation that refuses the all-seeing eye of the scientific gaze, that refuses her own dismemberment within the château's cartography of vision. It is not her Ideal I that Tamara must hold onto but an order of representation that she must disengage from. She, and not Blake, must become an eyewitness to her lack of power as a subject divided by gender, and encoded through sexual difference.

Thinking to herself, "I must inscribe an image in my mind—not lose the will to recall or I shall be dead," Tamara opens her eyes to embody a conscious I who has been able to slip out of the grasp of her father's inheritance. Like the medieval monks who constructed memory palaces in their minds to map an order of representation as a series of discrete visual images of their own choosing, Tamara draws upon a subjective faith in her own capacity to reconstitute another relationship between the body and the eye. It is at this moment, according to Coleman, that the story overtakes the prologue. Tamara, filling her coffin with photographic negatives, signals her refusal to remain a feminine hysteric frozen into a nineteenth-century paradigm of vision. Awakening from a fateful dream of symmetry that imposed upon her body a biological determinism mirrored in the architecture of her father, she returns to the château to remap her body from an interior point of view.

Now able to "see" from outside a dominant framework of power, Tamara descends to the bowels of the château which she knows "like the lines on the palm of my hand." There she encounters Clarisa, her stepmother, who swoons in fear of the "perfidious spirit" that has appeared. In this embodied encounter between Clarisa and the apparition of Tamara as a conscious seeing I who looks back from an unexpected place, the clause that voids the inheritance of her father and signifies a breach of faith is enacted. No longer caught into the lure of a visual certainty that conflates the universal eye of the observer with the invisible apparatus of the camera's gaze, Tamara sees from another vantage point than that which is inscribed by a unified field of vision. The last scene of the drama leaves Clarisa collapsed in Tamara's arms like a secular pietà, with Polly, the family servant, peering around the corner. The viewer hears the echoes of a disconcerting laughter that lingers long after the last projected image has faded into darkness. Signaling the disruptive presence of someone or something haunting representation, this lingering laughter points toward the importance of understanding the act of seeing as historicized and politicized.

In *Seeing For Oneself*, the "empirical immediacy of the body" is divided between the architectural body of the château and the gendered body of the heroine. The château becomes a topology for the all-seeing eye of power, a repository for patriarchy, biology, and positivism. On the other hand, Tamara's awakening from a fateful dream of symmetry suggests the potential to recognize systems of visual mastery as oppressive. For once the apprehension of knowledge is transposed from the classical order of the natural world to the "empirical immediacy of the body," an interrogation of the ways in which the subjectivity of the observer's body is elided by the camera's disembodied gaze becomes important for an understanding of how representation and power collide. An interrogation of the ways in which the objectivity of a scientific eye displaces other ways of seeing becomes important for an understanding of how representation and knowledge intertwine. Like Polly, who peers around a pillar with "one eye open, with one cheek pressed against the wall—a curious perspective to a familiar scene," Tamara learns to see through the cracks of representation, to see from the margins of power. Taking control of her own self-representation, Tamara embodies an act of seeing that cannot be dismembered from a body politic.

In Coleman's recent slide projections, *Background* (1992–93), *Lapsus Exposure* (1993), and *I N I T I A L S* (1994), it is this intertwining of the body and the body politic within and in between the screens of representation that is explored. For with the transposition of vision from a classical model of apprehending the natural world to that which is mapped upon the body of the observer, vision not only divides along the lines of sexual difference but also fractures along vectors of cultural specificity. In *Seeing For Oneself*, Coleman's interrogation of the act of seeing unveils gender as a blind spot of the embodied eye of power. The architecture of the château refers to a perfected topography of the Enlightenment body, the voice-over narrative entangles the viewer in a web of vanishing bodies and multiple viewpoints. In *Background, Lapsus Exposure*, and *I N I T I A L S*, the interrogation of the act of seeing unveils the embodiment of vision as a repository of identity and of memory. Cultural frameworks are offered up as the containers for a complex interweaving of language and gesture. The voice-over narratives are fragmented, disjointed, as if some of the words had been lost to interference or noise during transmission like a radio station that comes in and out of signal.

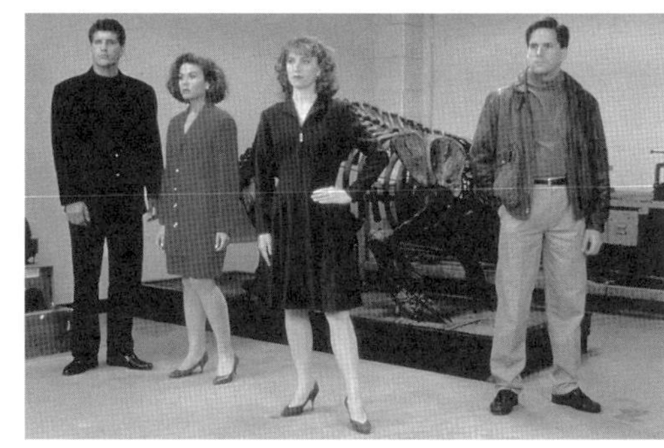

James Coleman, *Background*, 1992–93.

Background, the first of the related works, is set in the basement of the Carnegie Museum of Natural History, where the relics of classificatory science (fossils, skeletons, stuffed birds) are arrayed as monuments to the Enlightenment's Great Chain of Being. The voice-over narration alludes to the interaction of four figures—two men and two women—who are framed by the skeletal structure of a giant sloth. In each of the projected slide images, these figures appear slightly off-balance, as if they had walked accidentally into a field of vision and were caught off guard by the click of the camera's shutter. As a backdrop to their awkward gestures, the sloth becomes a negative imprint of history, in which the scientist chips away at a plaster encasing to get a positive image of display in the present. By contrast, the figures in *Background* become negative imprints of culture, a metaphorical reenactment of turn-of-the-century chronographs. But unlike the quest of Étienne-Jules Marey's chronography to represent the invisible aspects of movement, to map the body as a whole on a representational screen, the succession of images in *Background* appear to be missing pieces—much as the bones of the sloth are missing the living, breathing fabric of flesh. Isolated as gestures rather than as movements, the figures pose on the edge of representation, occupying a spatial location in the cracks and gaps between images, between communications.

From information the viewer can glean from the voice over, it seems that the figures represent workers in the museum. Or perhaps their disjointed staging stands in for workers in a culture obsessed with looking and evidence. The narrative speaks of a black raven, never seen, that is moved in its case from room to room. Snippets of conversation reveal a romance between the figures that has eluded them, much like the freedom that has eluded the mysterious raven. Holding Polaroids that have captured the sweet smiles of a fleeting passion, the figures struggle to communicate the memories of emotions and embraces. As fragmented and disjointed as their gestures, their dialogue recounts the story of a raven they found, almost dead, that would fly ahead on outings at a moment when a union of flesh was still possible. But the raven, a trickster and messenger in North American indigenous cultures, has been captured and placed within the clinical gaze of a Western science. The figures' eyes, locked into the task of cataloguing representation, no longer meet. The voice over laments, "I do not want this inheritance / I am afraid of / of time racing / or stopped / Polaroids fading." As in *Seeing For Oneself*, the inheritance of an Enlightenment model of classificatory nature and the embodiment of vision through the clinical eye of science are called into question. Instead, the viewer is left with the suspicion that photographic evidence masks the shadows and heartbeats of culture. For, just as the sloth is a fabrication of wholeness constructed from the "dry bones of the dead," so perhaps the image is an illusion of completeness in the present constructed from the elision of the past.

In *Lapsus Exposure*, it is not a repository of the artifacts of classificatory science that provides the backdrop but a repository of popular culture evoking the dreams and echoes of Hollywood and a corporate music industry. Placed amid a tangled web of studio lights and electronic musical instruments, the

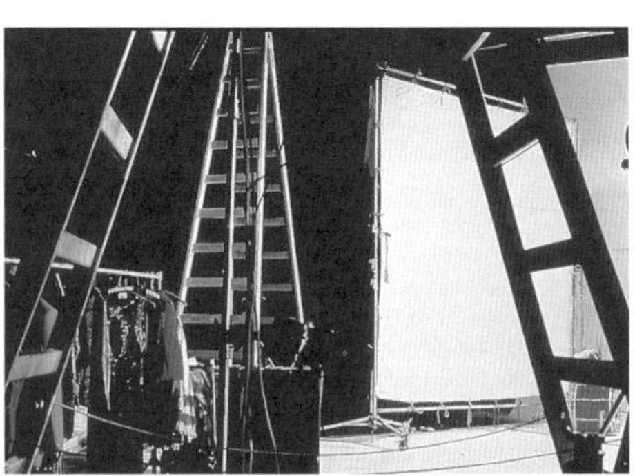

James Coleman, *Lapsus Exposure*, 1993.

young figures in the images appear to occupy a music studio or a film set. As with *Background*, the stilted gestures of the figures contribute to the sensation that something or someone is missing from the staging of representation. The viewer is left with the impression of film footage cut up frame by frame and reedited with sections of the narrative missing. The shards of a voice over lead the viewer to believe that perhaps a music contract is being negotiated or a studio gig is in process. Yet the viewer does not hear music, nor do the band members ever pose for a studio shot. This is a film shoot in which the participants have no place at the center of representation; it is a studio recording session in which the musicians never play an instrument. Hanging around the margins of popular culture, hey are engaged in an interminable process of waiting. Holding Polaroids in their hands, they are waiting for the promised inheritance of self-representation.

A fleeting reference in the elliptical voice over of *Lapsus Exposure* to the distortion of an amp and to replay alludes to a relationship between noise and communication, interference and silence, that finds its roots in information theory. For, in Coleman's fracturing of the voice over, the fragmentary nature of the speech acts parallels what the philosopher of science Michel Serres describes as the drift from order to disorder in information transfer. In his view, communication becomes a contradictory process in which noise is both what is needed for meaning to take shape and that which must be excluded from the act of speaking. Thus, just as the observer is caught in a paradoxical doubling of looking and seeing in a unified field of vision, so the observer is caught into a paradoxical doubling of speaking and hearing in the field of communication. As in the deadly encounter with the gaze, in which the embodied eye of the observer is elided by the act of seeing, so an encounter with the noise that underlies the audible lines of communication reveals the embodied voice of the observer elided by the act of speaking.

By structuring communication as interference, Coleman positions the viewer in between language and noise, whereby "the observer as object [and] the subject as the observed, are affected by a division more stable and more potent than their antique separation: they are both order and disorder."[11] Here, the unraveling of the act of seeing into blindness is interwoven with the unraveling of communication into noise. The allusion to the camera obscura through the enclosure of the viewer in a darkened room becomes a model for what Serres terms the black box of the unconscious: a site of repression in which the filtering of noise renders chaos as intelligible, and transforms randomness into the symbols of culture. For, we are, according to Serres,

> the voice of this hurricane, this thermal howl, and we do not even know it. It exists but goes unperceived. The attempt to understand this blindness, this deafness, or, as is often said, this unconsciousness, thus seems of value to me. We have eyes in order not to see ourselves, ears in order not to hear ourselves. The observer observes nothing, or almost nothing.[12]

Confronted with that which eludes vision and a regression of language into noise, the viewer in *Lapsus Exposure* struggles to "understand this blindness, this deafness." She or he becomes an active participant in the ordering of meaning from the disjointed screens of representation, piecing together the fragments of vision and language into a fabric of seeing and hearing.

In Coleman's *I N I T I A L S*, the backdrop serves as a repository for science's clinical gaze, in this case, the deserted rooms of an abandoned hospital. Here, the figures of representation are mapped onto a site of objectivity where the body is dissected and rethought as code through DNA genetics. Yet the figures are not immediately related to the setting, as were the museum workers in *Background* or the young musicians in *Lapsus Exposure.* Rather, they are actors who appear to be rehearsing for a play, rehearsing the act of communication. From this disjuncture between the scientific and the poetic, the voice over, that of a young girl, enters language diffidently, with hesitation. Trying to com-mun-i-cate, she struggles to reconcile language and the body. As she gains confidence, first spelling, then articulating the words, she moves from information to feeling, casting the embodiment of logos and vision into sharp relief.

Like Polly in *Seeing For Oneself,* who functions as the third eye in vision, the voice of the young girl in *I N I T I A L S* functions as the third term of language. She becomes, in Serres's words, a weaver, who "untangles, interlaces, twists, assembles, passes above and below, rejoins the rational, the irrational, namely the speakable and the unspeakable, communication and the incommunicable."[13] Bridging the disjunctures between objectivity and subjectivity, she conjoins the embodied eye of technology with the liminality of dreams; she connects the crevices and gaps of representation through an evocation to language and vision as forms of expression rather than of domination. The questions the young narrator poses —questions about the gaze and about the shadows haunting representation—are enveloped by the specificity of a cultural longing. In her voice can be heard the echoes of another voice, that of the Irish poet and playwright W. B. Yeats. Spoken with a passion that is visceral, haunting, the words of Yeats that emerge from her gasping entry into language conjure a poetic phantom from Irish history, materialize Irish ghosts that have been stalking each of these three works.

In each, allusions to Yeats's play *The Dreaming of the Bones* haunt the frozen gestures of the figures; the words of Yeats's characters are embedded in the voice over's disjointed communications. In *Background*, the figures dance around the sloth, reenacting a deathly dance that occurs in *The Dreaming of the Bones*. In *Lapsus Exposure*, the opening line of the play—"why does my heart beat so"—reverberates in the studio. But the portent of Yeats's poetic vision is occluded by the cataloguing of photographic evidence in *Background* and by the "noise" of global culture in *Lapsus Exposure*. It is only in *I N I T I A L S*, set amid the ruins of a temple to scientific objectivity, that the historical resonance of Yeats emerges from the cracks, and gaps, of representation. With the voice of Yeats punctuating the young girl's struggle toward language, his poignant tale of tragic lovers and the politics of betrayal in *The Dreaming of the Bones* permeates the fabric of seeing and hearing in *I N I T I A L S*.

Set in County Clare in western Ireland, *The Dreaming of the Bones* tells the story of a young man's encounter with a pair of ill-fated lovers from Irish history. Like the invisible man haunting the image in *La Tache Aveugle*, the young man is roaming the countryside seeking refuge. But unlike the invisible man, it is not the firing line of vision he is fleeing but the occupying forces of the British police. His crime is not a crime of science but a crime of colonial resistance; he is sought for his involvement in the taking of the General Post Office during the Easter Rising of 1916. In the twists and turns of the lonely country roads, he meets a stranger and a young girl who offer to hide him in the haunted ruins of the Abbey. The stranger tells him that while "no living man shall set his eyes upon you; I will not answer for the dead."[14] In County Clare, dry bones are not safely contained within museum walls as at the Carnegie, but are flung down in some forgotten place conjuring shadows of the dead.

Arriving at the summit overlooking the Abbey's ruins with the stranger and the young girl, the young man is told a tale of ancient ghostly lovers. Seven hundred years ago, the young girl laments, the intrigues of the lovers' passion brought internal strife to Ireland and the alien English to Irish shores. Condemned by history as a "most miserable, most accursed pair who sold their country into slavery,"[15] the phantom lovers wander County Clare side by side, cursed with a double glance, for "though eyes can meet, their lips can never touch."[16] If one of their race forgave them, the young girl tells the young man, "lip would be pressed upon lip."[17] The young man declares that the lovers will never be forgiven, then realizes that it is the lovers who have guided him to the Abbey's ruins. "Why do you dance?" he asks the ghostly figures with puzzlement and sadness in his voice,

> Why do you gaze, and with so passionate eyes,
> One on the other; and then turn away,
> Covering your eyes, and weave it in a dance?
> Who are you? what are you? you are not natural?[18]

With this same puzzlement and sadness, the young girl asks of Coleman's assembled cast of figures in *I N I T I A L S*, "Why? Why do you gaze? One on the other, one on the other, and then, turn away?" In her question, there is a poignancy, an urgency, that raises the specter of the blind spot of vision as a blindness of modernity to the complexity of history that lies outside the reach of the camera's disembodied eye. Just as the ruins of the Abbey in *The Dreaming of the Bones* harbors the passion and betrayal of the ghostly lovers, the deserted hospital rooms of *I N I T I A L S* harbor the masks of history. The cast of figures that Coleman has assembled slip in and out of the roles assigned them, embodying a present and a past simultaneously. Superimposing a blueprint of history upon a blueprint of science, Coleman evokes a complex web of what can be spoken and what is silenced, what is hidden and what is revealed when the universalizing gaze of science and a poetic resonance overlap, when the roles of the observer and the subject of observation are blurred.

In one of the images, a young woman stands over a table covered with a bolt of cloth in her hand, leading to the speculation that perhaps she is a costume designer for the play the actors are rehearsing. Yet, the voice over's breathless evocation of weaving and of walls concealing that which is drained and famished summons other memories enfolded in the images: memories of textile workers and cottage industries, of the ravages of English imperial policies and the Great Famine of the 1800s that led to the depopulation of County Clare, and the upheavals of mass emigration. In other images, the figures don the white laboratory coats of doctors; an older woman, dressed for the theater, appears at a doorway of one of the abandoned rooms. A patrician actor and a young man with long flowing hair pose with a paint box in between them; a younger woman poses with a paint can and a roller, preparing to renovate the canvas upon which the theater of history unfolds. Posing together against a pale blue wall in which the cracks have been plastered over, these characters stand before a backdrop in which the cracks of representation are now visible. The young narrator not only echoes the words of *The Dreaming of the Bones*, but summons the material traces of local culture, still growing, in the crevices of memory. Throughout *I N I T I A L S*, she alludes to the skin of the Autograph Tree, still growing, in Coole Park, County Galway, where the Irish poets and playwrights of the early twentieth century had carved their initials.

In *I N I T I A L S*, the ghosts and looks that have haunted the visual fabric of Coleman's oeuvre, slipping out of grasp, catching the viewer off guard, materialize as the politics of "seeing" from the margins of Western culture. Juxtaposing the clinical framework of an abandoned hospital with the specificity of Irish culture, Coleman locates within a field of vision a subjectivity that has eluded modernity's ordering of representation, with its faith in the invisible apparatus of the camera's gaze and the universalizing eye of science. That sudden moment of horror in *Charon (MIT Project)* when the quest for a visual certainty reveals a monstrous void is countered here by embodiment of the conscious seeing (I) within a fractured field of language and vision. The ghost in the machine that startles the viewer in *La Tache Aveugle* is no longer the invisible man of science seeking power and immortality but a mosaic of history and memory. For, in *I N I T I A L S*, the intertwining of the body and the eye, the observer and the natural world, leads not to a ferrying of images as presence and absence but to an affirmation of a theater of masks and screens that can weave meaning from the cracks, and gaps, of representation.

In so doing, Coleman offers the viewer a glimpse in *INITIALS* of an entangled web of representation that cuts to the heart of the dilemmas confronting Western culture. Like another great weaver of labyrinths and paradoxes, Jorge Luis Borges, Coleman warns of the phantoms of disorder that haunt the quest of Western culture to dominate the flux of time and death through an ordering of representation. Structuralist in form, and enigmatic in content, Coleman's work is like Borges's Library of Babel, in which a visual image of the universe as a geometrically precise ordering of representation shields a profound indecipherability. In his play with that which eludes the surface authority of signs, Coleman conjures the suspicion that the Western ordering of space and time does not reflect natural laws or a priori meanings but masks a profound incommensurability. He becomes the eternal traveler in Borges's Library, who, after centuries of crossing the library in every direction, "would see the same volumes repeated in the same disorder (which, thus repeated, would be an order, the Order)."[19]

As a traveler in Borges's Library, Coleman finds a companion in Michel Foucault, who sought to trace the discontinuities that underlie the formation of modernity. On reading a passage from Borges, Foucault says he erupted with a laughter that shattered "all the familiar landmarks of my thought...breaking up the ordered surfaces and all the planes with which we are accustomed to tame the wild profusion of existing things."[20] An echo of the disconcerting cackling that reverberates in the bowels of the château in *Seeing for Oneself,* Foucault's laughter provoked the realization that "there is a kind of worse disorder—that of the incongruous, the linking together of things that are inappropriate; I mean the disorder in which fragments of a large number of possible orders glitter separately in the dimension, without law or geometry, of the heteroclite."[21] Foucault then set out to study the rupture between the natural order of classicism in the 1700s and the empirical imperative and romantic transcendentalism that codified an order of representation and knowledge in the formation of modernity. But while the beginnings of capitalist accumulation and the rise of social sciences form the parameters of the grid he redraws in his analysis of the dissolution of the Great Chain of Being, he never mentions another grid intruding upon Western culture: the mapping of the colonial periphery.

Coleman, by contrast, takes up the heteroclite haunting Western representation from a vantage point that "sees" from outside a dominant framework of power. Positioned as was Borges, an Argentinean, "on the limits between cultures...a marginal in the center, a cosmopolitan on the edge,"[22] Coleman interrogates the unconscious and conscious structures of representation through the politics of gender and cultural difference. Bringing to an archaeology of knowledge the third eye and third term of language as the terms of an embodied vision and identity, he not only unravels the act of "seeing" but also deterritorializes the knowledge and power embedded in an order of representation.

May 19, 1994

Notes

I would like to thank Dia Center for the Arts for the invitation to deliver a lecture on James Coleman's work, the Ontario Arts Council for providing funding toward the research and writing of this essay, and James Coleman, for generously sharing his work and his insights.

1. Jacques Lacan, *The Four Fundamental Concepts of Psycho-Analysis,* trans. Alan Sheridan (London: Penguin Books, 1979), p. 73.
2. Ibid., p. 106.
3. Ibid., p. 101.
4. Ibid.
5. Jonathan Crary, *Techniques of the Observer: On Vision and Modernity in the Nineteenth Century* (Cambridge, Mass.: MIT Press, 1990), p. 24.
6. Ibid., p. 41.
7. Ibid., p. 24.
8. Ibid., p. 5.
9. Ibid.
10. Jacques Lacan, "The Mirror Stage as Formative of the Function of the I as Revealed in Psychoanalytic Experience," in *Écrits: A Selection,* trans. Alan Sheridan (New York: W. W. Norton, 1977), pp. 1–7.
11. Michel Serres, "The Origin of Language: Biology, Information Theory, and Thermodynamics," in *Hermes: Literature, Science, Philosophy,* ed. Josué V. Harari and David F. Bell (Baltimore: John Hopkins University Press, 1982), p. 82.
12. Ibid., p. 77.
13. Michel Serres, "Language and Space: From Oedipus to Zola," in *Hermes: Literature, Science, Philosophy,* p. 52.
14. W. B. Yeats, *The Dreaming of the Bones,* in *Plays and Controversies* (London: MacMillan and Co., Ltd., 1923), p. 385.
15. Ibid., p. 393.
16. Ibid., p. 391.
17. Ibid., p. 393.
18. Ibid., p. 394.
19. Jorge Luis Borges, "The Library of Babel," in *Labyrinths: Selected Stories and Other Writings* (New York: New Directions Books, 1962), p. 58.

20. Michel Foucault, *The Order of Things: An Archeology of the Human Sciences* (New York: Vintage Books, 1970), p. xv.

21. Ibid., p. xvii.

22. Beatriz Sarlo, *Jorge Luis Borges: A Writer on the Edge* (London: Verso, 1993), p. 6.

Contributors

Stephen Bann is a cultural historian concerned with the representation of history in museums and collections, as well as a critic of contemporary art. He is Director of the Centre of Modern Cultural Studies at the University of Kent, Canterbury, England. He is also the author of *The True Vine: On Visual Representation and the Western Tradition* (Cambridge University Press, 1989), *Under the Sign: John Bargrave as Traveler, Collector, and Witness* (University of Michigan Press, 1994), and *Romanticism and the Rise of History* (Maxwell Macmillan International, 1995).

Antje von Graevenitz, a former lecturer in modern art at the University in Amsterdam, became a professor of art history at the University of Cologne in 1989. She has published widely in both museum catalogues and art journals, and has lectured extensively in Europe. A noted authority on the work of Joseph Beuys, Dr. von Graevenitz delivered a lecture at the Hamburger Kunsthalle, entitled "The Ritual Strategies of Joseph Beuys," part of that institution's series, "Beuys in the Context of Time."

Anne Rorimer, an art historian and former curator of twentieth-century art at the Art Institute of Chicago, is now an independent curator, specializing in art of 1960s and 1970s. She has published widely in both art journals and museum catalogues, and lectures frequently in the United States and abroad. Ms. Rorimer has known the artist Lawrence Weiner for many years and has been closely involved in several of his projects.

Stephan Schmidt-Wulffen is an art critic and curator at the Kunstverein in Hamburg. He is a widely recognized authority on contemporary German art, and has published a book on German aesthetics. Schmidt-Wulffen is the curator of numerous exhibitions including "Aperto" and "Venice Bienniale, 1986."

Maureen P. Sherlock has taught philosophy, critical theory, and art history at a number of institutions. Her essays on contemporary art have been published in a variety of books, anthologies, catalogues, and journals in the United States and Europe.

Susan Stewart is a critic and poet. She is the author of the critical works *Crimes of Writing: Problems in the Containment of Representation* (Oxford University Press, 1991) and *On Longing: Narratives of the Miniature, the Gigantic, the Souvenir, the Collection* (Johns Hopkins University Press, 1984). Her poetry is featured in *The Hive* (University of Georgia Press, 1987) and *The Forest* (University of Chicago Press, 1995).

Dot Tuer is a writer and cultural critic who has written extensively on the visual and new media arts. She teaches at the Ontario College of Art, and has presented lectures on contemporary art in North America, Europe, and Australia. She has curated a number of film and video exhibitions, and has written catalogue essays on many of Canada's leading video artists. She also writes on issues of postcolonialism and Latin American history and culture. Currently, she is researching a book on issues of technology and utopia that examines the relationship between the emergence of cultural modernism, colonialism, and European projections of the "New World."

John Vinci, architect and principal of the Office of John Vinci, Inc., has been on the faculty of the Illinois Institute of Technology since 1972. He is a fellow at the American Institute of Architects, a board member of the Society of Architectural Historians, and advisory board member of the Landmarks Preservation Council of Illinois. He has received two national awards from the American Institute of Architects and five from the Chicago chapter. His projects include restoration of the Art Institute of Chicago's Michigan Avenue Lobby and Grand Stair, restoration of Frank Lloyd Wright's home and studio, and restoration of the Trading Room at the Art Institute of Chicago. Vinci is renowned for his exhibition design for many artists at the Art Institute, the Renaissance Society, and elsewhere.

Jeff Wall lives and works as an artist in Vancouver, Canada, where he was born in 1946. His work has been widely shown in Canada, the United States, and Europe in both solo and major group exhibitions (Carnegie International, Pittsburgh; Documenta, Kassel). A trained art historian with a degree from the Courtauld, Wall has delivered numerous lectures and is the author of several articles on contemporary art.

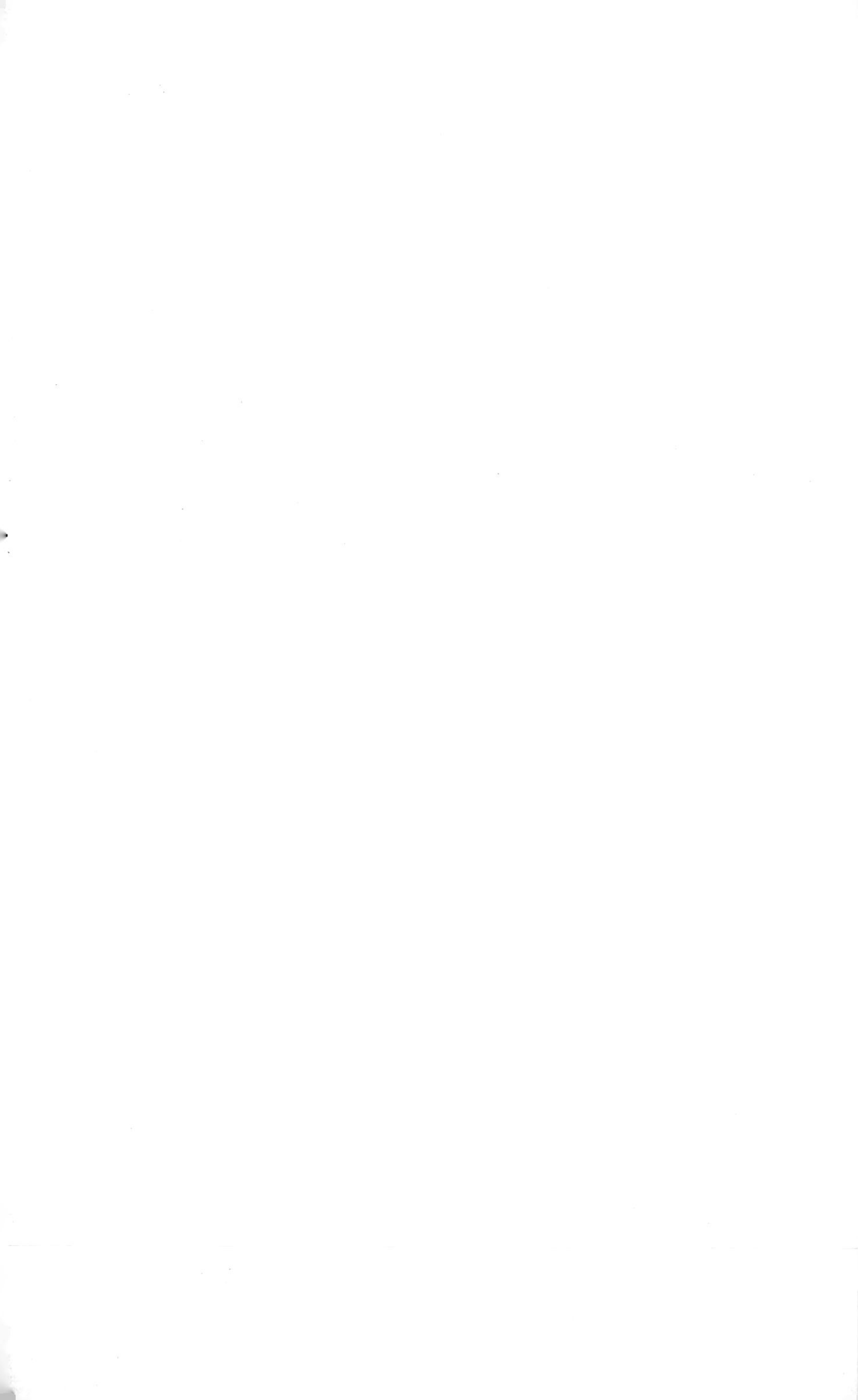

Photo Credits

Page 1, 7, 8, 9, 10, 11, 109 (top), 110, and 117 photographs by Bill Jacobson Studio, New York; pages 2 and 3, photographs by Douglas M. Parker, Los Angeles; pages 4, 5, 12, 13 photographs by Cathy Carver, New York; page 6, photograph by Todd Schroeder; pages 14, 15, and 162 photographs by Thibeault Jeanson; pages 16, 17, 179, 184, 189, and 190 courtesy of James Coleman and Marian Goodman Gallery, New York; pages 20, 21, 30, 31, 32, and 33 courtesy Lawrence Weiner; page 28 photograph by Peter Moore, courtesy Leo Castelli Gallery, New York; page 34 photograph by Christian Wachter, courtesy Lawrence Weiner; page 44 photograph by Zindman/Fremont, Collection Patrice and Elizabeth DeLaage, Paris; page 45 photograph by Zindman/Fremont, Collection Owen Morrisey, New York; page 46 photograph by Zindman/Fremont, Collection Helen Marden; page 48 photograph © 1996, The Art Institute of Chicago, all rights reserved; page 49 © 1994 Museum of Fine Arts, Boston, all rights reserved, courtesy Museum of Fine Arts, Boston; page 52 (top) photograph by Zindman/Fremont, Emily and Jerry Spiegel Family Collection; page 52 (bottom) photograph by Zindman/Fremont, Collection Virginia Museum of Fine Arts, gift of the Sydney and Frances Lewis Foundation; page 54 photograph by Zindman/Fremont, Collection Musée National d'Art Moderne, Centre Georges Pompidou, Paris; page 59 photograph by Bevan Davies, courtesy Mary Boone Gallery, New York; page 63 courtesy Heiner Bastian; page 68 courtesy Manfred Leve; pages 70 and 71 courtesy Anny De Decker; page 74 courtesy Edition Staeck; page 76 photograph by Peter Gauditz, Hannover, courtesy Kestner Gesellschaft, Hannover; pages 80, 82, and 101 courtesy Dan Graham; page 84 © 1996 FLW FDN, courtesy, The Frank Lloyd Wright Archives, Scottsdale, Arizona; page 85 (top) courtesy The Mies van der Rohe Archive, The Museum of Modern Art, New York; page 85 (bottom) courtesy Leo Castelli Gallery; pages 88 (top) and 97 courtesy Marian Goodman Gallery; page 88 (bottom) photograph by Richard Payne, courtesy the photographer; page 91 photograph by Lawrence S. Williams, courtesy Venturi, Scott Brown and Associates, Inc; page 93 photograph by David Hirsch, courtesy Venturi, Scott Brown and Associates, Inc; page 96 photograph by Mark Cohn, courtesy Venturi, Scott

Brown and Associates, Inc; page 103 Collection Le Consortium, Dijon, France, courtesy Marian Goodman Gallery, New York; page 109 (bottom) Philadelphia Museum of Art: gift of the Cassandra Foundation, photograph by Graydon Wood, 1995; page 113 courtesy of Photofest, New York; pages 114, 115, 116, 124, and 125 courtesy of Robert Gober; pages 130, 131, and 133 courtesy of Katherina Fritsch; page 132 courtesy of Luhring Augustine Gallery, New York; page 137 Museo Nacional Del Prado; page 138 (top) Städtische Kunsthalle Mannheim; page 138 (bottom) Museo Nacional Centro de Arte Reina Sofia; page 140 copyright © ARS, NY, courtesy Leo Castelli Gallery, New York; page 142 (top) The Museum of Modern Art, New York, purchase, photograph © 1996 The Museum of Modern Art, New York; page 142 (bottom) The Museum of Modern Art, New York, gift of Mr. and Mrs. Ben Heller, photograph © 1996 The Museum of Modern Art, New York; page 143 courtesy Carnegie Museum of Art, Pittsburgh, gift of the Friends of the Museum; page 144 Tate Gallery/Art Resource, New York, copyright © ARS, NY; page 145 copyright © 1996 Jasper Johns/Licensed by VAGA, New York, NY, courtesy Leo Castelli Gallery, New York; page 146 Oeffentliche Kunstsammlung Basel, Kunstmuseum/The Andy Warhol Foundation for the Visual Arts, photograph by Martin Bühler; page 154 courtesy of Gerhard Richter; page 157 photograph by Richard Nicol, courtesy Ann Hamilton and Sean Kelly Gallery, New York; page 158 courtesy Ann Hamilton and Sean Kelly Gallery, New York; page 159 photograph by D. James Dee, courtesy Ann Hamilton and Sean Kelly Gallery, New York; pages 164 and 171 photographs by Ted Hardin, courtesy Ann Hamilton and Sean Kelly Gallery, New York.